Praise for *Another India*

"With his latest book *Another India*, author Chandan Gowda delves into the diverse narratives that have shaped the country's cultural evolution, while challenging readers to broaden their understanding of the rich cultural and historical landscape." —*The New Indian Express*

"…the essays (in this book) are tentative in spirit, openly dependent on the author's personal encounters with books, authors, actors, farmers, and films, and free of the dogmatic closure of any one ideological commitment. As with Montaigne, the profundity of some of their arguments never compromises the clarity of their prose." —*The Wire*

"*Another India*…presents a fascinating amalgamation of aesthetic, spiritual and moral streams that represent both our cultural ethos as well as our democratic sensibilities." —*Deccan Herald*

"Equal parts storyteller, historian, sociologist and anthropologist, Gowda writes with remarkable restraint and economy, holding back judgement while offering generous glimpses into India's moral and religious traditions and shining a light on mythmaking as cultural history…" —*Open Magazine*

"…Chandan Gowda manages to carve out a niche…these are short essays representing the diversity of a nation within the microcosm of Karnataka, with threads of its language, its film industry, its epic literature, its cuisine and its gods connected into a cohesive portrait." —*The Telegraph*

"Modernists often see tradition as hidebound, conservatives tend to glorify the past. Chandan Gowda's new book of short essays, *Another India*, makes a charming case for the fact that neither can be right…" —*The Mint*

"It is impossible to do justice to each essay…Whether he recounts stories of devotion to village goddesses, snippets from the lives of eminent leaders, folk tales, and tales for children, Gowda holds our attention." —*The Hindu*

"Chandan Gowda's *Another India* transports the reader to a simpler India, unboastful, secure in its rich traditions and its people…" —*The Book Review*

ANOTHER INDIA

Events, Memories, People

Chandan Gowda

**SIMON &
SCHUSTER**

London · New York · Sydney · Toronto · New Delhi

First published in India by Simon & Schuster India, 2023

Copyright © Chandan Gowda, 2023

No reproduction without permission.

® and © 1997 Simon & Schuster, Inc. All rights reserved.

The right of Chandan Gowda to be identified as author of this
work has been asserted by him in accordance with
Section 57 of the Copyright Act 1957.

3 5 7 9 10 8 6 4 2

Simon & Schuster India
818, Indraprakash Building,
21, Barakhamba Road,
New Delhi 110001.

www.simonandschuster.co.in

Paperback ISBN: 978-81-946430-6-7
eBook ISBN: 978-93-92099-75-5

Typeset in India by SŪRYA, New Delhi
Printed and bound in India by Replika Press Pvt. Ltd.

To

UR Ananthamurthy
DR Nagaraj
Siddalingaiah
Lee Schlesinger

for their deep affection,
for the care they brought to ideas

CONTENTS

Preface   *xi*

COMING INTO FOCUS

A People without a Stereotype   3
Where Have All the Animals Gone?   6
Two or Three Things about Rajkumar   9
A Wedding Called Mantra Mangalya   13
The Democratic Imagination of a Poem   16
Barbers and Hairstylists   19
Shakespeare after Shakespeare   22
The Lure of the Literary   25
It's Christmas!   28
The World of Village Deities   30

MODERNITY ON TRIAL

Tales of Modern Mythology   39
Of Hustling and Other Such Seductions   42
Farmers in the Modern Imagination   44
The Sriniketan Experiment of Tagore   46
The Secure Selves of the Past   50
The Myth of a Single Home   53
A Different Journey for Millets?   56
Protest in Indian Tradition   59

SCENES FROM NOW AND THEN

Sri Raghavendra Swamy and the Nawab of Adoni 65
Three Miracles and a Riddle 68
The Case of the Women Sufis 71
A Disciple and His Guru 74
The Community Vision of a Maharaja 76
Repositioning Nehru 78
The Writer and the Census Report 81
The Discreet Charms of Akhadas 83
Challenging Sri Sathya Sai Baba 86
Styles of Welcoming Life 89

JANAPADA/WORDS OF THE PEOPLE

The Episode of Sankamma 93
No Place for Immoral Power 97
The Epic Tale of Junjappa 100
The Servant Girl and the Goddess 106
The Adventures of Puttakka 109
A Sacrifice for a Tank 112
Two Animal Stories 115

SOME IDEAS

Ambedkar's Ideal of Maitri 121
Kuvempu's Vision of Vishvamanava 125
The Passions of Lohia 129
Jayaprakash Narayan and the Idea of Sampoorn Kranti 139
In Pursuit of Cultural Sight 145
Let Us Become Shudras 148
The Matter of a Mela 150

EXCAVATIONS

A Few Devotees of Shiva   155
The Various Births of Ganesha   160
The Story of Gajakumara   162
Three Moral Stories for Children   164
The Chess Match   167
The Irish Connection   169
Around a Land Survey   171
Gandhi as Moral Presence   174
Tall Tales about Ambedkar   179
Lohia's Travels in the USA   182

A FEW BOOKS

Manasollasa: A Sanskrit Encyclopaedia   191
Half a Life from Mughal India   195
Gandhi's Tracts of Freedom   198
"…And the Beautiful Tree Perished"   204
The Scavenger of the Cosmos   207
In Search of Dignity and Justice   210
Hundred-Mile Communities   212
The Ramayana on the Human Condition   215

PERSONALITIES

To the Ocean of Struggle, Flow a Thousand Rivers   221
The Gandhi of Malnad   224
U.R. Ananthamurthy: The Attractions of Metaphor   228
The Figure of O.V. Vijayan   231
Ramchandra Gandhi: A Philosopher's Sojourn in the City   234
The Ethical Stance of Kadidal Shamanna   238
The Importance of Professor Kalburgi   241
D.R. Nagaraj: The Wonder of Retrieval   243

The Humanism of Siddalingaiah   248
Ksheerasagar: A Friend of the Adivasis   251
The Gesture of Nissar Ahmed   254
Nadoja Sara Aboobacker   257
Puneeth Rajkumar: The Last Kannada Icon?   260
A Farmer Called Narayana Reddy   263

Author's Note and Acknowledgements   266

PREFACE

*A*nother *India* has been in the making over the years. My writings, which took various forms—interpretative essays, narrations of little remembered historical episodes, retellings of mythic and folk tales, sketches of personalities, among others—sought to celebrate the living moral and aesthetic imaginations occluded in modern culture. I hoped that the sharing of these cultural memories would reveal the limitations of the modern ideas of progress and development which make people settle for thin views of the world amidst a plentitude of rich cultural visions all around. This exercise was as much about myself learning to see better.

In carrying out my task, I drew upon my own sense for the matter at times and reached out to kindred voices at other times. Anything that came in handy was fine: books, films, controversies, life-experiences. Since logical and analytical reasoning overwhelms public discussions, I preferred to offer narrations with minimal interpretive commentary, and hoped that they would reveal themselves to the readers as they had done to me: as alternate pictures of community interactions, of spiritual imaginations, of mythic worlds.

Both the modern as well as the orthodox imaginations tend to distort the traditional past. If the former fears it as a house of illiberal attitudes, the latter celebrates it as a glorious state of affairs. Several of the folk stories I retell in this book reveal traditional society raising uncomfortable questions about itself, and make those voices our co-travelers as we probe our own existential predicament in the present. Besides, there is the richness of the oral narrative imagination. Several stories in this book illustrate the stunning versatility in the imaginations residing outside the dominant cultural spaces.

The wish to set aside the power of modern ideas, either Western or the revivalist kind, is to allow for proper descriptions of Indian social realities. Parts of this book will show that the experiences of faith in the country are such that the term "religion" cannot properly describe them. Other parts of the book will show that several political leaders and creative intellectuals have—in their own distinct ways—tried to craft a culturally rooted democratic politics. In a free relationship with the civilizational moral inheritance, their creative imaginations also put on trial the ideas of modernity that have only grown in power since colonial times.

The rich reflections on virtuous conduct, justice and human suffering, seen in Buddhist, Christian, Hindu, Islamic, Jain, Sikh, tribal and other moral traditions are a living presence. The secular indifference to these moral conversations that have flowed over centuries is truly unfortunate. It has meant a shrinking of moral imagination in the present. This book goes over several exciting efforts that have sought to address contemporary concerns through a creative engagement with different traditions of moral thought. Moving beyond the binaries of the secular and the religious, the modern and the traditional, and the written and the oral, it suggests, will nourish intellectual and moral creativity in the present.

A rich range of aesthetic, spiritual and narrative streams flow together to form our cultural ethos, our democratic sensibilities. In engaging the contemporary predicament, we will need to give the effort everything we have. *Another India,* I hope, offers a sense of the excitement and the challenges in possessing everything we have.

COMING INTO FOCUS

A PEOPLE WITHOUT A STEREOTYPE

It is impossible to miss the large, floor-to-ceiling close-up shots of coy Indian brides and grooms on the restroom corridor walls at the New Delhi airport. Couples in Bengali, Kashmiri, Maharashtrian, Malayali, Punjabi and Tamil wedding finery are paired across the wall shared by the restrooms for men and women. Unsurprisingly, the Kannadigas have gone missing in this cute visual scheme of federal unity. In the national imagination, there are few images, sounds or smells that help create a recognizable presence for them.

Telecast ad infinitum on Doordarshan in the late 80s, *Mile Sur Mera Tumhara*, the national unity song, affords another instance. The video strove to bring an authentic fit between the regional landscape, dress and personalities and the various Indian languages found in the song's lyrics. Wearing a saree in the Gujarati-style, Mallika Sarabhai sings a line in Gujarati, and actress Revathi is draped in a Kanjeevaram saree while being all ears to Balamuralikrishna singing a Tamil devotional song.

A couple in traditional Coorgi attire lend visual support to the Kannada line in the song. In the absence of a nationally recognizable Kannada dress, the video director settled for a Coorgi symbol since Coorg is inside Karnataka. The irony is that the Coorgis have their own language, with many of them not seeing themselves as Kannadigas.

While locally specific dresses exist across Karnataka, no single attire has come to be ethnicized as uniquely Kannadiga either inside or outside the state. The same goes for food. Udupi and Kamat restaurants will serve vegetarian food from southern Karnataka, places like Swagath in Delhi non-vegetarian fare from coastal Mangalore. But what one might call Karnataka cuisine does not exist the way a state cuisine does for Bengal, Kerala or Punjab.

The unavailability of a codified image of how a Kannadiga speaks or acts will pose difficulties for any intrepid film director hoping to use a Kannadiga as the stock south Indian figure. How does one show a Kannadiga in Hindi or even Tamil and Telugu films? The missing resources for generic self-expression find positive summation in the Karnataka state tourism department's motto: 'One State, Many Worlds'.

Durable associations with Karnataka do of course exist outside: the pleasant climate and the hip IT sector of Bangalore, cricket stars like GR Vishwanath and Rahul Dravid, music legends like Kumar Gandharva, Gangubai Hangal and Mallikarjun Mansur and, in intellectual circles, figures like M.N. Srinivas, U.R. Ananthamurthy and Girish Karnad. Standard views about what Kannadigas are like as a people though do not exist. There is no sense of a Kannadiga student, for instance, on campuses at JNU, the IITs and the IIMs.

Consider a few images: the enterprising Malayali with the great survival instinct; the Bengali who is tenacious about his language; the fun-loving, ostentatious Punjabi. These views are of course gross caricatures and will run up against exceptions all the time. But the stereotypes exist and their absence in the case of Kannadigas—as well as numerous other communities in the country—is real. Community stereotypes thrive through jokes, gossip and anecdotes. Colloquial descriptive labels give them anchor: Mallus, Bongs, Gultis, and Gujjus, to name a few, all evoking confident certitudes about those communities. Stereotypes of communities will more likely emerge when their styles of being and doing get noticed and talked about in ways that add up and cohere in the minds of others. While these encounters can be social, or even simply textual, where people have views of others without ever having met them, what is clear is a community has to invite enough attention towards itself to generate standard impressions.

Historically, the Kannada speakers have not moved out much; and, the ones who did have not aided in the creation of generic impressions about themselves. When the Udupi restaurants in Bombay faced violence from a nascent Shiv Sena in the 1960s, the latter thought they were attacking South Indians and Madrasis, and not Kannadigas.

While stereotypes justly set off alarm for their potential for stoking wicked fun, harm and even death, the lack of it presents a peculiar predicament. Being a vague, inchoate presence in a system of federated stereotypes can summon unease and a sense of failure. While anonymity can be a source of pleasure and freedom, invisibility conveys a lack of power for those who wish to mark their presence in India's repertoire of sub-regional images. The non-arrival of a generic Kannada identity is also a triumph of its heterogeneous nature. None of Karnataka's chief cultural zones, that is, the old Mysore region, coastal Karnataka, Coorg, Mumbai-Karnataka, and Hyderabad-Karnataka, has been able to stand in for the Kannada community image. Amidst the unpredictable twists in a fast-transforming India, a Kannadiga stereotype might yet emerge. At the moment, however, being an amorphous presence in the national imagination should mean a delicious freedom.

WHERE HAVE ALL THE ANIMALS GONE?

One of the delights of Dadasaheb Phalke's silent film, *Kaliya Mardan* (1919), is the child Krishna's tussle with Kaliya, the deadly snake, in a river. Since the early days of Indian cinema, animals have appeared as characters in films across several genres: historical films (horses, elephants), mythological and devotional films (swans, peacocks, parrots, deer) and social dramas (dogs, snakes, monkeys, cows).

Not always an incidental part of the cinema's landscape, animals were often moral agents discharging right or wrong action in the film's narrative. They gave up their lives to save their masters or to avert disaster, or helped lovers meet or reunite, or were a source of trust and friendship. And those which aided in the misdeeds of villains were duly punished for siding with evil. The stuffed leopards and tigers inside mansions gave off clear clues that the masters of the house were dangerous. Besides, on many an occasion, animals sought revenge in reincarnated form.

Films with animal characters were of course continuing an old narrative tradition. For centuries, the stories in the Panchatantra, the Hitopadesha and the Puranas, as well as in the less exalted world of folklore, have included animal characters as moral beings.

Mainstream film makers have felt confident in linking up with this old tradition and cast animals in moral roles in their films. Big hits of the late twentieth century like *Hum Aapke Hain Hain Kaun* (1994) and *Maine Pyar Kiya* (1989) featured a Pomeranian dog and a pigeon, respectively, as important characters in them. Filmmakers in art or parallel cinema though do not seem to have felt as comfortable as their colleagues in mainstream cinema. Animals of course do appear in art cinema. In his essay, "The Humanism of Ray," T.G. Vaidyanathan, the critic, noted, "Ray's compassion and understanding are not only reserved for men but seem to extend also to Nature. Consider the animals that throng his films. There are cats and dogs in nearly everyone (of them)." Ray's films, he continued, express "pervasive sympathy for the entire order of animal creation."

Animals have also appeared as metaphors and allegories in art cinema. In *Elippathayam* (The Rat Trap, 1981, Director: Adoor Gopalakrishnan), the rat trap becomes a metaphor for the prison house of landlord culture in rural Kerala with the landlord being likened to a rat. In *Ondanondu Kaaladalli* (Once Upon a Time, 1978, Director: Girish Karnad), a couple enact the metaphor of being a tiger in bed: the wife becomes a growling tigress to show that she could be as tiger-like at love making as her husband. In *Koormavatara* (2013, Director: Girish Kasaravalli), the cracked surface design on the shell of a pet tortoise, which the Puranas explain as having appeared when Vishnu, in his tortoise-avatar, bore the Mandara mountain on its shell to prevent it from sinking while the Devas and the Asuras churned the ocean for nectar, offers a mythic allegory to the crushing experiences of the film's protagonist whose newly awakened Gandhian sensibilities make the world hard to endure.

Kummatty (The Bogeyman, 1978, Director: G. Aravindan) might be a lone exception in Indian art cinema in having an animal as protagonist. In this extraordinary film, a wandering magician and entertainer turns a boy into a dog. The boy's parents treat the dog as their son until the magician turns it back into a boy the following year. In an unforgettable scene, the first act of the freed boy is to set the caged bird in his house free.

But animals have not appeared as moral actors in Indian art films. The hold of secular thought over art cinema is so strong that its worldview routinely presumes a world under the charge of humans.

Dubbed into several languages, a recent hit Kannada film, *777 Charlie* (2022, Director: K. Kiranraj), which features the affection between Dharma, a lonely young man, and Charlie, a female labrador that succumbs to cancer in the end, cautions against incestuous dog breeding. The allusion—through the hero's name—that the companionship between the two film protagonists is like the one seen between Dharmaraya (Yudhishtra) and the dog towards the end of the Mahabharata though is a strained one. Unfolding against a landscape of pet food, animal welfare activists, no-dogs-allowed signboards, a veterinary clinic and a dog competition, 777 Charlie works with a diminished biological view of animal life.

The previous readiness in working with animals as moral characters has surely waned in mainstream Indian cinema. Alongside laws that make it difficult to use animals in films these days, something else might have brought about this decline in interest: the changing sensibilities of urban middle class audiences in India and abroad which do not resonate with films with animal characters and, indeed, with older conventions of social melodrama. The end of such films will mean Indian cinema's farewell to metaphysical views of animals as moral actors. Animals are likely to continue to be found in oral narratives and children's literature and television, but their departure from mainstream cinema as moral characters signals an impoverishment of worldview.

TWO OR THREE THINGS ABOUT RAJKUMAR

Understanding Rajkumar as a cultural phenomenon is a seriously difficult task: the dimensions of his presence in Karnataka are so many. A moral icon, a folk hero, a voice, a force, a *natasarvabhouma* ("the Emperor of Acting"): these familiar ways of pinning him down convey the complex cultural persona of the Kannada superstar.

It is unlikely that another film actor in the country has matched the variety of roles Rajkumar played. Appearing in 220 films across five decades, he did lead roles in historical, mythological, devotional, romance, action and espionage thrillers, and family melodrama, among other film genres. In what is surely an uncommon cultural fact, Kannada film viewers have experienced a diverse range of genre settings through the figure of Rajkumar: they have seen them through his eyes; they have felt them through his body.

Between 1953 and 2000, the release years of his first and last films, *Bedara Kannappa* and *Shabdavedi*, respectively, Rajkumar can be seen forging continuities between the past and the present and the future of Kannada society. The continuities in the community selfhood run through political-military episodes, exemplary lives of saints, mythological drama and the so-called social films.

The past was more squarely the past of Karnataka in the case of historical figures from this region—for example, Krishnadevaraya, the emperor of Vijayanagar, Kaivara Tatayya, the saint, and Ranadeera Kanteerava, the king of Mysore. Then there are the figures that Karnataka could lay claim to as being part of a sub-continental region—for example, Kalidasa, Kabir, and characters from epics like Arjuna and Ravana. The films of Rajkumar supplied durable images and sounds for numerous historical and mythological episodes. Indeed, popular memory in Karnataka recalls the visual images of Satya Harishchandra and Immadi Pulakesi, the Chalukya emperor, from his films. While history books reached schools and colleges as a set of dull details of dates and proper nouns, the historical, mythological and devotional films of Rajkumar brought the past to life for large numbers of people in a resonant way. The sets were grand; the dialogues were grand; the acting was grand: they vivified the past in ways that bewilder sober historians. Initially a theatre actor at the famous Gubbi Nataka Company, the timing and pitch of Rajkumar's delivery of stylized speech in these films was unmatched.

In films set in contemporary times, Rajkumar moves smoothly across both modernity and tradition. He visits temples, does puja at home, does the duties expected of a son, a lover, a husband and a parent. In other words, he is not embarrassed about traditional ways of being in the world. At the same time, he is comfortable in suits, in modern professions, in using modern technology, and more generally, in navigating modern spaces without melancholy, pathos, nostalgia or anxiety.

In his most famous film, *Bangarada Manushya* (Man of Gold, 1972), for instance, he deploys tractors and bore-well drills to make dry land cultivable for modern agriculture. Again, in an earlier film, *Operation Jackpotnalli CID 999* (1968), which was inspired by the James Bond thrillers, the Secret Agent's secretary asks the Police Chief to call back later as he was doing yoga at the moment. And, Rajkumar's ability to speak in English in modern day film settings is never in doubt. What he will never let pass though is anyone using English for status games, for making Kannada appear an inferior language.

At a broad glance, Rajkumar's films, in particular, those that he did after acquiring superstar status, work as a custodian of Kannada morality. Whether set in the historical or mythic past or in the rural or the urban present, the characters played by Rajkumar will affirm the values of self-restraint, kindness, humility, justice, tolerance, compassion and respect for others and refute arrogance and violence. They will be non-elitist and hold up the value of civility and refrain from peddling hatred. Being courageous rarely lapses into militant self-pride.

Not aligned with any denominational religion or sect, these values are worked out in a general sense in Rajkumar's films. A crucial feature of these films pertains to their edificatory content. A Kannadiga NRI parent in the United States once told me that he had made his young son watch *Gandhada Gudi* (The Sandalwood Shrine, 1973), where Rajkumar plays an honest police officer, several times as that hit film imparted good values. The director of a documentary on the film superstar admitted that the motive behind the film was to impart good values to Kannadiga children, especially in NRI families. Clearly, Rajkumar's films are not wholesome entertainment alone: they also extend lessons in self-edification. It would be incorrect however to view Rajkumar's films as affirming a consistent set of values. On occasion, the roles he played held out moral lessons within the framework of *karma siddhanta* and divine predetermination ("Adene bandaru avana kaanike/Whatever happens is His gift," is the refrain in a famous song in *Premada Kaanike* (A Token of Love, 1976)). On other occasions, they exhort the audience to take charge of their lives without an accompanying idea of karma. The famous song from *Bangarada Manushya* is a good illustration: "Aagadu yendu, kailaagadu yendu, kai katti kulitare, saagadu kelasavu munde, manasondiddare margavu untu/Saying it can't be done/saying it can't be done by us/if we don't do anything/the work won't get moving/Where there is a will, there is a way. Apart from the lyrics, heeding the work of the scriptwriter, cameraman and the director will all form a part of the task of grasping the film phenomenon, "Rajkumar."

Rajkumar's films show a care for building a Kannada *samaja* (society), and not a Kannada *rashtra* (nation) as such. He played the roles of royal personages many times but hardly ever that of functionaries of the modern state. Apart from the occasional role of a mayor, in *Mayor Muthanna* (1969), or that of a police officer, Rajkumar is not found playing a politician or bureaucrat or judge in ways that emphasize the value of the modern state or the rule of law.

In *Raajakumara* (2017), when its hero and Rajkumar's son, Puneeth Rajkumar, is asked to join politics, he replies: "Father always used to say: 'Those who rule over people need political power. We care for people. Willpower suffices for us.'" This response strove to explain why his father stayed out of electoral politics. Following his support for the Gokak movement in the early 1980s, which sought primacy for Kannada language instruction in state-run schools and job reservation for Kannadigas, Rajkumar became a symbol of the activist dreams of the Kannada movement. He desisted however from moving towards party politics.

Through the mysterious process which frees individuals from their community identity in people's eyes in India, Rajkumar, who came from the Idiga community, a toddy tapper caste, belonged to all. When held hostage inside a forest by Veerappan, the smuggler, for over three and a half months in 2000, the uncertainty over his safe return kept everyday life in the state tense the entire time. No one else could have drawn such levels of concern.

As superstar, as voice, as image, Rajkumar is an intimate presence in the lives of Kannadigas. Whether they admire him or not, he remains a deeply familiar point of reference, a point of entry into a world of belonging.

A WEDDING CALLED MANTRA MANGALYA

Purnachandra Tejasvi's biography of his father, Kuvempu, the great Kannada writer, recalls:

> Father knew full well that even idealistic youth surrendered to hidebound orthodoxy at the time of their marriages. This is why, during the seventies, he addressed the youth thus: 'Don't try to reform the world, or society, or orthodox tradition. Nothing will change if your minds do not change. If you are individuals with integrity, try to follow a small suggestion of mine for reforming yourselves: avoid dowry, blind ritual conformity and ostentatious wedding expenditure. These might not seem revolutionary. But you will experience the beauty and joy of doing what you believe in.'

Avoiding grand weddings, Tejasvi adds, his father ensured that the marriage ceremonies of his children stayed simple.

Kuvempu evolved a distinct model of marriage that he later called Mantra Mangalya (MM). It was an organic extension of his ethical ideal of *Vishvamanava* (universal man), which, briefly put, views all community identities as artificial and limiting on one's experience of the world.

The MM wedding recognizes marriages across the lines of caste and religion. Dowry, bride-price and horoscopes have no place in it. The wedding expenses need to stay minimal and only close relatives and friends are invited. Wedding music is absent as the marriage occasion demanded introspection among everyone present. Family elders and well-wishers of the couple, and not priests, officiate over the MM ceremony.

Tejasvi was the first to get married in the *Sarala Vivaha* ('Simple Wedding,' as MM was initially called) way. Many family members and friends came to opt for it over the years. It soon acquired popularity.

At this time, Kuvempu published a booklet titled, *Mantra Mangalya*, which included a selection of Sanskrit mantras from the Vedas and Upanishads and of hymns of goddesses, Sri Ramakrishna Paramahamsa and Sarada Devi along with his Kannada translation of these excerpts. Composed by "our rishis, *darsanikas* and saints," he explained, these mantras sought the highest virtues from humanity.

Later, Kuvempu added twenty "messages of fundamental freedoms" (*vivaha samhite*) to be read out at the wedding ceremony. He discussed these with Tejasvi and M.D. Nanjundaswamy, the farmers' leader, who then gave them final shape. (The involvement of the latter perhaps explains the blunt formulations of a few of the messages). While there is freedom to choose from among the mantras, the *vivaha samhite* is to be read out in full at the wedding.

The first few messages, which seek to unshackle the mind and spirit of the couple, note that they are neither superior nor inferior to any community (*jati*) in the world and that they were now free from all narrow religions.

The division of time as auspicious and inauspicious, which allows for much ritual manipulation in the country, is then rejected since all time is auspicious.

The couple are also asked to reject any religion that proclaims the superiority of men over women. The bride is then declared to be as free and independent as the groom. The equality between the couple is reaffirmed when they sign the *vivaha samhite* in a gesture of mutual consent.

Kuvempu's idea of religion is plural and open-ended and not dogmatic; there can be as many religions as there are individuals. The experiences of individuals could make them believe in a God, or not believe in one, or leave them unsure—all were valid stances.

The MM weddings became more widespread through the farmers' organization, Karnataka Rajya Raitha Sangha (KRRS). Since wedding expenses are a frequent source of farmers' indebtedness and the MM ideals resonated with its own, the KRRS made it an integral part of their activist work. It encouraged thousands of couples to opt for the MM wedding.

The MM's ideals of simplicity and social equality are directed at society at large. Compare its conviction about its universal relevance with the narrow ethics of Aamir Khan who suggested in his hit television show, *Satyamev Jayate,* that those who could afford high marriage expenses could do so but the poor should go in for "sherbet marriages" (where guests are served only sherbet) and save their money.

The MM opposes ritual practices which reduce religion to a need-based experience where a puja, homa or yagna is done to seek worldly well-being. The wisdom of the past is welcomed in the present, but not community identities and priestly intermediaries. The MM wedding remains an exciting moral experiment.

THE DEMOCRATIC IMAGINATION
OF A POEM

On December 20, 2003, at the centenary celebrations of Kuvempu, the Karnataka Government consecrated his poem, *Jaya He Karnataka Maate* (Glory be to Mother Karnataka, 1928), as the *Naada Geete* ("the song of the land"). No one could anticipate that the poem which saw Karnataka as "a garden of peace for all communities" would soon stir a controversy.

In the song rendition of the poem issued by the state government, Madhvacharya, the 13th century dvaita (dualism) philosopher, did not figure among the iconic spiritual figures invoked in it. Sri Vishvesha Tirtha Swamiji of the Pejavar Matha, one of the eight mathas (monastic orders) that Madhvacharya had founded in Udupi, objected to the absence. How could the official song of Karnataka mention philosophers from outside the state like Shankaracharya and Ramanujacharya, he argued, and leave out Madhvacharya, a native philosopher of the state?

While Madhvacharya's name had not figured in the poem when it was first written in 1928, the President of Kannada Sahitya Parishat (KSP) clarified, Kuvempu had inserted his name in his poem in 1971, in response to "popular demand." Although evidence of Kuvempu's consent to including Madhvacharya's name does not exist, a former president of KSP testified that the poet had indeed consented to the revision and that an anthology of Kannada poems published by the Kannada Development Authority in 1971 contained the revised poem. (*The Complete Poetry of Kuvempu*, published by Kannada University Press, Hampi in 2000 however retains the poem in its original form.)

In response to the Swamiji's objection, Purnachandra Tejasvi, the Kannada writer and son of Kuvempu, argued that Madhvacharya's omission in the poem was fully justified. His father, he said, had disapproved of the philosopher's view of Shudras as "nitya narakigalu" (people who lived eternally in hell) and as "thamoyogyaru" (people deserving darkness) and therefore as not being "muktiyogyaru" (people deserving spiritual liberation). Whereas the philosophies of Shankaracharya and Ramanujacharya at least admit possibilities for the Shudras to unite with God, Kuvempu had felt, Madhvacharya's did not. When this was the case, Tejasvi asked, how can we sing praises of such a philosopher?

Outraged at Tejasvi's comments, the Swamijis of the dvaita monastic orders in Udupi issued angry, sometimes contradictory, statements in self-defence. Sri Vishvesha Tirtha Swamiji challenged him to prove that Madhvacharya denied spiritual liberation to the Shudras. Madhvacharya, he argued, only believed that anyone, irrespective of caste, who had "tamo guna" (the quality of darkness) could not attain liberation. Since Shankaracharya and Ramanujacharya, like Madhvacharya, had also offered justifications for the four-fold varna social order, he also argued, it was only proper that their names were deleted from the poem as well.

Charged opinions on this controversy poured out in the pages of newspapers, magazines and websites: Could anyone edit a poem after its author had died? How could one object to the inclusion of Madhvacharya's name as he was only interested in "the development of mankind"? Critics as well as lay readers dug out evidence from old interviews with Kuvempu to Madhvacharya's own writings in support of their views.

Drawing attention to the social service he had done among the Dalit communities of Udupi, the Visvesha Tirtha Swamiji also noted that his matha was open to all castes. Tejasvi, in his view, was promoting inter-caste enmity and breaking the unity of Hindus. In response, Tejasvi asked whether the Udupi mathas had ever declared the caste system as socially and philosophically illegitimate or revised any of Madhvacharya's philosophical tenets. The latter's philosophy was conceptually so interconnected, he continued, revising any part of it could undo the entire whole.

A month after its official announcement, the Karnataka Government declared the revised poem as the *Naada Geete*. The Pejavar Swamiji thanked the Chief Minister for this decision. And Tejasvi refused to accept the insertion of Madhvacharya's name in his father's poem.

In an unforeseen way, a world of theological references on the human relation with the cosmos had claimed space alongside factual discussions of current affairs in the news media. Unlike the English media, the Kannada newspapers gave ample space to the controversy disclosing thereby a powerful public arena where the intellectual credentials required for participation were of an entirely different order.

A critical public attention on three terms—*nitya narakigalu, tamoyogyaru* and *muktiyogyaru*—could fluster the orthodoxy in Udupi and incite passionate debates revealing that conceptions of equality, fairness and justice other than those found in modern political discussions are a living force in many parts of the country. Only prior homework in Madhvacharya's philosophy and the commentarial literature surrounding it would let anyone participate in them. Otherwise, one was shut off from an important political constituency.

During this episode, the Kannada weekly, *Lankesh Patrike*, consulted the latest edition of Madhva's writings and published excerpts to show that the philosopher denied women access to the Vedas and forbade marriage between lower caste men and upper caste women. Since philosophers like Madhvacharya freshly interpreted sacred texts in their time, the custodians of his theology could be expected to make their cherished texts speak to the new political moralities in the present. These are spheres for democratic activism that do not directly concern the state even when large numbers of people are gathered in them. To participate here, an intellectual preparedness other than the one enabled by higher education institutions in the country becomes vital.

Activist concerns alone need not take us to literary and philosophical texts from the past. A casual probe into the etymology of our names could disclose a world of competing visions of the divine and diverse takes on the meaning of life.

BARBERS AND HAIRSTYLISTS

A few years ago, the Karnataka Savitha Samaja*, an association of traditional barber castes, demanded that the government prohibit the use of the word, "hajjam."

Originally a Persian word for a barber, *hajjam* has long been part of the Kannada lexicon. It can easily acquire shades of ridicule and mockery. It is not uncommon to abuse someone as a *hajjam* or to say, "Am I doing *hajjamat* here?" to assert that their work was valuable.

The low status of the barber profession in India goes way back. The Buddhist *Jataka Tales*, which are dated to the fourth century B.C., narrate a story of a barber's son who falls in love with a girl from the high Licchavi clan. His father reminds him of their low social status and assures him, in vain, that he will help him find a bride from his "own place and station" (in W.H.D. Rouse's 1895 translation). The son dies longing for his love.

A toxic tale from the world of Tenali Rama, the poet and jester in the court of Krishnadevaraya, the emperor of Vijayanagar, is also illustrative.

Krishnadevaraya's barber once gave him a fine shave while he was asleep, and spared him much discomfort. Delighted with the shave, the emperor granted the barber a wish. The latter asked that he be made a Brahmin. The emperor then summoned his Brahmin priests and asked them to confer a Brahmin status on the barber. He promised to exempt them from taxes in return. Unaware of the requisite rituals for enabling the barber's wish, they turned to the wise Tenali Rama for

---

* According to myth, Savitha was a sage who used to cut the hair of gods.

guidance. Agreeing to help, the poet-jester asked them to assemble on the riverbank along with some ritual paraphernalia.

At the appointed hour, Tenali Rama brought a black dog to the riverbank, bathed it and walked it around the ritual site. When Krishnadevaraya asked this bizarre spectacle to be explained, he replied that he was trying to turn the black dog into a white one. The emperor refused to believe him. The jester argued that if a barber could become a Brahmin, then the dog's coat could as easily be changed. The emperor now saw reason: the high and the low could never change places.

In an essay on the meanings of hair in the sub-continent, Patrick Olivelle, the Sanskritist, observes that discussions in ritual literature have consistently held hair as an impure object. This is a probable reason for the hair-related service occupation being accorded a low social status. The fact that barbers also performed minor surgeries and played musical instruments did little to alter their status.

Although rulers like Mahmud of Ghazni and Mohamed bin Tughlaq are known to have recruited from among Muslim converts from the barber castes for high positions in the army and administration, the status of barbers has been low among Indian Muslims too.

Untouchability adds another layer of complexity to the matter. The village barbers usually serve upper castes and Dalits with separate sets of instruments. The barbers can even refuse to serve Dalits, forcing the latter on occasion to cut their own hair.

More than a decade ago, the Salon and Beauty Parlours Association (SBPA) in Maharashtra protested against the term 'barber' in the title of the Shah Rukh Khan starrer, *Billu Barber* (2009). They pointed out that 'barber' was a translation of Nai, a Hindi word for the barber caste, and amounted therefore to an insult. Asking that the film's title be changed to "Billu Hairdresser," they elaborated: "We choose hairdressing as a profession because it is an art. Also, there are many women hairstylists. If *Billu Barber* becomes a hit, women hairdressers will be called barbers too!" Admitting innocence, Shah Rukh Khan agreed to have white paper pasted over the offending word in the film's posters since reprinting them was costly.

The SBPA's demand for language censorship stems from concerns other than those of the Karnataka Savitha Samaja. At present, the hair and beauty industry takes home 36,000 crores annually. In the expanding salon and spa sector, which smells of moisturizers, styling gels and money, hair work is an activity in style and loveliness. The elaborate new salon terminology shakes free from older associations of impurity with hair work. Asking that hair-dressing be viewed as an art, the SBPA wishes that the workers in this sector are termed hairstylists rather than barbers. Professional associations like them wish to merely steer clear of the old stigma of hair work and, unlike the Karnataka Savitha Samaja, show little interest in fighting the sources of such stigma. More crucially, they have themselves created new sources of humiliation and difficulty for traditional barbers.

The lack of economic capital will not let traditional barbers invest in air-conditioned state-of-the-art hair salons and spas. And the hip salon language and demeanour elude them. Those with class and community privilege are then perfectly positioned to reap the new profits. It is perhaps unironic that a leader from a barber caste recently wondered whether an occupation confined to them for centuries should not be set aside for them in the present too.

SHAKESPEARE AFTER SHAKESPEARE

Shakespeare, according to my Kannada teacher in high school, was born in India. The Bard, he insisted, was none other than Kalidasa. His claim left me unmoved.

A serious regard for Shakespeare prevailed at home. My father, S.N. Murthy, who had taught English literature before joining the state civil services, was a student of Professor C.D. Narasimhaiah (CDN), the distinguished literary critic who had awakened a critical regard for Shakespeare among generations of students in Mysore. An address CDN made to his students in Mysore in 1966, which appears in his autobiography, *N for Nobody* (1991), offers a glimpse of his passions for the Bard: "For to have laughed with Falstaff and to have suffered with Lear and Cordelia is not only to know the joys of the earth but the secrets of the grave and the felicity of heaven." J.C. Rollo, a British Professor of English at Mysore University (1928-1943), had been "a great teacher" to him. Famous for his classes on Shakespeare, Rollo was well known all over South India. It was due to him, CDN explains, that most colleges in South India continued to use "unabridged Shakespeare."

In an essay, *College Days* (1951), R.K. Narayan, offers a vivid glimpse of Rollo in the classroom: "He created an absolute enchantment with his voice and gesture and movement when he read us Shakespeare; he paced up and down with his text in hand and we saw almost in the flesh Lear and Falstaff and Macbeth, we watched mighty episodes unfolding before our eyes."

Shakespeare had found ardent local subscribers all along. His plays were frequently performed at the Maharaja's College Dramatic

Society (MCDS), which had been founded in 1914 by Thomas Denham, an English Professor of History and Principal of Maharaja College. He had got a new stage built with curtains and side wings. Kerosene lamps lit the stage as electric illumination did not yet exist in the college. The Maharaja and his European guests were occasionally found among the audience at the MCDS. The student troupes were often invited to enact scenes from *As You Like It*, *The Merchant of Venice*, *Much Ado About Nothing*, and *Julius Ceasar* in the palace and gifted special editions of Shakespeare's plays in return. Theatre activities were pursued with greater vigour after Rollo became the head of MCDS.

Local admiration for Shakespeare goes further back in time. Founded by the Maharaja of Mysore in 1881, the Palace Theatre Company spurred the translation of several of his plays into Kannada. The early translations gave local names, settings and illustrations to the ones found in the original. Actors wore locally recognizable costumes as well. Otherwise, theatre historians have observed, they would alienate the local audiences. In any case, the early translations show a keen awareness of the richness of the original plays and a clear confidence in adapting them to local audiences.

Arriving as part of the British colonial enterprise, Shakespeare stood in for the English talent, but he did not remain its symbolic possession.

In the hit melodrama, *Eradu Kanasu* (Two Dreams, 1974), Ramachandra Rao, an English lecturer—played by the superstar, Rajkumar—holds the low priced, thick hardback of the complete works of Shakespeare, that the English Language Book Society published in 1964 to mark the Bard's 400th birth centenary, in several scenes, including the charged evening of the nuptials, where he nervously flips through its pages on sensing his bride approach him from behind. He has married her to please his ill mother and continues to be melancholic about losing the girl he had loved due to her father's opposition.

The book appears in an even more poignant scene, when Rao, dressed in a suit, lectures his students on the last Act of *Romeo and Juliet*. Reading several of Romeo's stirring lines extempore, he translates them into Kannada before interpreting them to the students.

Explaining how the families of the young lovers had placed obstacles in their path, an overwhelmed Rao mistakenly calls Juliet, "Lalitha," the name of his lost love. The students break out in laughter. Realizing the slip, a distraught Rao dismisses the class.

Shakespeare might have smiled at the predicament.

THE LURE OF THE LITERARY

A few years ago, I found myself flipping through the back issues of *The Illustrated Weekly of India* from the 1980s. I had grown up with the *Weekly* and seen its rise and decline under the editorship of Pritish Nandy. My father had got all the issues of the *Weekly* (and *Frontline*) bound since he felt they would make for good reading at any time.

The essays by Claude Alvares, Rajni Kothari, Ashis Nandy and O.V. Vijayan and the cartoons of Mario Miranda still held out a refreshing political sensibility. It was wonderful, too, to notice that Pritish Nandy had carried a translation of a short story, or an excerpt from a novel, originally published in Indian languages in just about every issue. Absolute surprise however had to wait for a short story in English titled, *The Image-Maker* (April 17, 1988), which had appeared with the byline: "An unusual short story from one of the country's greatest sociologists, M.N. Srinivas."

It isn't clear when *The Image-Maker* was written. It is set in Kodigehalli, a village near Mysore where M.N. Srinivas did his fieldwork in the late 1940s and which is more familiar to the world under the pseudonym, Rampura. The narrator of *The Image-Maker*, a sociologist doing fieldwork in a village, reports a story he had heard from Thimma, a priest from a potter caste. In narrating how he became a priest, Thimma offers an account of his loss of faith in God during childhood after his prayers hadn't saved his mother from giving in to cholera and of his regaining that faith when he noticed that one of Lord Ganesha's eyes had closed partially after he had finished making his statue. In making space for the manifestation of a miracle in the world,

Srinivas' complex story disclosed a realm of experience that a secular academic enterprise like sociology cannot partake in in the manner of a believer. His awareness of the intellectual limits that inhere in social research inquiries stayed private though and never surfaced in the corpus of his academic writings.

Srinivas is among the few sociologists in the country who have shown care about their writing style—his prose is usually warm and elegant. R.K. Narayan is said to have urged literary critics to include his most remembered book, *The Remembered Village* (1976), in the canon of Indian writing in English. Srinivas had written this book mostly from memory since his notes and other research materials collected over two decades of fieldwork in Rampura had got destroyed by arsonists protesting the Vietnam war at Stanford in 1970. The result is a book in sociology with the narrative attractions of literary fiction.

Srinivas and Narayan had been friends in Mysore. In his *Indian Society Through Personal Writings* (1996), which is dedicated to Narayan, Srinivas writes: "I am privileged to have been the first to read the typescript of his first novel, *Swami and Friends*. I was lucky to have read it when I was young enough to look at the world through Swami's eyes. I have also had the pleasure of walking the streets of Mysore with Narayan, listening to the stories he was planning to write." He had published his first, and the only other story he wrote, *The Legend on the Wall*, in the debut issue of *Indian Thought*, a journal that Narayan had launched and edited in 1941. Unlike *The Image-Maker*, this story, which features an encounter between an orthodox Brahmin priest and an educated Dalit police officer, expressed rational disdain for the stubbornness of superstitious belief. In a long essay titled, *Bangalore as I See It*, which he termed "an idiosyncratic if not capricious account of the city," Srinivas devotes four pages to discuss the major Kannada writers of his time and their works.

Clearly, Srinivas made time for literature. It is intriguing therefore that his scholarly writings on the themes of caste dominance, sanskritization, modernization and urbanization, to name a few, do not engage literary works anywhere. This avoidance is especially striking since many of the writers in Indian languages of his time were grappling with the very themes that preoccupied him. A plausible explanation is that he took disciplinary boundaries seriously. In his self-conscious quest to establish the academic profession of sociology in India, he might have felt it his responsibility to play by settled boundaries of knowledge creation. In hindsight, the separation of social science from literature, which the work of Srinivas and his colleagues in sociology, helped sustain, seems to have cost our intellectual life dearly. An engagement with the literary works in Indian languages would have likely shaken up the modernist framework of Indian sociology, reshaping its sensibilities and routing its curiosity in novel directions. Social science discussions might then have acquired enhanced appeal in the country. They might have acquired a soul.

IT'S CHRISTMAS!

The excitement of Christmas has never slipped past. Since my school days it has inspired enthusiasm. The festival vibes would become manifest a couple of weeks before Christmas, with the appearance of a Merlin comic strip on the pages of *Deccan Herald*. Soon thereafter, newspaper ads for Christmas cakes, restaurant dinners and greeting cards thickened the sentiments, with the images of Santa Claus and Christmas trees adorned with bells and star-shaped paper lanterns adding to the visual sense. Closer to the festival, the Christmas jingle played softly in some shops and restaurants on MG Road, Brigade Road and Commercial Street. The commercialization of Christmas seen in Bangalore then—and even now, for that matter—was of course nowhere close to the phenomenon found in the West.

In the early 1980s, a chance encounter with the Nilgiri's plum cake with almond icing, which was available only during the Christmas season, got the whole family hooked to it. From then on, I would dutifully make my way to the Nilgiri's store on Brigade Road to pick one up for Christmas day.

At some point in my middle school years, I started attending midnight mass at the St. Thomas Church near home in Jeevan Bimanagar. Done at first out of curiosity more than anything else, these visits became an annual regularity. With the winter evening cold outside, being inside the brightly lit church full of people dressed in their best was a warm affair. Although the liturgical rituals were mystifying, listening to the choir and the midnight mass sermons in Kannada and Tamil was an experience.

Jesus Christ had been a familiar image all through. My kindergarten years were spent at St. Joseph's School in Madikeri. Christ figured among some of the stories that my mother, Subhadra Murthy, who had also studied in a Jesuit school, told me. And, with a desire to instill a humanistic outlook in me, no doubt, my father would occasionally remark that the Buddha, Christ and Mohammed were great historical figures. A student of literature, he also reminded me, at times, that the Bible and Shakespeare had generated a bulk of the figures of speech in the English language.

A Christmas Carol, Charles Dickens' story of the recovery of love for the world was a story I often returned to. The transformation of a miserly misanthrope into a person "as good a friend, as good a master, and as good a man, as the good old city knew, or any other good city, town, borough, in the good old world," is a fable whose narrative and moral force remains undiminished.

I still try to attend midnight mass at a church in my neighbourhood. In recent years, a police vehicle is always parked outside the churches, with weary policemen in crumpled uniform standing guard.

Photocopied handouts with select Biblical hymns and carols are not found at the church entrance these days. Instead, slides with the details of the hymns and carols and the languages in which they will be sung—Kannada, Tamil, Telugu, Malayalam, Konkani, Hindi and English—are projected on a big screen that hangs down from the ceiling, on the left side in the front, above where the choir stands. The non-evocative Kannada renderings of the English hymns has intrigued me. Rev. Ferdinand Kittel, a German missionary, who wrote *Kathamale* (A Garland of Stories, 1862), a book of episodes from Christ's life composed in high quality metrical verse in Kannada, and later compiled the first, and still excellent, modern Kannada dictionary, had laid down an inspiring model of translation.

My encounters with Christmas are generic and unmindful of the rich theological differences seen inside the Christian tradition. But this doesn't affect the spirit of the event. The children, who walk up and down the aisle, dressed as angels, as Joseph and Mary and their donkey, and the energetic choir would have done enough to secure the festive cheer.

THE WORLD OF VILLAGE DEITIES

Siddalingaiah, folklorist and Dalit leader, could talk about village deities for hours. His extensive research and travel within Karnataka had acquainted him intimately with their myths and festivals.

The devotees of a goddess were once keen to build a small temple for her. But the goddess spurned the idea. The perplexed devotees begged her for an explanation. She asked them: "Does everyone have a house?" One of the devotees said he did not have one. She then replied, "I don't want a house until all of you have one."

Village deities cherish freedom. A goddess once discouraged her devotees from building a shrine for her. She wanted to be left free to wander as she pleased whereas the shrine door would restrict her movements. The doorless shrine her devotees then built for her still exists on the outskirts of Bangalore.

The devotees of another goddess, Bisilamma, were also keen to build a shrine for her. The goddess pleaded with them to build one without a roof. She clarified: "I want to shiver in the cold, burn in the sun and get drenched in the rains." Identifying with the hardship of those struggling for shelter, she invited suffering for herself.

Siddalingaiah realized at a young age that the god-human relation was more intimate and humane among the lower castes and villagers. Usually, purohits are the intermediaries between the gods and the upper caste devotees. Only they are allowed inside the inner sanctum of a temple while the devotees offer their respects to the deity from a distance. In contrast, Siddalingaiah observed, the distance between the god and the devotees in folk religion is much less, if not non-existent. There is freedom to scold, criticize and even condemn gods. An elderly person once asked a deity on behalf of the local people: "Where were you all these days? Have you forgotten us?" The goddess retorted, "Is yours the only village? I need to look after the seven worlds. Do you know how difficult my work is?" The elderly person persisted, "We work so hard. Don't you see that?" The goddess shot back, "Am I working any less?"

Deities from different villages can be siblings or enjoy any other kin relation. Siddalingaiah's study, *Grama Devategalu* (Village Deities, 1997), records a story of sister deities. The childless deity, Madduramma, visited her sister, Patalamma, who had a hundred and one children, in the neighbouring village. She wanted to ask her to let her adopt one of her children. On learning of her sister's intentions, Patalamma hid all her children. One of her children, Sidiranna, though, was seen playing outside. Taking this child with her, Madduramma turned all the hidden children into stone. The villagers still worship the stone idols of these children. Sidiranna visits from the neighbouring village to offer respects to his mother first before doing so for his foster mother.

Deities of different castes can be related too. For instance, Kalamma is a deity of the craftsmen, Banashankariamma of the weavers, Hattimaramma of the Dalits: they are all sisters. Anjaneya is their brother in a few villages. Upper castes consider him their deity in some villages.

During festivals, the deities weep when their brothers or sisters do not arrive in time. Until the arrival of her sister, Beechnalliamma, from the neighbouring village, Haleooramma does not take a step at her festival. Festivals are sometimes organized to let sister deities meet.

"Affection, love, and large-heartedness," Siddalingaiah noted, "are the primary qualities of village deities." In the festivals of village deities, different castes come together to celebrate it as a community festival. The central thought behind these festivals is the well-being of all. And, he added, there is the celebration: "the festivals of village deities celebrate the grandness of life."

Urban migrants in cities usually visit their villages for the festival of their deities. In cases where migrant families from the same village live in the same neighbourhood in Bangalore, they arrange for their village deity to visit them in their area.

In the accounts of folk religion that he gathered for the monthly magazine of *Samudaya*, the influential left theatre movement in Karnataka, in the early eighties, which were published later as *Avataragalu* (Incarnations, 1982), Siddalingaiah sought to demystify local religious practices. In Gulbarga district, young women freely abuse a male deity called Kui once a year. And, in Bidar, women line up to thrash a male deity called Nathuram with chappals. Both of these deities, Siddalingaiah explained, were known to have lusted after the wives of other men and now live in fear of their devotees. Making the gods a part of the social world and denying them their divine status is another of his logical attempts at unmasking religious life as a worldly affair, as a social delusion. In the past, Siddalingaiah noted, it was common to see gold coins falling out of Lakshmi's hands. In recent times, rupee notes have taken the place of the gold coins. If the coins and rupees are phased out of the economy, he writes, there can be no doubt that cheque books will fall out of the Goddess' hands. Again: Gods address the lower-class individuals in the singular, and the rich with terms of respect. This sort of conduct, Siddalingaiah wrote, is seen in police stations. What then is the difference between the police and our Gods?

Folk religious practices left Siddalingaiah puzzled at times. After possessing a devotee, a deity called Doddaswamy would start whistling with his fingers in his mouth. His devotees are expected to address him only through whistles. Another deity from Gulbarga district, Gajalakshmi, expected her devotees to bare all their teeth in her presence.

I have translated below, in shortened form, a few of my favourite accounts of village deities found in Siddalingaiah's *Avataragalu*.

*

In Aradavalli village, a devotee was greatly disappointed that his God hadn't granted his wishes. His disappointment soon turned into anger. He ground dried chillies into a powder and carried it with him to the deity's temple. "God hasn't solved my problems. I'll make him suffer now. I'll rub chilli powder on his body." He threatened those who tried to dissuade him. "I'll rub this on your faces if you try to stop me." His resolve pained many of the devotees. While a few became curious about what might transpire, a few others could barely hold back their tears.

After reaching the temple, the aggrieved devotee stepped inside and began to rub the chilli powder all over the deity's idol. Within moments, someone outside started howling in pain. The frightened devotees soon realized that the deity had possessed one among them. They held him tightly, "Who are you?"

God: "Me?! I'm the God who is being attacked with chilli powder."

Devotees: "What do you want from us?"

God: "Stop putting chilli powder on me!"

Devotees: "Why?"

God: "It hurts a lot!"

Aggrieved Devotee (AD): "You said you would help me. Why didn't you keep your word?"

God: "Stop hurting me first. I'll take care of your problem later."

AD: "You are lying."

God: "I'm God. I never lie."

AD: "I don't believe you! I'll put some more chilli powder on you."

God: "I can't bear this pain anymore."

AD: "I'll give you one more week."

God: "Guaranteed! Stop rubbing the chilli powder!"

The possessed spirit slowly took leave. Everyone made their way home with much joy and relief. The discovery of a new way of having their wishes fulfilled also filled them with a secret delight.

*

A Dalit neighbourhood in Bangalore had once organized a ceremony for Goddess Annamma from the Majestic area. Revered and feared by her devotees, she was often invited by various neighbourhoods. It cost thousands of rupees to have her visit from her temple in Majestic.

The evening was grand and festive. The entire neighbourhood was decked up for the ceremonious occasion. Every household was filled with joy. The devotees surrounded the goddess with lamps. While the stately goddess sat under a pandal on the main road, everyone was scurrying around, attending to some task or another. Hundreds of people partook of the ceremony that began at ten in the night. The celebrations continued all night.

Around four in the morning, a man was seen rushing towards the deity. His eyes were wild. He was gnashing his teeth.

The devotees somehow managed to hold him back. It soon became clear that another deity, Village Annamma, had possessed him. He then ran towards the Kabaddi ground opposite the main road. The others followed him as he led them to a small shrine in a corner of this ground. It had been built with four small stone slabs. A small stone planted on the ground inside this shrine was the idol of Village Annamma.

Village Annamma (VA): "Fools! Have you forgotten me?"

Devotees: "No, we haven't! Can we ever forget you?"

VA: "You haven't come to me in so long. And now, all this special attention on the bitch from Majestic!"

Devotees: "Please forgive our mistake, mother. We will give you your due soon."

VA: "Don't I see how you are paying your due to me? I'll show you what I can do!"

Devotees: "Please don't punish us. We are your children, all said and done."

The devotees quickly set about tidying her shrine. They offered her a cock in sacrifice. The Goddess was placated somewhat at their response.

At this time, Majestic Annamma possessed a devotee. She rushed towards Village Annamma's shrine, "I'm a city deity. All the village deities should be under my control. Who is that speaking against me?"

The devotees were bewildered. Restraining Majestic Annamma wasn't easy.

A scuffle between the two deities followed. A little later, the person whom Village Annamma had possessed was found with his teeth broken and the one possessed by Majestic Annamma was in tattered clothes.

*

In Srirampura, God Muneshwara possessed a man regularly. He had numerous devotees.

An elderly devotee would visit him every week to seek his help to solve a problem faced by his son. Before taking leave, he would give two rupees as a token offering. One day, the deity became furious, "Two rupees won't do!"

Devotee: "What is this? I've always offered you two rupees."

Deity: "Dirty fellow! I've no choice but to ask for a bigger offering. Put down three rupees at least."

Devotee: "Why raise it all of a sudden?"

Deity (roared): "Why raise it?! Any idea how much a kg of rice costs? Do you know the cost of kerosene these days? Even a cinema ticket costs a lot now. If you only offer two rupees, how can I lead my life?"

Devotee (searching his pockets): "I see your point, my Lord."

*

Kariyamma, a deity in Chikmagalur, asked her devotees for a pen and some paper. She wanted to write a letter to her elder brother, Lord Manjunatha at Dharmasthala. The devotees never knew that the deity had a brother. She hit back, "What had you thought of me? I've relatives all over. Even in far off places like Bengaluru and Bombay."

The deity made a series of scratch marks on the paper. She would pause to think before making each one of those marks. After the letter was done, it was mailed to Lord Manjunatha at Dharmasthala. The devotees were delighted to see a letter passing between Gods. A reply from Dharmasthala arrived two weeks later. The deity was jubilant. Everyone gathered to read the letter. The reply turned out to be brief: "Please send a letter only if you can write in Kannada. Do not send meaningless scratch marks."

The deity had wished to brag that she was literate. After this episode, she kept out of letter writing altogether.

*

Never high-decibel, and always gentle, affectionate and witty, Siddalingaiah's accounts of folk religion end up being a moving experience more than anything else. Since his early writings on village goddesses, he came to show less interest in viewing religion as a cover for social games and care more for the deeper meanings behind it.

In an interview I did with him several years ago, Siddalingaiah explained: "Mockery was central to *Avataragalu*. Because of my rationalist background, I used to make fun of gods for a few years. But I don't think like that anymore. For example, people suddenly start lashing themselves with a whip. I would have probably made fun of this earlier. I would like to look at it differently now. This person is inflicting self-violence (*sva-himse*). Why is he doing this? What are its origins? I would ask such questions now."

MODERNITY ON TRIAL

TALES OF MODERN MYTHOLOGY

A foreign country sought the legendary engineer and Dewan of Mysore, Sir M. Visvesvaraya's assistance in building a dam. He however was willing to offer it only on the condition that India's map be displayed near the dam site: the involvement of an Indian in the dam project needed to be publicly acknowledged. The foreign client did not agree. Sir M.Visvesvaraya (Sir MV), however, assented. After the dam was built, the client asked him, "How did you agree to work for us even when we didn't accept your condition?" Sir MV replied, "Come with me. I would like to show you something." He took his client in a helicopter and let him have an aerial view of the dam. The letters, I-N-D-I-A, were written into the dam's upper surface!

*

Another foreign country sought Sir MV's help in building a dam across a turbulent river. The force of the river flow had made it difficult for them to build one. Sir MV accepted the request. He started getting a dam built beside the river. His clients were confused: "Why are you building it there?" Sir MV only counseled patience. After the dam was built, he got dynamite installed in strategic places around it. When the dynamites exploded, the dam shifted up in the air and settled down over the river. The incredible feat amazed everyone!

*

Before taking up his appointment as Dewan of Mysore, Sir MV convened a meeting of all his family members and told them, "I will accept the appointment only if you promise to never ask me for official favours." The relatives agreed to abide by his request. Sir MV now felt comfortable about becoming the Dewan.

*

During his entire career, Sir MV carried two pens on him, one of which belonged to the government and the other to him. He always used the former pen for office work and the latter for personal work.

*

On one of his visits to his native village, Sir MV was asked to give an impromptu speech at the local school. Never one to speak without prior preparation, he felt later that his speech had not gone well. He did not rest content until he went back to that school with a fully prepared speech.

*

During a visit to Bangalore, Nehru arrived at Sir MV's home an hour ahead of their meeting time. Sir MV refused to meet him as he had planned to be dressed for the meeting only by the scheduled meeting time.

*

When Sir MV died, many foreign countries were eager to buy his brain. They were in fact willing to pay any amount for it, but our government flatly refused.

My teacher in middle school had shared these tales in class. Her narration was so vivid and self-sure that they have still stayed with me. She recounted another tale, which did not involve the figure of Sir MV, but belonged to his world, no doubt:

An Indian and a Japanese man bought sugarcane on the railway platform before boarding a train. The Indian chewed on his sugarcane and spat it out after sucking in the juice. The Japanese man however carefully peeled off the sugarcane rinds with his teeth and kept them aside. The Indian was repulsed to see him retain something that had come in contact with his mouth. When he got off the train, he was taken aback to see that the Japanese man had made tiny toy umbrellas with the sugarcane rind and was looking to sell them!

These tales bear memories of course of India's tortuous encounters with Western modernity. The boastful tales of Sir MV's technical wizardry are countering the old Western accusation that non-Westerners were lacking in matters of science and technology. The other tales strive to convey the essential values for modern society: punctuality, official probity and prior preparation were necessary virtues and nepotism in office a vice; and, the ritual hang-ups about contact with saliva, which pre-empted the creation of economic value out of the sugarcane rind, were better laid to rest. And it is not a coincidence that the Indian saw a Japanese man in the train, and not someone from any other country. Deeply admired in colonial India, Japan was an Asian country that had not been colonized and seen to have done very well therefore in matters of economy and technology. Its defeat of Russia in 1905 refuted the claim of the superiority of the West and projected Japan as a model worthy of emulation for Asian countries.

The tales recalled above probably circulate less in schools nowadays. But if we look around, their narrative partners are everywhere.

OF HUSTLING AND OTHER
SUCH SEDUCTIONS

Sir M Visvesvaraya (Sir MV) travelled a lot during his long life (1860-1962). Getting a hold on India's problems was a primary preoccupation of his travels.

During a visit to the United States of America in 1920, Sir MV's friends arranged a meeting with Herbert Hoover, the US Secretary of Commerce, and later US President, in Washington, DC. He recalled asking him what he thought was wrong in India and why my countrymen were so backward." Hoover had a ready diagnosis: "You people have no hustle in you." Narrating this episode of civilizational dimension in his autobiography, *Memoirs of my Working Life* (1951), Sir MV clarifies that this remark "meant, of course, that Indians were slow, sleepy and easy-going."

In his address to the Mysore Chamber of Commerce, in 1927, Sir MV recalled a lengthier and more severe version of Hoover's remark: "I cannot speak hopefully of India's future. You do not seem to feel you have to hustle to make a living." He then followed up with his own grave comments: "The tragedy of the whole situation is summed up in the absence of this 'hustle.' Hustle implies love of initiative, a craving to invent, and a desire to push forward and advance. It is for lack of this quality that we are where we are…"

For Sir MV, Hoover's word "hustle," which held up entrepreneurial pushiness as a virtue that let people thrive in the United States, perfectly captured what he had known all along. If India had not achieved economic progress, he held, the habits of its people had a lot do with it: they were not punctual; they were not disciplined; they did not work throughout the year. He did not recognize that the habits he cherished had emerged through a violent process of industrialization.

Sir MV's comparative lessons though did provoke local imagination. Here's a sample of local reportage from 1927: "Sir MV asked his countrymen to adopt a policy of hustle and action…the traditional apathy of the East has been replaced in Japan and China by the Western character of 'hustle' and action. And what those countries have done, countries like India including Mysore, can also do."

The conversation between Sir MV and Hoover had traded powerful falsehoods of the time: the people in the West were industrious and disciplined while those in the East were lazy and undisciplined. The East therefore had lessons to learn from the West if it wanted to become modern. And colonial rule was truly helpful in this matter. In all of this frenzied drama, the educated Indian elite rarely wondered whether the colonial claims might be spurious.

But the drama has not ended.

A doctor friend once observed that Abdul Kalam had helped her see a basic truth: "India will develop when people learn to stand in line." The temptation to view an alleged personality deficit as *the* single cause behind the problems of the country continues to be great. Indian Prime Ministers have asked on occasion that Indians give up the *chalta hai* attitude if they wished to see a developed India. This style of catch-phrase causal thought can hold innocent acts guilty. A whole range of activities where people show tolerance and sympathy and get along somehow can seem culpable of the *chalta hai* attitude. An obsession with discipline and order all too easily clears the path for high-handed action.

The models of development that identify cultural habits as an obstacle are better put on trial first. And not the other way around.

FARMERS IN THE MODERN IMAGINATION

Images of rural society in colonial India held Indian villages as historically unchanging and backward. Rooted in social evolutionist ideas, which held that *all* societies moved from being agricultural to industrial, these images saw local villagers as ignorant and lacking in reason and who resisted scientific methods and new farm technologies. The idea that industrial progress was the inevitable destiny of all societies guided the work of the agriculture departments. In this understanding, England and America had reached the end point of the historical timeline.

For the British, establishing private property in land was a necessity to bring about capital accumulation. To achieve this aim, 'primitive' ideas and customs had to be overcome and a new society with utilitarian principles built.

Why did the figure of the Indian farmer—always male—pose a problem in the utilitarian view? He did not have a strictly economic relation to land. He was willing to pay tax on even uncultivated land but would not consider selling it. Considerations of dignity and family honour, attachment to ancestral land, and hope of better days prevented the local farmer from viewing land as merely property the way people did in 'enlightened' countries. Further, the farmer did not use his 'time and energy' all through the year. In this view of time as a resource, a farmer ought to employ his time 'profitably' to maximize his earnings.

In the official view, local agricultural methods were old fashioned and not very productive. Farmers lacked a calculative attitude in another sphere as well: they did not keep accounts of their transactions and crop returns. Keeping accounts, the agriculture officers held, would give them a better idea of whether their 'business' was paying or not.

The figure of the farmer, in short, conveyed so many challenges for achieving the goals of agricultural development. For several decades, the agriculture departments across colonial India wished to reform the farmer: make him learn accounting, adopt new implements, raise 'improved' cattle, among others. There was little recognition that the farmers might be rational in their own way, and have their own intelligence to offer.

The world of folk stories and songs offered different images of the farmers all along: they are hard working, they are wise, they are responsible. The official and the non-official images of farmers though ran parallel, with little contact. A century later, the divide continues to persist, with the narrow technocratic and economic attitude of the government and the agri-business sector having much, much more power than before. The suicides of nearly 400,000 farmers and agricultural labourers over the last three decades reveal the catastrophic policy indifference towards the fate of rural India. Two years ago, tens of thousands of farmers had to sit in protest outside New Delhi for twelve months to be heard by the government.

THE SRINIKETAN EXPERIMENT OF TAGORE

Not nearly as known as his work at Shantiniketan, Rabindranath Tagore's work at Sriniketan shows his reform passions towards rural society. Founded at Sriniketan in 1922, the Institute of Rural Reconstruction (IRR) was his attempt to put to work his ideas on 'village reconstruction'. His stint as a manager of his family's agricultural estates in East Bengal in the 1890s, Tagore recalled, had allowed a "town-bred" individual like himself to recognize the "sorrow and poverty of villagers."

Released in Pabna (now in Bangladesh) in 1906, Tagore's 15-point Village Reconstruction Charter saw the ideal of village autonomy running through its entire canvas: it was necessary to use "indigenously made goods"; all village disputes had to be settled internally through a process of village arbitration; a community grain bank was necessary to guard against famines. Further, in a clear gesture of regard for women's autonomy, the Charter asked that "housewives" be trained in a trade that enhanced the family income.

In desiring autonomy for villages, Tagore didn't wish that they remain isolated. It was necessary for "brotherhood" to evolve between "hamlets, villages and districts."

Several of Tagore's concerns reflected the village reform imagination prevalent at the time. Colonial officials and reform-minded Indians were also asking that science and history be taught in village schools and that demographic data be compiled meticulously for every village. A few of Tagore's concerns though were unique. His Charter, for instance, valued harmony between communities and asked that the essence of all religions be taught in schools.

The IRR was founded on the seven acres of land that Tagore bought near Shantiniketan in 1912. At his encouragement, his son, Ratindranath Tagore, his brother-in-law and a friend's son studied agriculture and dairy farming at the University of Illinois, Urbana, in the United States. Unfortunately, the three of them came down with malaria upon their return to Sriniketan and could not continue to work there. Tagore then invited Leonard Elmhirst, an Englishman who had studied agricultural economics at Cornell University to help build the IRR. Elmhirst did much of the founding work on the IRR between 1921 and 1923. He also helped get an American philanthropist to extend financial support for the nascent rural institute. At his request, his American Quaker friends sent a doctor who worked for three years to control malaria in the villages near Sriniketan. Other idealists from inside and outside the country joined in the work at Sriniketan over the years.

The work at IRR unfolded through various departments. The education department included a school for boys above eight years from all castes and a school for training teachers in music, agriculture and hygiene. Both the students and teachers had to learn a village craft. The agriculture department experimented with new crops and held demonstrations of their work for local farmers. It also tried to promote modern animal husbandry. In order to help supplement local incomes, the industries department introduced new cottage industries. The village welfare department, whose work covered fifteen villages, focused on issues of road, tank and school maintenance and also ran a circulating library. A weaver's co-operative was founded at Sriniketan in the mid-1930s. Picnics, games, theatre and socio-religious activities were also organized to combine work with joy.

The local zamindars are known to have been indifferent to Sriniketan while the responses of the small farmers and artisans to it remain unclear.

Tagore's early experiment in village reform awaits close research. Modest in relation to the scope of Gandhi's efforts to mobilize rural India through khadi and other measures for achieving self-reliance in villages, his work however shares a rare and valuable vision of symbiosis between cities and villages. His 1924 essay, *City and Village*, offers a wild elaboration of that vision.

The villages and the city will see "harmonious interactions," Tagore wrote, when communities do not wholly subordinate individuals or when individuals break their bonds with communities. Villages supply "food and health and fellow-feeling" to cities and the cities share in return "gifts of wealth, knowledge and energy." The rapacious materialistic civilization, which "maintains constant feasts for a whole population of gluttons," had undermined the unity between the cities and villages. It had "shut the gate of hospitality" and done away with the "social responsibility" that was tied to the possession of wealth in the past. The possession of wealth was an opportunity for self-sacrifice. In the past, Tagore observed, "most of the public works of the country were voluntarily supported by the rich."

Only the ideals of co-operation and self-sacrifice, for Tagore, enabled a mutually supportive relation between the cities and villages. He contrasted the figures of Kubera and Goddess Lakshmi to distinguish the wealth of olden days from that of modern cities: Kubera, whose "figure is ugly and gross with its protuberant belly," stood for the pursuit of wealth without moral responsibility, whereas Lakshmi symbolized prosperity for all and only dwelt "in that property which, though belonging to the individual, generously owns its obligation to the community." In modern cities, Tagore rued, Kubera had displaced Lakshmi and become their "presiding deity." And, unlike the towns seen in Kalidasa's play, *Meghaduta*, which expressed the "love and hope of man," modern cities lacked "a central spirit of Unity." Delhi and Agra, he added, "were a product of "the self-respect of man."

The prospect of high profits through machine production had turned urban individuals greedy. Not contributing to the village and luring villagers to work in factories, the cities were draining the villages: "The artificial lights of the town are ablaze—lights that have no connection with sun, moon or star—but the humble lamps of the village are dead."

For Tagore, the key aims of village reform included making villagers become self-reliant and self-respecting and free of fatalistic beliefs. Referring to the work in Sriniketan, he stated: "Our object is to try to flood the choked bed of village life with happiness. For this, the scholars, poets, the musicians, the artists have to collaborate."

An apocalyptic scenario set on the moon helped Tagore stress the ecological side of the crisis in the world. He often imagined, he wrote, that life appeared on the moon before it did on the earth. Like the earth, the moon "had her constant festival of colour, music, movement." However, the arrival of a race endowed with "a furious energy of intelligence," and "animal spirit," which "began greedily to devour its surroundings," ended life on it: "They exhausted the water, cut down the trees, reduced the surface of the planet into a desert riddled with pits… At last, one day, like a fruit whose pulp has been completely eaten by insects which it sheltered, the moon became a lifeless shell. My imaginary selenites behave exactly in the way that human beings are today behaving on this earth."

The dreams of an urban future engulf the contemporary policy imagination. Indeed, an economist committed to a future for rural India is hard to come by. Exposing the violence and obscenity of this state of affairs, Tagore's vision asks that the ideals of village self-reliance and of city-village co-operation firmly belong in our imaginations of the future.

THE SECURE SELVES OF THE PAST

Episode 1

During the construction work on the ambitious and dreamlike Krishnarajasagara (KRS) Dam across the river Cauvery, in the second decade of the twentieth century, the workers found a tablet with a Persian inscription. Tipu Sultan, the legendary ruler of Mysore (1750-1799), had issued it in 1794.

The English translation of the inscription reads thus:

YAFATTAH!
IN THE NAME OF GOD, THE COMPASSIONATE,
THE MERCIFUL.

ON THE 29TH OF THE MONTH TAQI OF THE SOLAR YEAR SHADAB 1221, ONE THOUSAND TWO HUNDRED AND TWENTY ONE, DATING FROM MOWLOOD OF MUHAMMED (MAY HIS SOUL REST IN PEACE) ON MONDAY AT DAWN BEFORE SUNRISE UNDER THE AUSPICES OF THE PLANET VENUS. IN THE CONSTELLATION TARUS, HAZRATH TIPPOO SULTAN, THE SHADOW OF GOD, THE LORD, THE BESTOWER OF GIFTS LAID THE FOUNDATION OF THE MOHYI DAM ACROSS THE RIVER CAUVERY TO THE WEST OF THE CAPITAL, BY THE GRACE OF GOD AND THE ASSISTANCE OF THE HOLY PROPHET, THE CALIPHS OF THE WORLD, AND THE EMPEROR OF THE UNIVERSE. THE START IS FROM ME BUT ITS COMPLETION RESTS WITH GOD.

ON THE DAY OF COMMENCEMENT THE PLANETS, MOON, SUN, VENUS, NEPTUNE, WERE IN THE SIGN ARIES IN A LUCKY CONJUNCTION.

BY THE HELP OF GOD, THE MOST HIGH, MAY THE ABOVE MENTIONED DAM REMAIN UNTIL THE DAY OF RESURRECTION LIKE THE FIXED STARS. THE MONEY AMOUNTING TO SEVERAL LAKHS WHICH THE

GOD-GIVEN GOVERNMENT HAVE SPENT IS SOLELY IN THE SERVICE OF GOD. APART FROM THE OLD CULTIVATIONS, ANY ONE DESIROUS OF NEWLY CULTIVATING THE ARABLE LAND SHOULD IN THE NAME OF GOD BE EXEMPTED FROM VARIOUS KINDS OF PRODUCTION WHETHER OF CORN OR FRUITS, OF THE ONE FOURTH PART LEVIED GENERALLY FROM OTHER SUBJECTS. HE WILL ONLY HAVE TO PAY 3/4 OF IT TO THE BENIGN GOVERNMENT. HE WHO NEWLY CULTIVATES THE ARABLE LAND, HIMSELF, HIS POSTERITY AND OTHER RELATIVES WILL BE THE MASTERS OF THE ABOVE AS LONG AS EARTH AND HEAVEN ENDURE. IF ANY PERSON WERE TO CAUSE ANY OBSTRUCTION OR BE A PREVENTER OF THIS PERPETUAL BENEVOLENCE, SUCH AN INHUMAN BEING IS TO BE REGARDED AS THE ENEMY OF MAN-KIND, AS THE ACCURSED SATAN AND THE SPERMA HOMMIS OF THOSE CULTIVATORS, NAY OF THE ENTIRE CREATION.

On the inaugural occasion of the KRS dam in 1932, Nalvadi Krishnaraja Wadiyar, the Maharaja of Mysore (1884-1940), had this inscription installed along with its Kannada and English translations on the walls of the arched entrance doorway to the new dam.

Episode 2

In 1932, the farmers of Mandya protested the new irrigation scheme launched after the KRS dam was built. They found the water charges high and the scheme's rotational scheme of using water impractical. *Baduku-Melaku* (1974), the memoirs of Veeranna Gowda, the chief leader of the protest, which later came to be known as the Irwin Canal Agitation, contains a valuable account of the struggle against the new irrigation scheme.

On learning that Dewan Sir Mirza Ismail had planned a secret visit to Mandya to discuss the irrigation scheme with a few local landlords who were likely to yield to the state's proposals, the leaders of the struggle urged the farmers from the surrounding areas to convene in Mandya during the Dewan's visit. Around ten thousand farmers had gathered there by the time of the Dewan's arrival.

The farmer leaders printed and distributed thousands of copies of the Kannada translation of Tipu's 1794 Persian inscription found at the entrance of the KRS dam. The Kannada translation of this inscription renders it within a local cultural idiom. "God," for example, becomes "Bhagavantha" and "inhuman being" is translated as "kroorathma (cruel soul)". The Latin phrase, "sperma hommis," is dropped altogether, owing perhaps to the lack of an equivalent local term.

The protestors found Tipu's inscription valuable, Veeranna Gowda explains, as it declared that the farmers availing the irrigation facilities in the area surrounding the KRS dam were to pay tax on only 12 annas for every rupee they earned (16 annas = 1 rupee) while it was the state's dharma to waive the tax on the remaining 4 annas "in the name of God." On the protest occasion, the farmers had offered a powerful reminder of a former ruler's commitment to the present ruler.

THE MYTH OF A SINGLE HOME

In *The Story of the Namdharis*, an essay written in 1922, a Christian missionary noted: "One matter of great interest is the fact that this community has already been converted twice." He was referring to the peasant caste—now familiar as Vokkaligas—which lived in the densely forested Malnad area in Karnataka.

The Vokkaligas in these parts of Malnad are known to have embraced Jainism in the 8th century after a Jain monastery was founded at Humcha, Shivamogga district. Were they a caste or a tribe previously? We cannot be certain.

As we know, Jainism forbids its members from practising agriculture as land cultivation hurts worms and insects in the soil. The Malnad Vokkaligas however became Jains without giving up agriculture. And hunting, fishing and drinking alcohol remained cherished habits. The orthodox Jains considered them inferior as a result.

In the 12th century, Ramanujacharya, the Sri Vaishnava philosopher, sought refuge under the Hoysala rulers of Mysore. The hostility of the Shiva-worshipping Cholas had posed a threat to his life. Myth has it that Bitti Deva, the Hoysala ruler, switched from his Jain faith to the Sri Vaishnava faith after Ramanujacharya cured his daughter of an illness. His then took on a new name, Vishnuvardhana ('the one who elevates the name of Vishnu').

The Hoysala patronage to Sri Vaishnavism made the Jain agriculturists of Malnad move over to the new faith. The discrimination by the orthodox Jains may have also mattered. Their new caste name, Namadhari Vokkaligas, refers to the new practice of wearing a *nama* on their foreheads. They set aside a portion of the ritual food for their Jain ancestors during festivals even now.

*

Palkuriki Somanatha's *Basava Purana*, a 13th century text on the life and times of Basava, the founder of Lingayat dharma, is replete with stories affirming Shiva's superiority over Vishnu. In these frequently violent accounts, the heads of those who don't believe in Shiva are cut off, or their temples destroyed, with unbelievable ease. Unlikely to be real life accounts, they offer a sample however of the imaginations of violence among rival faiths in medieval India. It is no surprise, that V. Narayana Rao's English translation of *Basava Purana* is titled, *Siva's Warriors*.

Rao explains that Somanatha's narrative conformed to the guidelines that Panditaradhya, another Shaiva poet, had laid down in *Sivatattvasaramu* such as (a) "One should not commit violence towards any living being, but yet the sinners who abuse Siva must be killed without hesitation" and (b) "Books that include words accusing Siva should immediately be burned without hesitation and their authors should be killed."

The Shaiva-Vaishnava rivalry was bitter throughout medieval times, their competition for converts intense.

In Lingayat philosophy, devotion to Shiva alone matters, not caste hierarchy. Various Lingayat mathas converted different castes into their faith in medieval times. Ironically, the effort to transcend caste differences later saw the emergence of the Lingayat caste. The matter however is not settled here. The seven decades old demand of several Lingayat mathas that the Indian government view them as a separate religion and not club them with Hinduism is still alive.

The banality of how religious conversion is talked about these days is truly embarrassing. The experience of conversion varies profoundly across different faiths, i.e., in terms of the changes seen in the outward and inner aspects of one's life and the freedom one has towards one's former faith. For instance, the Namdhari Vokkaligas retained their meat-eating and hunting habits while they moved across two faiths that shunned animal killing whereas vegetarianism stayed non-negotiable for the Lingayat converts.

Castes have lived in *ghars* (homes) we can never know about, renovated them, rebuilt them, and moved to new *ghars* at times, with or without their old belongings. Really, there is no one ghar in Hinduism or, for that matter, in any other religion. Any talk of *ghar vapasi* ('return home'), where Christian and Muslim converts are asked to return to their "original home of Hinduism" should make little sense.

A DIFFERENT JOURNEY FOR MILLETS?

On their way back to Ayodhya, after the victory in Lanka, Rama and his army stopped by the ashrama of the sage, Gautama. The sage served his guests several dishes made from nine different grains.

After finishing his meal, Rama asked Hanuman, "Which among these grains is the most excellent?"

Hanuman replied, "Every dish was delicious. To find an answer to your question, each of the grains will have to be examined closely." Bringing out the nine different grains, at Rama's request, Gautama singled out *ragi* (finger millet) as the most excellent of them all. Slighted by his judgement, the rice grain objected, "You know the essence of all religions. We have enormous respect for you. How can you slight me and a grain like wheat and view ragi as superior?"

The rice grain then turned to ragi in anger: "Are you my equal? A low-born like you have been elevated in front of Rama." The rice grain's scornful words presumed throughout that it was the food of the rich and ragi was that of the poor.

Ragi retorted, "You have maligned me without a sense for decent conduct in a gathering. You don't deserve a reply."

Unable to resolve the dispute, Rama had the rice and ragi put in prison for a test of endurance. After six months, he summoned them to Ayodhya. Indra and the other gods were present at the court.

Ragi had stayed fresh and vigorous whereas the rice grain had gone stale. Indra himself declared ragi the winner.

This is a brief summary of course of the sixteenth century saint, Kanakadasa's famous poem, *Rama Dhanya Charite*. The dispute between rice and ragi powerfully symbolizes the social tensions between the privileged and the non-privileged castes. Food appears here as an arena of social struggle, and not an innocent means of satisfying hunger.

Ragi triumphed in Kanakadasa's poem but its status in the real world has remained insecure. Ragi might evoke a deep emotional bond between their region, food and social identity for many castes in Southern Karnataka and in neighbouring areas in Andhra and Tamil Nadu, but rice has stayed the superior crop. The latter fetches more money; it is the preferred crop wherever irrigation is found; it is the default grain in restaurants in towns and cities. Further, most upper castes abstain from eating ragi. The white colour of rice has also mattered in keeping the status of the dark-brown ragi low. And, adding harsh irony to the grain rivalry, even the ragi eaters prefer rice dishes on festive occasions.

New allies have rallied behind millets in recent years, moving the rice-ragi dynamic to another phase. Nutritionists praise the high protein, calcium and iron content of ragi and other millets. The low cholesterol content of millets is making them seem ideal for combating diabetics and obesity. Newly awakened to the harms of gluten, the diet-conscious note with relief that millets are free from it. And, since millets grow in dry regions, ecologists see them as a valuable alternative to water-dependent food crops. They can withstand the threat of climate change too. It has taken the ills of modern life to bring a positive aura around millets.

Ragi and other millets were of course never without loyal enthusiasts. Several decades ago, "Ragi" Lakshmanaiah, a brilliant self-taught seed specialist in Mandya, created a variety of ragi seeds that could be sown in diverse climatic conditions.

A few years ago, Krishna Byregowda, the agriculture minister of Karnataka and a dear friend, showed an ardent commitment to create durable demand for millets across the state. Regretting that millets are routinely termed "coarse grains" and *truna dhanya* ("worthless grains,"), he sought to undo the enormous policy and research neglect towards them. His ministry offered higher prices to procure ragi and jowar from farmers and included them—for the first time—in the Public Distribution System. A chief aim of Krishna's campaign was to find novel culinary applications for millets like *ragi, navane, araka, sajje, korale,* among others, both in familiar local dishes and snacks as well as in newer food items like pizza and pasta: the millets should appeal to the palates of the better off and the not-so-better off, of the younger and the older generations.

When high prices weren't keeping the health-conscious ones away from expensive imported grains like oats and quinoas, Krishna felt that the equally virtuous local millets deserved better. He organized an ambitious trade fair in Bengaluru where farmers' groups met private companies, and food processing firms met retailers, and curious members of the public got a sense of the many uses of millets. His efforts inspired the Central Government to declare 2018 the National Year of the Millets which then laid the path for it to ask the United Nations to declare 2023 as the International Year of the Millets.

Will the new regard for millets mean good news for dryland farmers? Will the cities show more care for the villages? Will the visions of the powerless fare better in the modern world? The centuries old struggle between ragi and rice puts these questions at the centre of the table.

PROTEST IN INDIAN TRADITION

In the afternoon of December 26, 1810, around twenty thousand people deserted Benares and sat on a *dharna* outside the city. A new tax on houses and shops that the British had imposed on them, they had felt, was unfair.

A group of protestors had gathered a few days earlier but the British had dispersed them. The protestors' resolve showed a different strength now. The various Hindu and Muslim communities took an oath to cease work until the new tax was lifted. The blacksmiths, the barbers, the weavers, the tailors, the palanquin bearers and boatmen, all of them stopped work. The effects were soon visible. Without the priests to do the cremation rites, for instance, corpses were being thrown into the Ganga.

The protestors berated and penalized those hesitant to join them. The police could do little to protect them. A few who withdrew from the *dharna* were ostracized from their communities.

The blacksmiths, who had turned up in large numbers, kept up the pressure. Their refusal to work made things difficult for a large number of farmers: new implements for cultivation and harvesting couldn't be got nor the old ones get fixed.

Taking an oath not to disperse, the protestors sent a moral decree to every village in the province, asking all the families to send a member each to join them. Several thousand blacksmiths, farmers and weavers left their villages and joined the *dharna*.

Members of every community at the *dharna* joined in to help buy firewood, oil and other provisions needed to sustain the protest. They also raised a substantial sum of money to support those whose families depended on their daily work. Besides, the various religious orders did their fullest to keep the protestors united.

The protestors did not take to violence at any point. Being unarmed, they were certain that the British would not use violence against them.

Eight days later, the British succeeded in dispersing those sitting in *dharna*. The police seized the boats lying unused and made them government property. They cracked down on the traders supplying essential provisions to the *dharna* site and were especially brutal towards those recruiting protestors from the villages. Under pressure from the British, many landlords asked their farm labourers to return to their estates.

Shaken by the *dharna*—Patna, Saran, Murshidabad and Bhagalpur had also seen protests, albeit on a smaller scale—the British however exempted a few religious orders and the very poor in Benares from the new tax and did not impose it in new areas.

*

My retelling of the above episode draws from the British official correspondence at the time, which the Gandhian scholar, Dharampal, has compiled in his valuable book, *Civil Disobedience in Indian Tradition* (1971). These documents, which he found during his research at the India Office Library, London, in the mid-1960s offered support for an observation found in Gandhi's *Hind-Swaraj* (1909): "In India the nation at large has generally used passive resistance in all departments of life. We cease to cooperate with our rulers when they displease us." Besides Thoreau, Ruskin and Tolstoy, whose influence is acknowledged in *Hind-Swaraj*, Gandhi's philosophy of civil disobedience drew from his awareness of it as a living presence in Indian society.

The *dharna* that the British could only view as sedition, Dharampal notes, would have been morally intelligible to Indian rulers. Unlike the modern state, which only expects full compliance with the law and greets any non-compliance with penalty, the philosophy of civil disobedience sees the rulers and the ruled in a relation of mutual engagement and not in a frozen the-State-versus-the-People binary where the commands of the former are mechanically obeyed by the latter. It asks political authority to be sensitive to social suffering and stay open to revising its own conduct. Rather than a sign of weakness, this moral attitude emanates care, creativity and wisdom.

SCENES FROM
NOW AND THEN

SRI RAGHAVENDRA SWAMY AND
THE NAWAB OF ADONI

Asadullah Khan, the Nawab of Adoni, was enjoying himself in the company of women in his palace. A messenger interrupted them, "Dewan Venkanna wishes to see you." The women quickly exited the chamber.

"What news do you bring, Dewan-ji?" asked the Nawab.

"A messenger of God has come from heaven."

"Who? Mohammed Paigambar?!"

"No, his name is Guru Raghavendra Swamy."

"Ha, ha, ha! Not all maulvis and sanyasis are great souls. Anyway, give him something and send him away."

The visitor, the Dewan explained, was not an ordinary mortal. He had, he clarified, helped many people overcome their difficulties. "You must see him at least once and get his blessings. That's all I wish for."

The Nawab remained skeptical. "You people are so gullible… Anyway, arrange for me to see him tomorrow. Let me test his powers!"

Next day, the Nawab came to greet Sri Raghavendra Swamy. "Please accept the salaam of Nawab Asadullah Khan."

"Narayana! I'm very happy that we have met," the saint said.

The Nawab asked if he would accept a gift. Sri Raghavendra Swamy replied, "Sri Rama will accept anything given out of devotion." The Nawab's servant then placed a large tray covered with silk cloth on the table in front of the saint.

The saint turned to the Nawab, "Please do not conceal the gift that you have offered with love. Remove the cloth." Stepping forward, the Nawab lifted the silk cloth. The tray was laden with pieces of meat. Sri

Raghavendra Swamy's followers were shocked at the sight. Unmoved, the saint sprinkled some water on the tray. The tray was now laden with fruits! Everyone was amazed.

The saint turned to the Nawab: "Did you see, Nawab? Allah knows how to respect our God better than either one of us. He will keep correcting us whenever we err, isn't it?" The Nawab begged the saint's forgiveness. "Punish me, Allah," he cried. "Swamiji, please ask your God to punish me too!"

Observing that Sri Rama never punished the genuinely contrite, Sri Raghavendra Swamy asked whether Manchale village in the Nawab's kingdom could be gifted to him. The Nawab demurred. Manchale was located in a barren region. Couldn't the Swamiji, he asked, settle for a village in a fertile area? He also offered to give him as much gold as he desired. His God, the saint said, had asked only for Manchale. At this moment, the Dewan reminded the Nawab that that village had already been granted to the Kazi. "That doesn't matter," the Nawab replied. "Take it back from him and give him another village." "The palace," he declared, "will meet the Swamiji's daily requirements. He is not a Guru for only you and I but for the entire world. Jai Raghavendra Swamiji!"

I have reconstructed this episode from the Kannada film, *Mantralaya Mahime* (The Greatness of Mantralaya, 1966), where the superstar, Rajkumar, starred in the role of the seventeenth century Madhva saint, Sri Raghavendra Swamy. Among the famous miracles of Sri Raghavendra Swamy, this episode appears with minor variations in other film adaptations of his life. In another Kannada film adaptation, *Sri Raghavendra Vaibhava* (The Glory of Sri Raghavendra, 1981), for instance, the Nawab expresses his lack of enthusiasm in receiving the saint, "The gurus of Kaffirs (non-believers) make me very angry." And, the Tamil film adaptation, *Sri Raghavendrar* (1985), where Rajnikanth, the Tamil superstar, fulfilled his wish to play Sri Raghavendra Swamy in his hundredth film, has a louder dramatization of the Nawab's encounter with the saint. At the moment the silk cloth is lifted off the tray, a group of Muslim men and women look gleeful while the men and women devotees of the saint let their jaws drop. And when the meat turns into fruits, the former look defeated while the latter show cheer.

Belonging to the venerable list of episodes where saints, fakirs and other holy figures chasten kings and place the pursuit of spiritual life above that of worldly power, the encounter of Sri Raghavendra Swamy with the Nawab of Adoni holds out another moral lesson. The Nawab's contempt for a "Hindu" saint and the "kaffirs" gives way to great generosity towards them while Sri Raghavendra Swamy only expects that his God be recognized without insisting on the superiority of his faith. And whatever the style of its narration, the episode is unambiguous that religious faiths ought to respect each other.

THREE MIRACLES AND A RIDDLE

Rains failed once in Itagi village. The village elders sought Bhimavva's help for bringing rain. She said to them: "The rain god says he will come only when Kori Hanumavva weeps." This remark appeared strange. The elders had to abide however by the word of Dharma, the name of the power working through her and the author of her words and deeds.

How to make Hanumavva weep? The elders enlisted the help of a sentinel, who was passing through the village, for realizing their ploy. Hanumavva, a poor, old woman, lived with her two children. The sentinel came to her house and demanded to know her son's whereabouts. He told her that he had to be arrested for a horrible crime. A frightened Hanumavva broke into tears. It started to rain rightaway. The rougher the interrogation, the more she wept. And heavier became the rainfall. The earth cooled in the end.

*

A well needed to be dug for providing water to those living near Bhimavva's matha. Bhimavva would pay the well diggers with broken corn and some coins for their work. She ran out of corn and coins in a few days. She visited her devotee, Havalappa, a potter, and said: "Dharma is getting a well dug. There is no money to pay the workers. He has sent me to ask you for a loan of hundred rupees." Havalappa, who was very poor, expressed helplessness. She then asked him to dig the earth under his pottery wheel. An earthen pot filled with gold coins was found. Taking coins worth a hundred rupees, she left after advising the potter not to let the wealth make him arrogant or ostentatious or extravagant.

*

Chennaveeravva's young son had died from plague. On hearing about it, Bhimavva sent word for her. She told the bereaved mother: "Your son is really asking to drink *nucchina ambali* (buttermilk mixed with boiled broken corn). Borrow some from your neighbour and give it to him." She borrowed the corn-mixed buttermilk from her neighbour and poured it in her son's mouth. Showing signs of revival, he slowly began to gulp it down. The people grieving around him feared whether a ghost was behind it all. But the overjoyed mother told them that Bhimavva was behind the miracle.

*

Bhimavva spoke in difficult riddles at times. Ordinary expressions contained extraordinary meaning. Only Chayasaaba Hosamane could help make sense of them. A village messenger by profession and a Muslim by caste, he also worked as an administrator in Bhimavva's matha. Viewed as her shadow (*chaya*), therefore, he had seen Allah in Dharma and found liberation.

Anxious that the monsoon would be cut short abruptly, the villagers of Itagi rushed to Bhimavva. They had taken care to take along Chayasaaba with them. After a long silence, Bhimavva said: "Chaya?" "I'm here, sister," he replied as he moved closer to her. She asked: "Do you see two ants moving on top of Shantagiri Hill?" He said: "Yes, I can see them clearly." She asked further: "Does the one in the front have a bell around its neck?" He replied: "Yes, I can see it." She then turned to the others and asked them to leave. Understanding her perfectly, Chayasaaba assured the villagers that the sequence of rains would not be interrupted. And the rains came the way they always did.

*

Itagi Bhimavva is a revered goddess in north eastern Karnataka. Her life chronicler, KB Kambali, speculates that she might have been born in the early nineteenth century. The miracles narrated here are from around a hundred miracles that he has compiled and classified as pertaining to the overcoming of illness, penury, childlessness and other difficulties of those times.

I learnt about Bhimavva from Prasanna, the theatre director and founder of Charaka, a women's handloom co-operative, who launched a handloom satyagraha in her name in Gadag a few years ago.

Bhimavva's image shows her spinning yarn behind a charaka. The most remarkable feature of this image is that it shows her at work. She is unlike the other Hindu goddesses, who are either at rest or in combat, and, in any case, not involved in labour activity. While those goddesses tend to prefer silk, Bhimavva wears a green cotton saree with a red border. There is no jewellery or crown on her. She only wears a necklace made of black beads. Similar to a posture seen among rural women, one of Bhimavva's legs rests folded on the floor while the other is folded and upraised. Unlike mainstream goddesses, who sit on a throne or stand inside a lotus or on a cloud or ride a beast or bird, she is seated on a vacant floor. Affirming the values of physical work, simplicity and austerity, the image of Bhimavva quietly substitutes the symbols cherished by the better off.

THE CASE OF THE WOMEN SUFIS

Mastani Maa, a Sufi saint, was usually found praying or meditating or doing *zikr**. Her love of God was boundless. When her visitors found her doing *zikr*, they usually seated themselves opposite her and started meditating upon God.

One day, a group of men, women and children dropped by to see Mastani Maa. Finding her engaged in *zikr*, they sat down opposite her and began to meditate. They did not break for food or water. Around midnight, Mastani Maa opened her eyes. She was moved to see that her visitors had waited this late, without food or water, to meet her. Asking them to put the earthen pot, which lay in a corner, on the stove, she told them to fill it with the leaves, stones and soil from the courtyard and cook them in water. She then beseeched God for help. Soon afterwards, rice was seen boiling inside the pot. Mastani Maa's visitors looked at her questioningly. She reassured them, "There is nothing special about this. It is all God's love. He provides food through stones, soil and leaves, doesn't He?"

Mastani Maa lived in Bangalore. It isn't clear when she arrived here or where she came from. Since she belonged to the Majzoob Sufi order, she wore thick iron bangles and anklets. She gave her blessings to all, irrespective of the communities they belonged to.

Hazrath Khwaja Qaseer, a famous Sufi saint in Bangalore, had sent his disciples to attend her funeral. When they let him know that her face had turned yellow after her death, he felt certain that she was a great Sufi. Her tomb in the city continues to attract many of the faithful in the present.

---

* *Zikr*: A devotional exercise of rhythmic repetition of God's name or a short prayer.

I found these few details about Mastani Maa and her miracle in Kannada writer Fakir Muhammad Katpadi's *Sufi Mahileyaru* (Women Sufis, 2010). Little is known about the two dozen Sufi saints whose dargahs exist in different parts of Bengaluru. The lack of an adequate account of Mastani Maa, or of Saiyada Bibi and Saiyadani Maa, the other women Sufis from the city though is to be regretted a bit more since the traditional Sufi orders does not easily recognize women as Sufi saints.

The leadership of the various Sufi orders, where disciples learnt the techniques of attaining the mystical experiences of the divine, has usually resided in men. When women did become, on a rare occasion, the heads of any Sufi order, their powers were curtailed in various ways. For instance, they could teach but not initiate disciples, or, they were allowed to initiate only female disciples. The Bektashi order in Ottoman Turkey was the lone exception: men and women here had equal rights of spiritual apprenticeship and organizational leadership.

Women Sufi saints are found all over the Islamic world. Not all of them had received formal training within a Sufi order. Some women Sufis remained unmarried, several of them achieved sainthood alongside fulfilling familial obligations, as mothers, sisters, daughters.

Besides North Africa, Annemarie Schimmel, the reputed scholar of Sufism, notes, Anatolia and Iran have a large number of shrines of women saints. Women devotees visit there for help in resolving family problems. But the largest number of women Sufi saints, she adds, are found in India and Pakistan, especially in the regions of Sindh and Punjab. Men are not admitted to many of the shrines that have been built for these saints. Legends on the lives and deeds of these saints are very many. Schimmel records an unforgettable one: "As elsewhere in the Muslim world, we find in Sind whole groups of women saints, like the *haft afifa*, 'the Seven Chaste,' who escaped a group of attacking soldiers and were swallowed by the earth before their virtue could be touched."

In *Karnatakada Sufigalu* (The Sufis of Karnataka, 1998), Rahamath Tarikere, the Kannada literary critic, identifies several women Sufi saints in the state whose dargahs continue to be living spaces in the present. The policemen of Mangalore are fond of Saidaani Bibi. They celebrate her death anniversary (*urs*) every year.

On occasion, Tarikere notes, women who cannot be traced to any specific Sufi order, have come to be regarded as Sufi saints. Mastani Maa of Bagur exemplifies such an instance. When she was walking back to her house, the man she was betrothed to appeared in front of her. She was deeply embarrassed at this chance encounter. Failing to find a place to hide, she jumped into a well to avoid facing him and lost her life. The local people built a tomb for her right beside the well. Worship continues to be offered to her here. It is easy, Tarikere cautions, to conclude that the myth around her serves patriarchal ideals, but why people worship her as a deity is harder to understand.

A DISCIPLE AND HIS GURU

Govinda Bhatta, a revered Sanskrit scholar and an *advaitin*, arrived in Shishunala. Villagers rushed to see him. He was seated at the foot of a tree. Imam Saab, who was among the visitors, made his young son touch his feet and asked that he impart knowledge to him. Drawing the boy near him, Govinda Bhatta asked, "Who is your father?" The villagers were puzzled at the question. The boy replied, "Who else? Don't we have the same father?" Impressed by the boy's sense that everyone had the same creator, Govinda Bhatta made him his disciple and took him to his village, Kalasa. The boy later became Sant Shishunala Sharif.

Sharif's parents, Imam Saab and Hazamu, were poor agriculturists*. Imam Saab's guru was Hajaresha Khadiri, who had sought to synthesize Islamic and Hindu philosophical tenets. Shishunala had grown up in a milieu where the Quran, the Puranas, the Ramayana and the Mahabharata were all present.

Govinda Bhatta was an unorthodox Brahmin. He mixed with everyone. He ate with everyone. He drank alcohol, and smoked *bhang*, and wandered freely. Although repelled by his disregard for caste taboos, the orthodox Brahmins had to admit that he was gifted. His learning, his kindness and his simplicity made him an endearing figure across several villages.

One day Govinda Bhatta led his student disciples towards a Kali shrine at some distance from Kalasa. A thorny fence had to be crossed along the way. The guru, who had worn wooden sandals, was able to

---

* Sharif was born in Shishunala, a village in Dharwar district, two centuries ago, in 1819.

move ahead through an opening in the fence. But the barefoot disciples found it difficult to follow him. Sensing their problem, Govinda Bhatta flung his sandals across to them over the fence. The disciples couldn't bring themselves to wear their Guru's sacred sandals. Sharif though didn't hesitate. Putting on his Guru's sandals, he crossed over to the other side of the fence and reached the Kali shrine along with him. Sharif had not let external observances come in the way of getting a glimpse of the goddess.

Govinda Bhatta was once seated under a tree when Sharif happened to walk by. The Guru was overjoyed to see his disciple. He flung his arms around him and made him sit beside him. A few upper caste men rebuked him, "Don't you have any sense of propriety? Don't you know who should be treated how? He is a Muslim and yet you hug him! Why don't you perform the thread ceremony for him too?!" Govinda Bhatta laughed at their pettiness. "No one becomes a Brahmin by birth alone," he said. "Sharif is a truer Brahmin than all of you." He then removed his sacred thread and put it on Sharif.

Sharif never visited a mosque. Nor did he offer the daily prayers. The local cleric once chastised him for failing to do these rituals. "My body itself is a mosque," Sharif replied. "I dwell in it always. Where then is the need to make a separate visit to your mosque?"

Not letting community identities shrink their perception of the world, Sharif and Govinda Bhatta lived freely.

Sharif's widely loved moral poetry (*tattva pada*) hold out intense visions of humanism. A poem of his has a bamboo reed ask: "I became a rocking cradle for graceful mothers… I became the hunting staff for children… What do I not belong to? I became the sweet basket in large mathas… I became the flute in Krishna's hands… What do I not belong to?"

THE COMMUNITY VISION OF A MAHARAJA

At the inaugural ceremony of a newly built mosque in Mysore in 1922, Nalvadi Krishnaraja Wadiyar, the maharaja of Mysore, declared passionately in Urdu: "I look upon you all, whether Hindus, Mahomedans or others, as equally dear to me. I hope that you will bear in mind the fact that you are Mysoreans first and all the rest next, owing a duty to the State..."

The maharaja's education, which made him proficient in three languages—English, Kannada and Urdu—let him relate richly to the world. He gave fluent public speeches in each of these languages. He also acquired an acquaintance with Vedanta, Islamic, Christian, Jaina and Buddhist theologies as well as general Western philosophy.

Identifying himself as Hindu, and on occasion, as Ursu, the caste community he came from, Nalvadi Krishnaraja Wadiyar was fully secure in relating to the other religions around him. He was proud that his ancestors built a new Jumma Masjid in Mysore city. While laying the foundation stone for the first Young Men of Christian Association in Bangalore in 1912, he expressed confidence that "its influence, religious, moral and educational, will be all for the good, not only of its Christian members but also of the young men belonging to other religions who will pass their leisure hours within its walls."

Nalvadi Krishnaraja Wadiyar saw the significance of religion in the lives of Indians, but the Indian polity, for him, was above all religions. In his Chancellor's address at the first convocation ceremony of Banaras Hindu University, in 1919, he expressed an "earnest hope" that the new university would "attract by the quality of its secular education, the young of all religious persuasions in India. The institution should be Indian first and Hindu afterwards."

An ethics of reconciliation and mutual support anchored Nalvadi Krishnaraja Wadiyar's vision of achieving justice among communities. Expressing his "earnest desire to see all classes of my subjects represented in just proportion in public service," at a meeting of non-Brahmin leaders in mid-1918, he hoped that the measures of reserving posts in the government would not bring about "a cleavage" among the people. He exhorted the non-Brahmin leaders to ensure that their work "did not in any manner mar the unity and harmonious relations which have hitherto existed to a great extent among the different classes of my subjects" which were "an essential condition of all real progress." He continued: "I appeal to the Brahmin community also to behave likewise in a conciliatory and tolerant spirit towards the other classes" and felt certain that the "Brahmin officers" would "co-operate with my Government in advancing the interests of the other classes also in the State and show practical sympathy with them in their natural aspirations." In asking the upper and lower castes to realign themselves to the new demands of social justice, he had placed his faith in their moral capacity for acting selflessly.

On numerous occasions, Nalvadi Krishnaraja Wadiyar asked the better off communities to actively aid the not-so better off ones. It was "the sacred duty of the more advanced communities," he said, "to extend a helping hand to less fortunate communities." He also stood for "the promotion of inter-racial and international fellowship."

Taking all religions to be quests for "the same eternal truths," Nalvadi Krishnaraja Wadiyar expressed "sorrow" to see the clashes "over the externals of religion," in various parts of India and "rejoiced" that such a "spirit" of "following the shadow rather than the substance" was not found in Mysore.

REPOSITIONING NEHRU

Masti Venkatesh Iyengar (1891-1986), the Kannada writer, shared a variety of sentiments towards Nehru. He admired his ideals of non-alignment and world peace. He was angry at his disapproval of the idea of linguistic states. He was simply exasperated at his secularism.

In 1953, Masti's editorial in *Jeevana*, a monthly magazine he ran, recalled a newspaper reporting that Nehru would offer puja for Goddess Tulaja Bhavani in Maharashtra. The following day, that newspaper had clarified that he wouldn't offer puja there. While Nehru respected all forms of worship, the clarification had continued, he never offered puja at any temple. Why was visiting a temple, Masti wondered, such a difficult idea for "the dharma of our modern people?"

In an editorial from the following year, Masti argued that Nehru's remark made at the inaugural occasion of the Bhakra Nangal Dam that such an achievement ought to be "worshipped" shared the same attitude that long held that the rivers Ganga, Yamuna, Cauvery and Godavari be worshipped. A previous editorial of his had even claimed that the tolerance and generosity of Nehru were inherited from Hindu dharma.

Written soon after Nehru's death in 1964, Masti's essay of condolence provided a lengthy survey of the leader's life, virtues and achievements. The closing part of this essay shows him, yet again, refusing to read Nehru's secularism literally: "Jawaharlal had thought that he was indifferent to matters of religion (dharma). Does the self (atman) exist? Is it eternal? Do god and heaven exist?

These questions appeared unnatural to him." "But," Masti continued, "Nehru's actions were truly rooted in religion. The essence of religion is that one must secure the well-being of the world, without prioritizing one's, or one's family's, interest. Religions might preach this in the name of god while the modern mind might do so in the name of mankind. Although the act of achieving the goal might seem to differ a bit, the achievement is the same. A poet's spirit was at the bottom of it all." "This is why," Masti observed further, "Nehru overflowed with bhakti when he encountered persons with a noble consciousness such as Gandhi and Tagore."

In a speech delivered at a college in Madikeri in 1956, Kuvempu had tried to shake the student enthusiasm for Nehru's ideas of a modern India: "It looks like we are determined to live in a this-worldly (*loukika*) state and build factories, dams and harness electricity. But what use are these if our consciousness is not shaped properly, if it lacks light, radiance, guidance, and courage." The Kannada writer's confident skepticism towards Nehru's modern ideals came from his own philosophical convictions which owed to advaita vedanta.

Kuvempu's essay on Nehru's scientific vision and rationality, written a few months after the leader's death in 1964, offered an intriguing view. Dismissing any characterisation of Nehru as an atheist, he pointed out that an acknowledgment of a force larger than himself could be seen in Nehru's writings, speeches and letters and in his conduct and relations with elders. Anyone who saw the newspaper photos of Nehru and Vinoba Bhave at the Sarvodaya meeting in Mysore in the newspapers could not possibly mistake the former for an atheist. Nehru's body posture and facial gesture expressed sentiments that were impossible to describe fully. Older than Vinoba, and only second to Gandhi in relation to the leadership of the freedom struggle, and an internationally renowned statesman, and immensely read, Nehru had still bowed to Vinoba. Authority, power and honour had surrendered here to kindness, humility, charity and devotion. This proved beyond doubt, for Kuvempu, that it was wrong to view Nehru as an atheist. In matters of sacrifice, love for the country, courage, empathy, intelligence, oratory and writing talent, Kuvempu

felt Nehru was an "extraordinary man" and that "some great spirituality
was behind each one of these qualities."

Nehru might have openly sported his secular ideals and atheist
outlook but Masti and Kuvempu, in their own distinct ways, hadn't
taken it at face value.

THE WRITER AND THE CENSUS REPORT

Bhava, the autobiography of Masti Venkatesh Iyengar, quietly recalls that many newspapers in England had admired his *1931 Mysore Census Report*. One of them had noted that the *Report* presented a strange occasion where a government document seemed like poetry.

In his introduction to the *Report*, which he compiled during his stint as the Census Commissioner of Mysore, Masti writes that he had presumed that it would find readers "other than the students of statistics." Why? Because "a number of persons" had asked him to make the *Report* "interesting," which he says he had "tried to do." True, not being a statistician was "a disadvantage," but he felt he could make up for it by making the *Report* "intelligible to the layman." The result: a vivid account of local society filled with proverbs and literary allusions.

Composed in lively, patient and confident prose, the *Report* offers a panoramic picture of the time. A deeply personal document, it also shows Masti's affection for Mysore as well as his stance on the major issues of the day.

In the chapter on literacy, Masti wryly illustrates the "vogue" of English: "A conversation in Kannada between two Kannada people who both know English is generally a weird jumble of English and Kannada." Noting that English was "purely a means to secular knowledge" for the Indian student, he complains about the chief weakness of the country's education system: "The learning required for the soul and that required for the body are in different languages." Revealing the power of the modern belief that the future was urban, Masti describes the disappearance of numerous rural professions due to competition and changes in "taste" without emotion.

Masti's wit and sarcasm suffuse the *Report*. In noting the persistence of antiquated marriage rituals, for instance, he explains that the idea of the Kashi Yatre ritual among the Brahmin community was "that the young man having finished his Vedic studies is going on pilgrimage when the bride's father meets him and begs him to come and marry his daughter and lead a married life... Now with our young men studying English and dreaming of London rather than of Benares when they finish their studies in a University here, the ceremony is no more than a play."

Masti is defensive in places. Since households usually gave "great consideration" towards women, the advocates of women's reform exaggerated the "harsh treatment of women." When the daughters leave for their husband's home, he writes, "few fathers can be strangers to the feelings expressed by Kalidasa's Kanva when sending Shakuntala to her husband's house." The appendices in the *Report* include Masti's short summary of a recent book of folk songs on women. He asserts: "A study of these pieces gives a clearer idea of the kind of life the women lead than any disquisition of the position of women in our life."

The appendices also include a charming survey essay on the "literary activity in Kannada" over the last decade and a note comparing the physical features of "Brahmins" and "Non-Brahmins" of "the Kanarese speaking people at Bangalore." The latter note, which measured differences in the size and shape of the skulls, foreheads and noses between these two groups, was of course rooted in the pseudo race science of the 19th century. Masti felt that this note proved that the races were the most mixed in Mysore! Arguing that eugenics should not mean that only "the physically strong should be allowed to marry," he felt however that the "mentally defective" or those with a "heritable disease" ought not to marry. His interest in eugenics appears to have missed the attention of literary critics.

Masti does not lose a single opportunity to caution against the census simplifications. He lays bare the differences within castes, for example, to show how the census caste categories simplified them. His *1931 Mysore Census Report* is perhaps unlike any other census document.

THE DISCREET CHARMS OF AKHADAS

A wrestling match was raging in Bangalore. A large crowd had formed to watch it. The year was 1950.

Tall and finely built, both the wrestlers kept the fight going, matching technique ("dao") with counter-technique ("tod"). All the while, a man in a black coat and a black cap and with vermilion marks on his forehead shouted excitedly from the stage to encourage them, his eyes keenly following every movement in the *akhada* (arena). He rose suddenly and started making his way towards the wrestlers. One of the wrestlers, Ismail, who enjoyed fame as the Gama of Mysore, had just used the *tibbi dao* to bring down his opponent to the ground. As the crowd cheered, the man in the black coat took off his golden wrist watch and thrust it in the hands of the winner. This sports aesthete was Annayappa, a wrestling contractor in Bangalore whose integrity and commitment was known across Maharashtra, Punjab and Pakistan.

Annayappa's young daughter, Ramakka, was superbly skilful at swinging a metal baton with water sprinklers at its ends. Blown away by her talent, the Maharaja of Mysore offered to build a gymnasium for her if she wished to train girls in this skill. Her father had been diffident: "It's better that young children not shoulder big responsibilities."

In the early part of the twentieth century, around 1915, Pehlwan Amiruddin Qureshi, a wrestler from outside Mysore, had posted notices all over Mysore city challenging the locals to wrestle with him. By this time, he had already "shown the sky" to every local wrestler. The wrestlers and their gurus and fakirs went into a huddle: none among them, it became clear, could take on the challenge. A deep silence set in at the meeting. One of the wrestling teachers soon noticed a farmer's son returning from his farm in his bullock cart. Studying him at length, he felt certain that he could be trained to rise to the challenge.

A rigorous training regime followed for the farmer's son, Basavayya. He had to climb up and down the Chamundi Hill very early in the morning with two wrestlers on his shoulders. To keep him inspired during the exercises, his teacher sang alongside. Basavayya's body soon grew strong. He also learnt the secrets of various wrestling techniques. A date was then found for the contest with Pehlwan Amiruddin Qureshi. In the sold-out wrestling show that lasted several rounds, Basavayya pinned down his opponent. The defeated wrestler vowed never to wrestle again, and Basavayya went on to become a champion wrestler. Both of them became good friends.

Two years earlier, a heavily built wrestler from North India had thrown an open challenge on the popular wrestling arena inside Jaganmohan Palace in Mysore. None of the local wrestlers responded to his call. A tall, fair and sinewy man, Sardar Gopalaraje Urs, a member of the royal family, then stepped inside the arena and extended his arm to accept the challenge. His deep breaths made his chest heave, tearing the buttons off his shirt. Oddly, the other wrestler withdrew his challenge. Both a wrestler and a wrestling trainer, and admired widely for his impartial refereeing, Gopalaraje Urs ably oversaw the wrestling matches during the month long Dasara festivities for a few decades.

I encountered these thrilling episodes, among many others, in *Kustirangada Diggajaru* (The Giants of Wrestling, 2010) by M. Narasimhamurthy. His lively profiles of eight wrestlers, including brief asides about several other wrestlers, trainers and patrons, show traditional Indian wrestling to be a beautiful, open affair: trainers and the *garadis* (training centres) welcome anyone interested in the sport; and, community barriers do not exist in the wrestling competitions: Hindus and Muslims, high and low castes, meat eaters and vegetarians, North Indians and South Indians, everyone freely wrestles with each other, and make the *garadi* and the *akhada* truly unique cultural spaces. The audience, too, does not allow the social identities of the wrestlers to matter for their enjoyment: the man with the better talent wins, and that is that.

The world of wrestling sees a range of dietary conventions with differing ideas of how food relates to the body. Even within the same *garadi*, some eat meat, some put their faith in fruits and vegetables. But what the wrestlers eat never offers a basis for judging their performance.

With its own cartography of *garadis* and *akhadas* stretching across different parts of India over centuries, traditional Indian wrestling, which prizes technical finesse and keeps out brutality, and where the honour of the *garadis* and their gurus and fakirs matter so much, is still seen in small towns and cities, at a safe distance from the showy world of commercialized sports but in need of new sources of sustenance.

CHALLENGING SRI SATHYA SAI BABA

A group of devotees had gathered around a holy figure on a beach in South India. They started to recall the various names of the ocean found in Indian mythology. "Ratnakara," was one of them: "Lord of Precious Stones." The holy figure smiled, "The ocean should have some diamonds for us." He dipped his hand in the sea water and brought out a diamond necklace.

Sri Sathya Sai Baba (1918-2011) is the holy figure found above. Any account of his life will include episodes where he makes objects appear out of thin air. At an early age, he is said to have taken out fruits and flowers from an empty bag for his school friends. He also made pencils and other school items appear for his classmates who needed them. He made flowers appear for his family members all the time. Instances where he increased the quantities of food to make it suffice for a large group of his devotees are also very many.

Sai Baba was to make *vibhuti*, gold rings and necklaces appear in front of his devotees till late in his life. I doubt there is any other major spiritual figure in twentieth century India with whom the performance of miracles is as tightly tied to their persona.

By the early 1970s, Sai Baba was probably the most powerful spiritual guru in the country. His devotees in India and abroad numbered in lakhs. Around 1500 organizations—all accountable to the Sri Sathya Sai Central Trust—are known to have existed around this time.

In 1973, H. Narasimhaiah (HN), well-known Gandhian freedom fighter and Vice-Chancellor of Bangalore University, was invited to inaugurate a summer workshop on spirituality that Sai Baba had organized at his ashram in Whitefield. In his autobiography, *Horatada Haadi* (The Path of Struggle, 1995), HN, a trained physicist, recalls his hesitation about accepting the invite since he had long viewed Sai Baba's miracles as unscientific. Viewing it as an opportunity to directly share his views with him, he finally agreed to inaugurate the event.

The inaugural was a grand event. Around two thousand youth dressed in white were seated on the floor in a large auditorium. The elderly devotees were at the front. Two grand throne-like seats stood on an elevated platform: one for Sai Baba, the other for HN. A large lamp was beside them.

Delivered in English, the speech, which HN had worked hard at, argued that the spiritual seeker had to be socially sensitive and free from superstition. Admitting that he believed in God and in reincarnation, he clarified that he kept those private, without using them to exploit anyone. His speech concluded by asking Sai Baba and the audience to strive to end poverty, social exploitation and superstition and the system that supported them.

There was a stunned silence. The foreign women devotees in the front looked very anxious. Even the three friends of HN who had accompanied him did not applaud.

This was the beginning of HN's protracted effort to prove that Sai Baba lacked real powers.

In 1976, HN formed an eleven member "Committee to Investigate Miracles and Other Verifiable Superstitions." This committee did succeed in exposing a couple of small-time miracle men in the state. The Committee's most spectacular target was of course Sai Baba.

They wrote him three letters—over six weeks—asking him to let them scientifically inspect his acts of miracle making. Not getting a reply, they released the letters to the press, which then turned this episode into a raging national controversy.

Journalists asked HN: "If you met Sai Baba, what would you wish for?" "A pumpkin," HN replied. A point he stressed repeatedly was that Sai Baba only gave out palm sized objects. *Couldn't miracles bring out larger objects?* Further, the other miracle objects, like watches, were branded. *Didn't this prove that they were not really created by him?*

R.K. Karanjia, editor of *Blitz*, carried each of these objections to his interview with Sai Baba. In response, the latter asserted that he made objects appear without knowing what was being created. And, he did not give pumpkins or cucumbers as they were perishable and did not work well as talismans. Scientific methods, he added, could never understand his powers; only spiritual figures could succeed here.

I pulled out this old episode not to defend or repudiate Sai Baba or the efforts of HN, but to throw in relief a genuinely sticky issue.

From a modern perspective, the worlds of faith appear as oddities, and, worse, falsehoods. Its scientific styles of validating reality make that a natural view. Since the beliefs pertaining to faith and to the sciences of the natural world are rooted in different worldviews, using the same term, "belief," in both cases is indeed part of the problem.

Scientific, rational opposition to magic, superstition, and religious faith has been around in India since the nineteenth century. The intention is easy to appreciate: the number of victims of fake gurus is so huge. The hope of the rationalists that the followers of holy men and women will desert them when their miracles are exposed though is not always fulfilled. Since the positive attachments that the holy figures elicit in their devotees will not all hinge on miracles, the latter's faith in them might not diminish even when one or the other miracle is shown to be false. The well-meaning activist effort to keep people away from pseudo holy figures might be better off if it perused its own understanding of the nature of religious belief.

STYLES OF WELCOMING LIFE

When babies turn over on their own and when they cross the threshold of a doorway, it is a matter for celebration among many Muslim communities of Karnataka. On these occasions, they break a pair of coconuts and distribute pieces of coconut flesh along with sugar among relatives and friends. When babies in Shia families cross the thresholds, the thresholds are covered with red cloth before making them sit on them and sprinkling coconut water on their faces. In Bidar district, the families make the babies wear new clothes as well. In Bellary, they do not observe any ritual when their babies turn over, and only celebrate the occasion when they cross the threshold. They convey the joyous news to the maternal family who then come over with coconuts, mutton curry, *kichdi* and *karjikaayi* and other sweets to celebrate the occasion. The Shafis, one of the four Sunni communities, though, do not observe either of the rituals mentioned here.

In Bidar, Gulbarga and Chitradurga, parents take their expectant daughters from their in-laws' homes to their homes for delivery during the seventh month of pregnancy. In the Dharwar region, this event occurs during the fifth month of pregnancy. In Bagalkot, Bijapur and Hubli, the maternal parents visit their in-laws twice, during the third and seventh month of their daughters' pregnancy. Known variously as *satvas*, *godh bharna*, *choli karna* and *taulat*, the feasts offered on these ritual occasions vary across regions. The pregnant women usually wear green sarees and green bangles at these ceremonies.

Around the regions of Bengaluru, Mysore, Hassan, Chikmagalur and Coorg, on the day the expectant daughter-in-law is to leave for her parents' home, she dresses up in fine clothes and jewellery at her husband's home. Her favourite dishes are prepared that day. After her parents and relatives are served their food, a utensil containing the snacks brought over by her parents is covered with red cloth and tied into a one and half knot and then placed on her lap. She offers a prayer before untying the knot and eating the snacks inside. The guests at the ceremony then line up to rub sandal paste on her cheeks and offer her gifts.

The regional diversity in the rituals of welcoming new life finds an earnest discussion in *Karnataka Muslim Janapada* (The Muslim Folklore of Karnataka, 2000), a book by a scholar, Shahseena Begum, that documents the birth, marriage and funeral rituals and the festivals seen among the Muslim communities of the state. Proverbs and riddles found among them, many of which are seen among other communities, also find delightful mention. The book's uncovering of the dazzling variety of ritual practices among the Muslims of Karnataka—and the variety of imaginations of life behind them—takes us to the arena of lived practices and asks that we not stay with official theologies to understand the social and religious lives of communities.

Rahamath Tarikere, the Kannada literary critic, cautions that a term such as "Muslim folklore" is best avoided as that hides the creative confluence of images, metaphors and narratives found across community cultures. The Muharram festival, he remarks, is celebrated in many North Karnataka villages without Muslim residents. Tarikere's caution indeed holds true for a range of lived practices: the cultures of food, clothing, music, architecture, gardening and everyday conversation found among the communities of a region show the many layered mutual influence between them. Lifting the amnesia about the interwoven evolution of "our" culture and "their" culture reveals the beautiful intimacies in communities.

JANAPADA/WORDS OF THE PEOPLE

THE EPISODE OF SANKAMMA

After searching far and wide for a bride, Neelegowda, a Soliga*, came upon Sankamma. Her beauty and virtues won him over instantly. They got married. His sisters' malice towards Sankamma however made him move out of his family and set up a separate home.

Neelegowda had to go once on a month-long hunting expedition. The headmen of several villages were accompanying him. Uneasy about leaving his wife alone in the house during his absence, he asked her to take an oath of chastity.

Sankamma refused. She couldn't believe he was suspecting her.

"What wrong have I done? Why should I take an oath?"

"You haven't done anything wrong," replied Neelegowda. "I only fear you might do something wrong. I don't feel like leaving you all by yourself. My friends and relatives might come home asking for some light, for boiled water. They will fall for your beauty and take you away. And I've so many enemies who are waiting to destroy my reputation. They can easily cast a spell on you with their magical powers and take you away."

He continued, "A bangle seller might also come here. You will let him inside to look at the bangles. You will extend your arm for him to help you try them on. He will certainly fall for your looks and do all he can to win you over and take you away."

Sankamma replied, "Summon all my friends and relatives. Summon my mother-in-law and father-in-law. Summon all my sisters-in-law and brothers-in-law. Prove that I have done a wrong first and then ask me

---

* A tribal community in Chamarajanagar district, Southern Karnataka.

to take an oath. Isn't the bangle seller like a father? Aren't my brothers-in-law like my children? I left my parents' home twelve years ago and have lived with you, served you. And you still suspect me!"

"Listen, Sankamma! You haven't done any wrong until now. I'm asking you to take an oath so that you won't do a wrong while I'm away. You haven't borne a child yet. You continue to have such a fine complexion. What if someone takes you away? Can I then walk holding my head high?"

She fell at his feet and wept, "You mustn't ask me to take an oath."

He was adamant. "I won't go for the hunt without an oath from you. Shall I leave you at your parents' home?"

"There is no one to look after me there. My parents died soon after I was born. If you left me there, people will suspect my character. Let me stay here."

"Come with me! You are a devotee of Lord Madeshwara, isn't it? Let's see what powers he has, and what kind of a devotee you are!"

"Where are you taking me?"

He slapped her. She fell down crying, "Mahadeva!" He then dragged his unconscious wife by her hair. It was very late at night. No one saw them leaving the village.

Neelegowda and Sankamma crossed several forests before they reached a dense forest nested inside a hill range.

"Why did you bring me here?" she asked.

"You are Madeshwara's devotee, isn't it? Stay here until I return from the hunt."

"I'll stay here."

"Remove your clothes," he cried.

She pleaded with him, "My parents' family deity watches every step I take!"

He hit her again. She fell unconscious.

Neelegowda made a bed from the thorns found in the forest. After removing Sankamma's clothes, he placed her body on the bed of thorns. Afraid that she might return home if a wandering cowherd or a goatherd found her, he bound her mouth, ears and eyes with thorns. After tying her hands and feet, he placed a heavy, round stone on her chest. He covered her with leaves to hide her from sight.

Invoking his powers of magic, Neelegowda encircled the leafy hut with seventy-six mandalas. Still feeling uncertain whether someone else with magical powers could walk through the mandalas, he placed two magic dolls at the entrance. Bringing them to life, he armed them with sickles, "Kill anyone who comes this way."

Neelegowda then returned to his village to join his clansmen in the hunting expedition.

When she came to her senses, Sankamma grieved, "Mahadeva, my lord, look at what has happened to me." She remembered him day and night. Her cries reached him in his forest.

Wishing to free his imprisoned devotee, Lord Madeshwara rode his tiger to where Sankamma lay trapped. Neelegowda's protective measures were no match for his powers.

Sankamma rose up fully clothed. She looked around to see what might have happened.

A mendicant was standing outside the entrance, "Who is at home? Give me alms."

She fell at his feet, "No one has asked me for alms in my village. You are asking for alms in this forest. Who are you?"

"Didn't you recognize me?"

"No."

"People call me Madeshwara, Nanjundeshwara, Mallikarjuna..."

Lord Madeshwara granted Sankamma the boon of prosperity and children before she returned home. When he found her safely home and pregnant with child, Neelegowda put her to several ordeals to prove her purity. Surviving all of these tests, she turned her husband into a devotee of Madeshwara.

*

Among the six episodes that constitute the major tribal oral epic, *Male Madeshwara*, the episode of Sankamma, which unfolds through a mesmerising lyricism and breathtaking metaphoric power, graphically describes the power of men over women. Whether encountered in print or as song, there is little doubt that Sankamma is being wronged and that the poet admires her for refusing to take a chastity vow and standing her ground. In this powerful instance of tradition feeling uncomfortable about itself, Neelegowda's abuse of Sankamma doesn't ever risk being taken as male triumphalism. In the regions where the epic is a living force, the loving regard for Madeshwara found among women tacitly hosts memories of disapproval of male violence.

Madeshwara, a Saiva saint, lived in the 14th century. Running over 25,000 lines, the epic, *Male Madeshwara Kavya* (The Poem of Madeshwara of the Hills), which recounts this saint's struggles to establish his faith in the land, is hugely popular in the hilly regions of the southern tip of Karnataka, especially the region of Chamarajnagar. Different versions of the epic elaborate its six episodes in differing ways. The account I have translated in abridged form above draws mainly from a rendition of the Sankamma episode done by Mysore Gururaj, the famous folk singer.

NO PLACE FOR IMMORAL POWER

One day, in the valley of the Seven Hills, Mahadeva lay on a rock. Half of his flowing matted hair was spread as a mattress and the rest of it covered him like a blanket. Two wrathful deities, who were carrying pots filled with the milk of tigers and bears for Shravana, the king of Bankapura, walked hurriedly in front of him. He asked them, "Can you give me some milk?" They refused haughtily. Angered by it, Mahadeva tied them up and kicked at their pots. He then decided to visit the king.

Shravana was a mighty king: the very earth was in his hands. When he did a harsh penance, Shiva had granted him a powerful boon in admiration. With his newly enhanced powers, Shravana had stormed the celestial abode and taken captive the three hundred crore gods. An alarmed Brahma rushed to him to plead for their release. Amused by his visit, Shravana replied, "Dear Lord Brahma, I've made Lord Shani my cot and Goddess Ideyamma the mattress. Only a pillow was missing." He then seized Brahma and made him his pillow.

The arrogant king had set his eyes on Kailasa next. A terrified Shiva turned himself into a stone to conceal himself. So Shravana took his consort, Parvathi, captive instead. Seizing goddesses Lakshmi and Saraswathi alongside, he made them his servants in the palace. The Goddess of Fire was already working as a cook. And, Kangolli Mallappa worked as a sweeper while Vishnu was entrusted with the task of reading the almanac and Ganga herself washed the king's feet daily.

When Mahadeva appeared in his court, Shravana asked him for his name. The visitor shared his name. Mishearing it as "Maadaari," he took him to be an untouchable cobbler. So he asked Mahadeva to make him a pair of leather sandals: he wished to wear them while visiting his wives.

Agreeing to do the king's bidding, Mahadeva came to see Haralayya, a cobbler and a great devotee of Shiva, in Kalyana. Haralayya greeted him, "Sharanu!" Mahadeva said, "Sharanu! Sharanu!" On seeing that a superior Guru had greeted him twice, Haralayya anxiously asked how he could make amends for what he had done. Mahadeva said: "I need a pair of sandals. But they need to be made with human skin and their soles filled with lac and chillies." Ever a man of his word, Haralayya didn't hesitate to kill his wife, Kalyanamma, to procure human skin for the sandals. Moved by the devotion of the couple, Mahadeva brought her back to life immediately.

Mahadeva took the newly stitched sandals to Shravana. He suggested that he wear them in the presence of all the Gods. Shravana agreed. All the captive gods followed him as he made his way to the rock where the sandals had been placed. "When you slip your feet inside," Mahadeva advised, "imagine you are stepping on an enemy's chest." Putting on the new sandals, Shravana stamped his feet repeatedly. The sandals burst into flames. "Did you want to kill me, Maadaari? I'll destroy you now!" the king cried loudly. The frightened gods scattered everywhere. But Lord Mahadeva stood where he was. Becoming larger and larger in size, he tore out a large white tree from the ground and used it as a crutch as he crushed Shravana's head with his foot. At his behest, the Goddess of Fire burnt down the king's palace.

*

An allegory of the human lust for domination and its moral unacceptability, this story punishes the king with death for his power mania. Wielding power, it affirms indirectly, needs to be a moral affair. The story of King Shravana joins hundreds of other Indian stories that disapprove the limitless hankering after power. Enslavement also appears a wrongful act alongside. Besides, the leather sandals, the makers of which belong to the lowest of castes, find symbolic centrality as a means for ensuring justice in the story. The flame of the sandals is indeed a metaphor for the creativity of lower castes and tribes, which has seen them evolve mythic cosmologies with distinct moral and aesthetic values.

My narration of the King Shravana episode in translated and shortened form draws from three different versions of the tribal folk epic, *Male Madeshwara Kavya* (The Poem of Madeshwara of the Hills), compiled respectively by J.S. Paramashivaiah, P.K. Rajashekhar and K. Keshavan Prasad.

THE EPIC TALE OF JUNJAPPA

Chinnamma and Mallegowda were married for twelve years, but remained childless. They had lived apart from the beginning: she lived in a straw roofed palace while he lived afar, in a cattle-shed along with his cows and goats.

Their family deity and the Lord of Tirupati were unable to help Chinnamma have a child. When she turned to Gaurisandrada Maari, the daughter of Shiva, for help, the latter warned her, "Why do you want a child? A daughter will follow the birth of three boys. She will bring you ruin." But Chinnamma stayed firm: "Let it be born in the evening and die the next morning, if needs be, but I must have a child."

Maari fell at her father, Shiva's feet, and asked him to part with his son, Veerabhadra. Shiva and Parvathi had kept their son far away from Kailasa, inside a forest of flowers encircled by an iron wall: he was that unruly.

Maari, though, persisted. She wanted nothing less than a child with the power to rule the earth and the heavens for Chinnamma. The wild Veerabhadra agreed to be born on the earth only after much effort.

At Maari's suggestion, Chinnamma took food to her husband and made sure that his shadow touched her during the visit. He had broken into tears seeing her visit him: the path from the palace was filled with thorns; and, the summer heat intense. After returning home, Chinnamma ate the mango that Maari placed on her lap.

Three months later, Chinnamma was terrified to hear the child in her womb speak. Her seven brothers rushed over at her request. Disclosing himself as Shiva's son, Junjappa pacified his mother.

Junjappa spoke again after a few days: "Two other sons and a daughter will be born to you. You must kill the girl child. You will lose all the gold and cattle otherwise. You will lose your husband too."

At the end of nine months, Junjappa sprang out through the middle of Chinnamma's back and settled on an anthill. He told his mother, "Since you gave birth to me, you can feed me with your milk today. Don't ever make me drink your milk afterwards."

When Junjappa turned three months old, he asked his mother where she wished to get the ritual blessing done for him. Since she didn't know, he helped identify the appropriate deity and led the way to the latter's shrine in Chitradevara Hatti.

The golden cradle was heavy. Chinnamma could barely take a step with it. Junjappa shot off an arrow to Indra, with a demand for a horse written on a peepul leaf. Realizing that the sender was none other than the son of Shiva, Indra immediately sent a white horse to earth. This horse carried Junjappa and his mother across the sky and landed in Chitradevara Hatti. After hiding the horse, Junjappa shrank in size and got back into the cradle.

The seven priests in Chitradevara Hatti refused to bless the child: "The couple were never together even after twelve years of marriage. Who knows who fathered this child? Let us not bless them." They forbade everyone in the village from offering water or milk to Chinnamma and her infant child.

Junjappa prayed to the rain god. Heavy rains poured on the village for seven days. The rains though did not fall anywhere near Chinnamma and her son. When the wife of one of the priests tried to get a glimpse of the infant, Junjappa opened his blazing eyes. Wounded heavily by his look, she collapsed on the ground. When the priests brought her to the shrine, a flower dropped on the left side of the deity.

The terrified priests turned to a *koravanji* (a wandering female fortune-teller), who had just arrived there, for an answer. They offered her everything they had but her basket wouldn't become full. Utterly helpless, they prostrated themselves at her feet. Her basket then became full.

Revealing herself as Maari, the *koravanji* told them, "The infant is none other than Junjappa. If you don't bless him, he will burn your village into ashes. And, Chinnamma is a virtuous woman."

The priests begged Chinnamma and her infant child for forgiveness. The wounded wife of the priest recovered soon afterwards.

The entire village celebrated the ritual for Junjappa. Hundreds of shiva lingas were worshipped. Praising the child's valour, the priests named him Junjappa of the Gollas.

After returning to their home, Junjappa slipped into a deep, mysterious sleep. During this time, Chinnamma gave birth to twin boys. After he woke up, Junjappa named them Maaranna and Mailanna.

Chinnamma soon became pregnant with a girl child. Junjappa's repeated warnings were of no use. His mother kept the girl child, Maarakka, and concealed her from everyone in the initial months.

The festival for Maari arrived at this time. Wanting to celebrate it grandly, the village headman sent word asking the villagers to offer sacrificial goats to the deity. Junjappa knew that his father, Mallegowda, would die if he gave a goat in sacrifice. So he cautioned him about it.

Despite Mallegowda's efforts to avoid the headman's messengers, the latter managed to find him and ask him to offer his goats for the deity. Finding it difficult to refuse them, he offered them three kinds of goats.

Junjappa knew his father wouldn't live much longer. However, when he noticed Yama's messengers in the village, he warned them against taking his father's life. Mallegowda's life was spared for three days after his goats had been sacrificed. Soon after her husband's death, Chinnamma lost all her gold, cattle and goats. She and her children had to endure much hardship.

Chinnamma sold the cow dung her husband had collected. She then chopped firewood and collected fallen leaves in the forest and sold them.

One day, a malevolent wind blew away Chinnamma's saree. Breaking into tears, she hid behind a bush. A while later, her seven brothers, who were on their way home after trading their merchandise, passed near her. Spotting her behind the bush, the youngest brother offered his *panche* (dhoti) to her.

Deeply moved at Chinnamma's plight, her brothers took her to their home. Each of them gifted her a calf while their wives gave her sarees.

Chinnamma returned home with the gifts. A great suspicion about his mother's character now arose in Junjappa. He put her to severe ordeals in the presence of the elders. These elders were not ordinary people: they ate rice with milk; they ate rice with ghee.

Junjappa challenged his mother to break fourteen wooden pestles and pluck out the fibres from within them. Chinnamma met the challenge. Next, he demanded that she pull out a snake from inside an anthill, wind it into a coil and place it on her head to hold a sieve filled with water. She then had to circle the gathering of the elders nine times without spilling a drop. She passed this test too.

Chinnamma stirred her dead husband to life. He pleaded with his son: "She has not shared the cloth she spread for me with anyone else!"

Ignoring him, Junjappa lined fourteen curtains beside each other. Chinnamma's milk flowed through them to reach the mouths of her four children. Junjappa was now convinced of his mother's chastity.

For twelve years, Junjappa and his two younger brothers, Mailanna and Maaranna, tended cattle in pastures far away from their home. Chinnamma and her daughter stayed in their straw-roofed palace and lived under tough circumstances.

Chinnamma's brothers found a groom for her daughter, Maarakka. But the marriage had to wait for three years, until Junjappa and his brothers could be found. Their consent for the alliance was important for Chinnamma. After Marakka left for her husband's home, Chinnamma's fortunes improved. Money and gold filled her house. She resumed eating rice with ghee and slept on a comfortable bed again.

Junjappa soon raised a very large herd of cattle. With thousands of cows in his possession, he seemed an uncommon man to his uncles. They began to worry: "He doesn't fear us at all!" And, whenever they took their cattle to drink water in the lakes or to graze in the meadows, they found Junjappa's cattle there already. Resentful of their nephew's prosperity, they began to explore ways of checking him.

The seven uncles approached an evil magician for help in destroying their nephew. Using his powers, he poisoned the waters Junjappa's cattle drank from. Frightened at the reddened water, the cattle fled to their shed. After Junjappa's efforts to purify the water failed, he turned to Maari, the daughter of Shiva, for help. She cleaned the water of its poison.

The seven uncles hatched another evil ploy to hurt Junjappa. They let a diseased calf loose among his cattle. When Junjappa took the calf back to them, they refused to take it back, denying it belonged to them.

Taking the calf with him, Junjappa dipped it in seven lakes and then in seven wells, washed it with the water of Purasakka Lake and covered it with a black woolen blanket. He then broke a coconut, sprinkled its water on the calf and burnt its tongue with a twig of neem. The calf was cured!

Junjappa blessed the calf: "You have stars in your tongue and dignity in your horns. You must say what it is to be born and grow up in this world." He asked his cows to feed the calf and care for it. In three months, the calf grew as large as a hill.

After several other efforts to hurt Junjappa failed, the uncles decided to poison him to death. At their request, a potter prepared the poison. They asked Maarakka, Junjappa's sister, to aid them in feeding him the poisoned food. When she declined, they thrashed her and forced her to agree.

The uncles approached their sister, Chinnamma: "We have prepared a feast for the Billu Habba ('Festival of the Bow'). Send your sons with us. Otherwise, we will cut off our tongues and take our lives." She begged them to leave her sons alone, but they wouldn't listen.

Walking over to where her sons were grazing their cows, Chinnamma asked them to attend the feast at her brothers' home. Junjappa warned her, "They will serve us poisoned food. We should avoid the feast." But she insisted that her sons go: "They will kill themselves otherwise." Never the one to disobey his mother, Junjappa visited his uncles' home along with his brothers.

Marakka was in tears. Junjappa asked her not to hesitate and serve them the food. He gave the food served to one of his brothers to a dog. The dog died instantly. Asking his other brother to avoid his food, Junjappa ate his meal and died soon after.

After seven days had passed, Junjappa returned to earth. Going against his mother's words for the first time, Junjappa shot a flaming arrow from the top of a hill and destroyed Kambera Hatti, where his uncles lived. Only his sister and brother-in-law who lived there were spared.

Junjappa moved to Kalaveri village. The two daughters of his clansman, Ale Gowda, got wells built at the foot of Junjappa's Hill. One of the sisters groaned about the digging expense. Her well collapsed immediately. The other sister built her well with devotion. Water sprang out as milk in her well. Junjappa blessed her: "Let the water in this well last until the time of your children and grandchildren."

I have translated in shortened form the folklorist, J.S. Paramashivaiah's prose rendering of the over 23,000 lines long verse epic, Junjappa, that he encountered in Central Karnataka in the mid-70s. This epic poem of Kaadu Gollaru (literally, the cowherds of the forest) was compiled in full by Cheluvaraju a decade later (Junjappa, 1987, Kannada University Press).

THE SERVANT GIRL AND THE GODDESS

There was a village. It had a wealthy headman. Thimmi was a servant in his household. She would talk excessively as if she had lost her mind. No one in the village liked her.

The village had a tiny tank lined by a narrow bund. Taken in by the charm of this tank, a few stonecutters passing by built a small pandal on the bund. A few days later, a weary old woman, who rested in the pandal's shade, built a small stove under the pandal to let other wayfarers cook their food.

The following day, a potter, who was travelling in a cart loaded with pots, halted near the pandal to rest. Before resuming his journey, he placed a clay pot on the stove for other travelers to use. Other passersby that day also joined in: one of them filled the pot with water, another dropped rice grains into it, a third put some jaggery inside the mix and a fourth brought some firewood and lit the stove to let the rice cook.

Next day, Thimmi walked by the village tank carrying a headload of manure to the headman's banana grove. After she unloaded the manure inside the grove, which was beside the tank, a sweet fragrance made her stand still. Intrigued, she went inside the pandal and found a nicely cooked dish of jaggery rice inside the pot. Since she was feeling hungry, she decided to eat it. To avoid being seen by anyone, she thought of having the dish inside the Goddess Kalagattamma temple nearby. She spread the jaggery rice on a plaintain leaf that she had plucked from the headman's grove and started eating.

While she ate, Thimmi noticed the goddess looking at her. "How dare you look at me, Kalagattamma?" she cried. "Turn around, I say!"

The stone idol didn't move. "I came here to eat by myself, but here you are looking at me!" Thimmi continued angrily. "Turn around right now! Or, I'll scratch your face with a broom!" The goddess turned her back thinking, "Why should I get my face scratched by her?" Thimmi then finished her meal in peace.

Later in the day, the temple priest noticed the reversed position of the idol. Taken aback at this sight, he rushed out and raised an alarm all over the village. Everyone came running towards the temple. Try hard as they might to move the idol, it wouldn't budge.

Anyone who restored the idol's position, the headman announced, would be rewarded with the land attached to the temple. No one offered to do it. Thimmi then stepped forward, "I'll do it." People began to wonder whether she had gone mad. But someone among them said, "Let her also try."

A large group of people assembled outside the temple the next day. Thimmi alone went inside. She put the cooked rice she had brought along on a plaintain leaf and sat down to eat facing the goddess. Looking up at the goddess, she said: "I wanted to eat without being seen by anyone. But you are now staring at me. Turn around!" The idol didn't move. "Wait, I'll show you!" Picking up the broom from the corner, Thimmi threatened her, "Will you turn around? Or, should I thrash you with this broom?" The goddess thought, "Why should I let her hit me?" She returned to her original position.

Thimmi came outside. "Everyone can go in now." The villagers were thrilled to see the idol as it had always stood. They exclaimed, "No one is as truthful as our Thimmi!" The land attached to the shrine passed on to Thimmi. She then left the headman's household and lived a life of contentment.

*

The co-operative charity of the travelers, the goddess' recognition of Thimmi's moral worth as higher than that of her despisers, the affirmation of a life outside bondage, all of these narrative elements let us glimpse the imagination of a village community engaging fundamental ethical matters. Besides, Thimmi's desire to be left alone by the goddess, her intimidation of the goddess and her concealing of her thoughts from the goddess depart from the usual idea of God as all-knowing and all powerful and disclose an imagination of a freer, more supple human relationship with the divine.

The story which I have translated in abridged form is found in *Kannada Janapada Kathegalu* (Sagar Publishers, 1970), a classic anthology of folktales compiled by the famous folklorist, J.S. Paramashivaiah, fifty years ago. He had recorded this tale from Rame Gowda, a thirty-year old man from Ambala Jeerahalli, a village in Bellur taluk, Mandya district, two years earlier.

THE ADVENTURES OF PUTTAKKA

In a village lived a couple called Puttanna and Puttakka. Bright and beautiful, Puttakka could charm anyone. The village headman fell for her and a relationship started between the two. Whenever her husband was away, he would go over to her house. This carried on for a while. Soon enough, Puttanna smelt something was amiss. One day, he said to his wife, "Pack me some food. I'm going to the cattle fair in Subramanya." A pleased Puttakka swiftly packed food for him. Taking leave of her, he proceeded to sit watch on the peepul tree opposite their house.

Puttakka started preparing the syrup to make *kajjaayas*: she knew the headman would come over. In a little while, he entered the house stealthily and peeped inside the kitchen and saw her frying the sweet in a deep pan. "Let her finish making it," he told himself and lay down on the cot outside the house. He quickly fell into deep slumber.

Her cooking done, Puttakka came out of the house and found the headman snoring heavily. Before he wakes up, she thought, she might as well fetch some water from the well. While she was away, Puttanna climbed down the tree and went inside the house. He brought out the pan from the kitchen and poured the hot oil down the headman's nostrils. The headman resembled a radish in no time. Moving the corpse inside the house and propping it up against a wall, Puttanna thrust *kajjaayas* in the dead man's mouth and hands and quickly went back up the peepul tree.

On returning from the well, Puttakka was struck to see the headman inside the house. "What was the hurry?" She said after noticing the sweets in his mouth. She poked his chin. He fell on one side. She then poked his cheeks: he fell on another side. As she was beginning to see what had happened, Puttanna's voice was heard: "I'm back from Subramanya. Bring me some water. I need to wash my hands and feet." Feigning innocence, Puttakka said, "I had made *kajjaayas* and gone out to fetch water. And, this man has eaten them and fallen dead. What to do now?" "Don't worry," he said. He brought down a wooden chest from the attic and stuffed the corpse inside. He then said loudly, "I've put the chest under the cot. God's jewels are in it. So keep a close eye on the chest. I'll be away from the village for some time." It was already dark. Four thieves, who had overheard Puttanna, entered the house when Puttakka was asleep and made away with the chest.

On discovering the ploy, the thieves decided to punish Puttakka. They returned to her house and took away the cot on which she had lain asleep. Feeling the cool air on her face, and seeing the stars in the sky above, Puttakka saw what was happening. She clung to a low tree branch as the thieves passed under it. The thieves soon realized that she had outsmarted them. Noticing a mango grove nearby, they now decided to steal a few mangoes.

As it happened, Puttakka had sought safety on top of a mango tree in the same grove. When one of the thieves, who climbed up the same tree, recognized her, she hushed him, "Look, how about you and I become husband and wife?" He was thrilled. "Ask the others not to come here," she continued. "Tell them that Moogchoudi (a forest deity) is here." Obeying her happily, he warned his friends from coming anywhere near his tree.

The thief turned to Puttakka, "Okay, then. Let's become husband and wife." She replied, "In our village, when getting married, the tongues of the husband and wife need to touch each other. Let my tongue touch yours first. And then yours can touch mine." After her tongue had reached out to his, the delighted thief extended his tongue out towards her mouth. She quickly bit it very hard. The thief fell down screaming in pain. Terrified that Moogchoudi had flung him down, the other thieves hoisted him on their shoulders quickly and fled from there. They still haven't returned.

The complex amoral story admires the quick-witted heroine while staying non-judgmental about her actions throughout. Besides, the husband's overlooking of her affair with the headman contrasts with the more commonly found sentiments of injured male pride on such occasions.

The story I have abridged and translated here is folklorist J.S. Paramashivaiah's contribution to *Dakshina Karnatakada Janapada Kathegalu* (Sagar Publishers, 1979), his edited anthology of folktales.

A SACRIFICE FOR A TANK

Mallanagowda, the headman of Kallanakeri, had got a large tank dug in the village. But the tank bed stayed dry. The almanac could not help explain why water did not collect there. An astrologer assured them however that this wasn't the handiwork of either the Gods or the ghosts. The eldest daughter-in-law, he advised, had to be sacrificed to the tank. The headman's household decided that Bhagirathi, the youngest daughter-in-law, be offered instead as sacrifice.

Bhagirathi prepared to leave for her parents' home. "Come back soon," said her mother-in-law. When Bhagirathi reached her parents' home, her father met her at the entrance.

"Why are you here? You never visit us. Why the dull face? Why the tears?"

"My in-laws wish to separate me from them."

"Let them! I'll give you a farm and a house."

"Who needs your farm and house? Throw them away."

The mother asked, "Why are you here? Why are you crying?"

"My in-laws wish to separate me from them."

Her mother consoled her, "I'll give you a pair of earrings."

"Mother, throw them into the fire."

Bhagirathi's elder sister offered to send her children to stay with her. Declining her offer, she left her parents' home and went over to her friend's house.

The friend exclaimed, "I've never seen you cry before. What happened?"

"Do you really want to know, my friend?"

"Don't be afraid. Don't hesitate."

"My in-laws want to sacrifice me to the tank."

"Let them. We ought to do as we are told."

Bhagirathi returned to her in-laws' home. She had come back sooner than expected.

Tears rolled down Bhagirathi's face as she cleaned the lentils.

"I've never seen you cry before. What happened, Bhagirathi?" her father-in-law asked.

She replied, "The stones in the lentils struck my eyes."

She gave a similar excuse when her mother-in-law asked about her tears.

A big feast was being cooked that day. Water had been boiled in a large vessel and kept ready for everyone to bathe. The elder four among the five daughters-in-law made excuses to skip their bath. If they were freshly bathed and nicely dressed, Ganga would surely not let go of them: none of them wanted to risk that.

"Why don't you have your bath?" the mother-in-law asked Bhagirathi.

Bhagirathi bathed and got dressed. Holding a golden basket, she led the family to the tank. After offering worship on the dry tank bed, the members of the family ate their food and started on their way home. Along the way, they remembered that the golden bowl had been left behind. None of the four elder daughters-in-law were willing to fetch it from the tank bed.

"Why don't you get it, my young daughter-in-law?" the mother-in-law asked.

Returning swiftly to the tank, Bhagirathi picked up the golden bowl. As she climbed the first step of the tank, on her way back, Ganga came up to her feet. When she climbed the second step, Ganga covered her feet. Bhagirathi drowned completely as she climbed the fifth step. She became the sacrifice for the tank.

At this time, Madevaraya, Bhagirathi's husband, was away from the village fighting a battle. A nightmare where he saw his clothes burn and his house collapse made him rush home. He hadn't even saddled his horse. He was alarmed when his sisters-in-law offered him water to wash his feet. Where was Bhagirathi? She is away at her parents' home, they told him. When he reached his in-laws' home, they told him that she was visiting her friend. Bhagirathi's friend let him know the truth: "Your parents have sacrificed her to the tank."

A sorrowful Madevaraya rode his horse to the tank and drowned himself in the water.

*

I have adapted the above tale from *Kerege Haara* (A Sacrifice for the Tank), a famous folk song from North Karnataka. Unlike in the genre of sati stories which end with the sacrifice of women, Bhagirathi's husband dies after her death. Much of the action in *Kerege Haara* is not made explicit. Our imagination has to step in every now and then to connect the snatches of dialogue and the jumps in sequence.

In a well-known essay on *Kerege Haara* (1948), T.N. Srikantaiah, the reputed Kannada scholar, has explained that no one tells Bhagirathi that she is to be sacrificed. She has somehow become aware. In fact, her in-laws presume all along that she does not know of their design. Bhagirathi's parents do not show sufficient sensitivity to her predicament. Her sister's offer to send her children, which reminds us that she has not had children yet, is also not an adequate response. Only her friend, who asks her to do what was expected of her, offers genuine sympathy. The rest of the poem until the sacrifice occurs is a strengthening of Bhagirathi's resolve to do what was expected of her.

Kerege Haara has invited much critical discussion. For its poetic quality as much as for its controversial imagination of sacrifice. Noting the poet's sensitivity to Bhagirathi's sorrows, a few critics complain that he does not reject the ugly beliefs of his times. Others have asked that *Kerege Haara* not be read literally and be seen as affirming the value of individual sacrifice for securing the well-being of a community.

The moral binding of Bhagirathi haunts the mind.

TWO ANIMAL STORIES

Ninga and Basava lived in the same village. Basava was well off. Ninga was very poor: he and his family barely got by.

Early in the morning, after waking up, Basava would make his way to a pipal tree to get a glimpse of the eagle, Garuda. But Ninga would walk over to a hill and start his day with a glimpse of an owl.

Ninga continued to be poor. The owl asked him once, "Everyone begins their day with a glimpse of Garuda's face. Why do you start yours with mine?" Ninga pleaded, "Oh, Owl-King, lift me out of my misery."

Pondering a bit, the owl said, "Goddess Lakshmi will visit your home on Friday. Make sure you and your wife keep your home clean and tidy. And keep a knife handy. I'll come at the same time as Lakshmi. Cut my neck on the threshold of your house and spill the blood along its length." Desperate to get over the hardship, Ninga agreed to do as the owl said.

On Friday, Lakshmi and the owl arrived at Ninga's home around noon. Ninga did just as the owl had advised him.

Finishing her visit, Lakshmi tried to leave through the front door but halted on seeing the blood lined threshold. Ninga's miseries ended soon thereafter. He even became wealthier than Basava. Since the owl confined the goddess of wealth to one man's home, it is better to avoid looking at it.

*

Orphaned at a young age, a brother and sister grew up together in their family house. They both worked the field.

It rained very, very heavily once. The roof of their house got damaged badly. The brother had to stay back home to repair it. For several days, his sister worked in the field all by herself.

One day, she was surprised to see that the unfinished work from the previous day had been attended to. The same thing happened again the following day. Determined to get to the bottom of things, she stopped her work halfway the next day. She proclaimed loudly that she was tired and pretended to return home. She left behind the extra portion of food she had brought with her.

She then hid behind a tree to see what might transpire during her absence from the field. A monkey appeared a short while later and started working on the field. After finishing a large amount of work, he ate the food she had left behind.

This sequence repeated over many days. One day, the grateful girl came out from where she hid and made friends with the monkey. They worked together from then on.

She could tend the field easily on her own, she told her brother. He should therefore repair the roof, she assured him, without regretting that she worked the field all by herself.

The grateful brother soon started to suspect his sister's motives. *Might she have a lover?* He was keen to know.

Falling in love, the monkey and the girl had decided to marry each other. When she became pregnant, her brother was furious. He wanted to kill the man who had ruined the family honour.

For a few days, the brother wasn't able to find out who her sister's lover was. Finally, he discovered that it was a monkey, and not a human, who his sister had loved. He rushed from his hiding place and killed him with his spear.

Fearing that her brother wouldn't let her child live, the sister escaped into the forest as the time of giving birth drew near. Her twin children—a boy and a girl—grew up in the forest and made it their home. They were adept at climbing trees. Inheriting from their mother her fear of her brother, the sight of a man made them flee. They continue to do so even now.

*

The Prosperity Brought by the Owl and *The Monkey-Husband*, which were collected, respectively, by folklorist J.S. Paramashivaiah (Kannada Folk Stories, Sagar Publishers, 1970) and writer Eastern Kire (Naga Folktales Retold, Barkweaver and Keviselie, 2009) offer pictures of a social world where humans and animals relate to each other in richly meaningful ways.

Offering reasons why humans avoid owls and monkeys avoid humans, these complex stories at bottom make respectful place for animals in the social imagination: the owl and the monkey are ethical beings and strike kinship with humans.

Making prosperity exclusively available to one person seemed wrong, but the owl had chosen to give up its own life to help the only person who had faith in it. Sharing this background, the story rails against the ease with which the owl is seen as a bad omen, and an inauspicious sight. By brutally ending the monkey's loving relationship with his sister, the brother had acted in a dishonourable way. The hard-working monkey who earns the love of the sister goes against the usual images of monkeys as mischievous and destructive. The monkey-husband story might be endorsing women's ability to appreciate virtues in animal-like men or domesticate wild-natured men. A fear of female sexuality might also lurk in it. The most striking thing however is that both the stories judge animals with the same moral compass as that for the humans and offer them a dignified presence.

SOME IDEAS

AMBEDKAR'S IDEAL OF MAITRI

During a stay at Shravasti, the Buddha asked the *bhikkus*, "Suppose a man is preparing to dig the earth. Does the earth resent him?"

"No," the *bhikkus* replied.

"Suppose a man wishes to paint pictures in the air using lac and colour. Will he be able to do it?"

"No, he can't."

"Why not?"

"Because the air has no dark patches."

"Your minds also shouldn't have dark patches. They reflect evil passions. Suppose a man tries to set the Ganges on fire with a strip of burning fern. Will he succeed?"

"No."

"Why not?"

"Because the water in the Ganges is not inflammable."

"Just as the earth is not resentful, just as the air does not lend itself to any action against it, just as the River Ganges keeps flowing without letting the fire disturb it, *bhikkus* like yourselves must bear the insults and injustices done to you without letting them affect your *maitri* towards the offenders. It is your sacred obligation to keep your mind as firm as the earth, as clean as the air and as deep as the Ganges. No action will then be able to disturb your *maitri*. Those who hurt you will then soon become tired. Let your *maitri* be boundless and your thought vast and beyond feeling any hatred. According to my *dhamma*, practising *karuna* is not enough. It is essential to practise *maitri* alongside."

*

In the Buddha's advice to the monks, *maitri* ought to become intrinsic to human nature. Its presence in them should stay constant, like the unchanging substance of wind, earth and water. Whatever their opponents might do to them, the *maitri* residing inside them should stay firm, unaffected. Cultivating a solidity for the *maitri* in the self was nothing less than a sacred obligation: their *dhamma* required this of them. Kindness and compassion by themselves prove morally inadequate when unaccompanied by the sentiments of *maitri*. In this understanding, *maitri* appears a preserving and nurturing force for individuals as well as for a community. It protects them from giving in to hatred, vengeance and any other destructive sentiments and nourishes life-sustaining instincts in them. The Buddha's discussion also gives enormous agency to the powerless to direct their self-transformation in the direction of *maitri*.

The Buddha episode from Bhimrao Ramji Ambedkar's last book, *The Buddha and his Dhamma* (1957), which I re-narrated at the start, shifts the meanings of *maitri* as friendship and friendliness in Sanskrit—and as loving-kindness in Buddhist thought—in new directions. Earlier on in this book, Ambedkar (1891-1956) describes *maitri* as "fellow feeling to all beings, not only to one who is a friend, but also to one who is a foe; not only to man, but to all living beings." Could anything other than *maitri*, he asks, "give to all living beings the same happiness which one seeks for one's own self, to keep the mind impartial, open to all, with affection for everyone and hatred for none?" In asking that fellow-feeling, happiness and affection be offered impartially to all human and non-human life, and not allowing space for regarding the other as a foe or for hating the other, Ambedkar's ideal of *maitri* renewed the imagination of community as well as of social struggle.

In his later writings, Ambedkar clarified that he had used the term 'fraternity' earlier to mean *maitri*. In his posthumously published *Riddles of Hinduism*, he observed that equality and liberty were not sustained by law, but by 'fellow-feeling', and added that the proper word for this latter phrase was not what the French revolutionaries termed, 'fraternity', but 'what the Buddha called *maitri*'. Without *maitri* as the foundation, he continued, the pursuit of liberty undermined equality and vice versa.

The value triad, liberty, equality and fraternity, is indelibly tied of course with the French Revolution. Although the Revolutionaries saw fraternity as a founding secular ideal of the new Republic which symbolized the end of closed social arrangements, the term 'fraternity' was ambiguous enough to be defined variously in France later, from a civic ideal that restrained individualism to a religious ideal that enabled the proper exercise of liberty and equality.

Ambedkar too imagined fraternity differently, in relation to Indian society. In his famous undelivered speech, *Annihilation of Caste* (1937), he described fraternity as "another name for democracy." Besides a form of government, he continued, a democracy also meant a community life where individuals and associations freely pursued their interests and associated with whomever they wished: "It is essentially an attitude of respect and reverence towards one's fellow men."

Religion, Ambedkar continued, offered a moral foundation for fraternity. But Hinduism, which he viewed as a Religion of Rules, i.e., a ritual bound religion with which the believers had a mechanical relationship, could not offer it. Instead, a Religion of Principles, i.e., a religion in "the sense of spiritual principles, truly universal, applicable to all races, to all countries," was needed.

In *Annihilation of Caste*, where he still saw scope for a reform of Hinduism and the caste order, Ambedkar wrote that the Upanishads might be able to provide Hinduism "a new doctrinal basis" that was "in consonance with Liberty, Equality and Fraternity." Many years later, he acknowledged in *Riddles of Hinduism* that the philosophy of the oneness of reality found in a few of the Upanishads had "greater potentialities for producing social democracy than the idea of fraternity," but this philosophy, which he termed 'Brahmaism,' had no 'social effects' and let caste and gender inequalities as well as untouchability remain.

In making *maitri* the foundational ideal for his vision of a democratic community, Ambedkar had reached out to another inheritance of Indian civilisation, that is, Buddhism. He found in *maitri* a satisfying moral vision for the work of transforming Indian society. Departing from a human-centred idea of community, *maitri* gestures to the sentient world at large and fosters an expansive political consciousness where nation, religion, race, caste, gender and language, among other sources of social identity, do not come in the way of experiencing community life freely and vastly. The male-centred image of brotherhood implied by fraternity also makes way for a wider sense of solidarity encompassing human as well as non-human life.

Ambedkar's brief address made on All India Radio on 2 October 1954 clarifies several key details:

"Positively, my social philosophy may be said to be enshrined in three words: liberty, equality and fraternity. Let no one, however, say that I have borrowed my philosophy from the French Revolution. I have not. My philosophy has roots in religion and not in political science. I have derived them from the teachings of my master, the Buddha...Law is secular, which anybody may break, while fraternity or religion is sacred, which everybody must respect."

Only the prior presence of a fraternity, or *maitri*, where togetherness with all living beings formed the basis of community life, ensured that the free and egalitarian functioning of social institutions. People might freely violate secular law, but will hold back from violating a sacred phenomenon like *maitri*. Only a community founded on a theological vision, not secular reason, could attain a democracy. And Buddhism offered that sacred foundation.

The word 'fraternity', in the Preamble to the Indian Constitution, is running up against a truly rich moral horizon. How might the ideal of *maitri*, which abjures hatred as well as the idea of a foe, inspire new political creativity in the present. The transformation of the caste order in India was indeed uppermost among Ambedkar's reformist concerns. His universalist vision of the community however enriches the political imagination everywhere.

KUVEMPU'S VISION OF VISHVAMANAVA

Affirming the Kannada writer Kuvempu's observation that humans were born as *vishvamanava* (universal human) but grew up to become *alpamanava* (diminished human), Devanur Mahadeva, the great Kannada writer and activist, pointed out that if his readers shut their eyes for five minutes daily and imagined themselves to be vishvamanava, untouchability would be reduced significantly. Claiming Kuvempu as being among the early writers to voice the concerns of the oppressed, Siddalingaiah, the famous Kannada poet and activist, remarked, "His is a message that this land needs to understand. May his vishvamanava light up our lives." These robust endorsements of Kuvempu's philosophical idea convey as much about the regard that these profound Dalit writers have for him as they do about the appeal of the idea itself. In 2015, the Karnataka government declared Kuvempu's birthday (Dec 29) as Vishvamanava Day.

A distinct contribution to the moral thought of modern India, Kuvempu's idea of vishvamanava found an early articulation in a speech he made to college students in Mysore in the late 1930s: "It is true that I have been searching many years for a fundamental truth (*tattva*) that applies to different times, different countries and all people." Noting that he did not wish to hurt anyone, Kuvempu clarifies that his idea of vishvamanava emerged not out of "non-generosity or a desire for counter-violence or from reckless instincts" but out of "long standing synthesis, calm contemplation, and a pure anger (*satvik krodha*) that arose upon seeing acts of injustice and folly."

Kuvempu considered his moral vision not as a deviation from existing morality, but as being part of a proper moral evolution. He likened this task of renewing morality to that of science where Galileo's discovery that the earth rotates round the sun went against Church orthodoxy but allowed for knowledge to move ahead. If the new truths discovered by science can complete the old partial-truths, he asked, why cannot this happen in the world of dharma? He noted that, "The Veda is an unfinished book; its last chapter is not complete still. It will continue to be written in the present and in the future. The new Vedas of the new rishis need to be listened to. The right to submit everything to a severe and critical examination is always ours." He viewed the Vedas not as Shruti texts, but as texts written by rishis and which were open to be being revised by later rishis who had experienced *darsana*.

Briefly recapitulated, Kuvempu asked that humans unshackle their minds from the attachments of tradition and community identity and strive to experience *darsana*. *Darsana*, as an experience of seeing the whole truth, features prominently in his philosophical thought.* The possibility that *darsana* was available to all anchors his idea of vishvamanava. Everyone, he would argue, could be a seer, a vishvamanava.

In a 1933 lecture, "The Eyes of Poetry are the Poet's Darshana," Kuvempu argued that poets had to have a darsana of *jeeva* (life): "Darshana does not mean logical or rule-bound thought. Its feature is that it combines emotions, thought and imagination. Such a darshana can be achieved only through penance, contemplation and introspection." Pointing out that art cannot be justified for art's sake, he admitted that writing for him was a practice of spiritual attainment: "Spiritual achievement is what I have strived for; literature has emerged out of the experience of this *sadhane*."

Everyone, Kuvempu noted further, had to strive to attain poornadrishti (a vision of the whole):

> A partial vision lacks meaning. Poornadrishti is really a permanent darsana: "In such a darsana, science, politics, community, philosophy, art—all these parts are in harmony. A *shrestha kavi* has to have this darsana. Only then does he

---

* Sri Aurobindo was an influence on Kuvempu's understanding of *darsana*.

become a rasarishi. In his voice, the Vedas, Shastras and the arts come together... Nothing should be outside or other than this expansive embrace; nothing escapes it.

His epic poem, *Sri Ramayana Darshanam* (1949), offers salutations to Homer, Virgil, Dante, Milton, Firdousi, and a whole host of poets in Kannada. He did this, he says, in disregard for the differences between the writers tied to their land and time. Anyone can attain poornadrishti at any time and at any place.

The idea of poornadrishti led Kuvempu to criticize a discipline like history which views events only within the framework of time and space and fails to grasp the whole truth of experience which transcended the contexts of time and space. He asked that universities serve as spaces for imparting universal knowledge, fostering world friendship (*vishva maitri*) and creating possibilities for the emergence of vishvamanava.

As the only major non-Brahmin Kannada writer in his time— he was from the farmer caste of Vokkaligas—Kuvempu's efforts to practice a universal moral philosophy stand out as even more special. Not dismissing tradition as oppressive, his philosophical ideas, which drew from Vedantic thought, made him engage India's intellectual and moral heritage in a distinct way. His play, *Shudra Tapasvi* (The Shudra Ascetic, 1944), for instance, revised the Shambuka episode found in Uttara Ramayana since he was certain only a poet of a lesser vision, and not Valmiki, could have written it. In this play, Rama does not kill Shambuka and the Brahmin who had complained that his young son had died because Shambuka, a Shudra ascetic, had violated dharma by doing penance, realizes his mistake. His creative effort, Kuvempu felt, now offered an enjoyment that rose above the differences of caste, clan and wealth. In another enactment of the vishvamanava ideal, *Mantra Mangalya*, a form of wedding Kuvempu designed in the mid-60s, frees the married couple from all community attachments and sets them on a spiritual quest of their own.

Radiating across his fiction, poems, speeches and criticism, Kuvempu's philosophical vision has shaped the critical sensibilities of Dalit and Shudra communities as well as the Kannada humanist ethos at large in distinct ways.

In 1985, Kuvempu's inaugural address at the first World Kannada Conference in Mysore sought to codify the philosophy of vishvamanava. Released on this occasion, a booklet prepared by Kuvempu titled, *The Message of Vishvamanava,* observed:

> We bind them (children) into nation, caste, language, varna, and community. The primary aim of education has to be to turn them into a "Buddha," that is vishvamanava. Only then will the world survive and flourish. The *bhavanes* (sentiments) that applies to humans cannot be limited to a caste or any other community. We do not need the prosperity of a few individuals but of everyone. We do not need a reduced vision that distinguishes the worldly and the divine, but a *poornadrishti.*

A brief quote from Swami Vivekananda, "No man is born to a religion… Let there be as many religions as there are human beings in the world," which serves as an epigraph to *The Message of Vishvamanava,* acknowledges his influence on Kuvempu. This booklet specifies the seven articles (*sapta sutra*) of vishvamanava which ask that "distinctions like Brahmana, Kshatriya, Vaishya, Shudra, Shia, Sunni, Protestant, Catholic, Sikh and others must be done away with" and that each individual strives to arrive at his or her own religion, his or her truth (*darsana*).

Kuvempu wrote impassioned essays on the importance of Kannada as the medium of instruction in school and higher education in Karnataka. But languages, he felt, offered only a limited medium for experiencing the world. Being a vishvamanava was to go beyond all cultural distinctions, without prior submission to official religions or to community attachments.

Animated by a love for peace and a great daring to experience the world freely, the philosophical idea of vishvamanava is Kuvempu's passionate invitation to explore truth on one's own terms.

THE PASSIONS OF LOHIA

I. *The Political Self*

Rammanohar Lohia (1910-1967), the socialist thinker and politician, is remembered for his advocacy of land reform, of affirmative action for backward castes, religious minorities and women, of devolution of power to village panchayats, of Indian languages as sources of political and intellectual creativity in India, of international equality between countries and races, of global disarmament. Scattered across his voluminous writings, his exciting views on human nature and on the cultivation of the self among activists though are not remembered as much.

Lohia deplored what he termed "environmentalism", a view which saw legal and policy changes as sufficient to reform individuals. For him, political discussions that focused only on large structures such as the economy and the polity were inadequate since they offered scant attention to the moral selves of individuals.

In his famous essay, *Fundamentals of a World Mind* (1958), Lohia argued that "the eye must necessarily redden at an act of injustice and at the fact of poverty and inequality, but it must also shed a tear." The capacity for feeling angry at the sight of injustice and suffering is essential to see in *everyone*. It makes up, in Lohia's phrase, "social conscience."

Aided by general reflections such as these, Lohia scaled down the focus on the Indian predicament on several occasions. He often bemoaned the hypocrisy in India, where the pursuit of material prosperity went hand in hand with a life-denying stance. This disjunction between ideal and practice ought to make way for an affirmative attitude to life.

A disjunction between the ideal and practice in India, for Lohia, could also be seen in how metaphysical claims of the oneness of reality like the one found in Shankaracharya's *advaita* philosophy existed alongside active caste divisions. He asked the young socialist activist to put an end to this "sorry mental condition."

Lohia freely drew his ideas on cultivating the moral self from the Indian philosophical traditions. The idea of *nirvikalpa samadhi*, or a state where time stands still, plays a key role in his view of how a morally engaged individual orients herself to the world. Evolved from his experiences of torture during his imprisonment in Lahore in 1944, it asks that their struggle stay focused on the present without anxiety or fear or desire towards the future or the past.

An integral part of his views about evolving an independent relationship with the present, Lohia's concept of immediacy asks that moral justifications for activist efforts be sought in the immediate steps taken towards them instead of seeking them in either past actions or future outcomes. He invoked Gandhi's phrase, "one step at a time," for illustrating his model of the means-ends relation.

Lohia's recuperation of the philosophical ideal of *samata*, which values inward equanimity and outward equality at the same time, foregrounds the value of being attentive to the moral self amidst public struggles, and extends the discussions of equality in novel ways. In his essay, *The Meaning of Equality* (1956), he wrote:

> The modern mind has forgotten yet another meaning of equality, its most inward meaning. Man must strive to feel an inward quality between contrary conditions of pleasure and pain, heat and cold, victory and defeat. The ancients in India seemed to have sensed that inward equanimity and outward equality were two sides of the same coin, for alone in India's languages, does a single word stand for both meanings, Samata or Samatvan.

Arguing that attaining equanimity had "been possible in the past to those who have prepared themselves for it", Lohia felt that it could be attained under politically difficult circumstances in the present as well.

II. A Reading of Rama, Krishna and Shiva

'The myths of a people are a record of their dream and their sorrow, an inerasable register of their most deeply cherished and highly rated desires and aspirations as well as of the inescapable sadness that is the stuff of life and its local and temporal history.'

Found in *Ram, Krishna and Shiva*, Lohia's wild essay from the mid-1950s, these prefatory words clarify the socialist leader's regard for the mythological life of communities before inaugurating an original effort at evolving a civilizational self-portrait as well as a political philosophy through a delineation of the differing personalities of the three gods.

Noting that India's "great myths have for centuries exercised an unbroken hold on the mind of the people," Lohia observes that the Buddha and Emperor Ashoka won't be familiar to more than a quarter of all Indians whereas the names of Rama, Krishna and Shiva will be known to "everybody," and "their doings vaguely known to almost everybody or at least one in two of the population" and "one in ten would know the details of their acts and ideas."

These three gods, for Lohia, are "India's three great dreams of perfection": "Ram is the perfection of the limited personality, Krishna of the exuberant personality and Siva of the non-dimensional personality." Lohia's elaboration of these "categories of perfection" is an absolute delight.

Rama stayed loyal to Sita. He never set his eyes on another woman. And when the washerman casts doubt on Sita's chastity, Rama banishes her to the forest. These examples, Lohia observes, clarify that Rama was bound by rules, a constitution. Despite his love for his wife, he had to abide by the rule that any complaint from the subjects ought to receive a hearing and find a remedy. Obliged to act within rules always, Rama is a limited personality. Lohia offers a counter-factual to illustrate this point. Rama could have abdicated his throne and accompanied Sita. (*He should have!* Lohia says). But his people would have then asked him to waive off the rule and stay on. And a person bound by a constitution will not want such a waiver of rules under any circumstance. For a limited personality, the obligation to rules is not just an external demand; he or she is inwardly attached to them.

On the other hand, Krishna, the exuberant personality, recognizes rules but feels free to depart from them "when they prove irksome."

Lohia lays out brilliant comparisons between Rama and Krishna. Rama does not speak much: and, when he does speak, he seems to have listened to the other closely. Things are different with Krishna. He is a great talker but listened "only so that he could talk yet better…"

Rama breaks down and cries a couple of times, but never Krishna.

Rama does not perform miracles; Krishna performs many. Then the Lohia spin comes in. Rama who went to the forest with his wife and brother managed to put down an empire, while Krishna, who "dazzled the world with his deeds," only oversaw the transfer of a kingdom from "one wing of the ruling dynasty to another." It is Rama, in other words, who achieved "a political miracle."

Unlike Rama and Krishna who "led human lives," Lohia points out that Shiva "was without birth and without end." Characterizing the formless (*nirakara*) and attributeless (*nirguna*) Shiva as "non-dimensional," he points out that he is both infinite and a part of events occurring in time.

The compassionate side of Shiva holds great appeal for Lohia. After destroying Kama for disturbing his meditation, he is moved by Rati's sorrow at her husband's death and restores his life. Shiva's intense love for his wife, Sati, also stands out for the socialist thinker. His mourning at the death of his beloved wife takes on a demonic character: placing her corpse over his shoulders, he kept walking until her body fell off part by part across different parts of the country. "No lover, nor god, nor demon, nor human," Lohia remarks with amazement, "has left such a story of stark and uninhibited companionship."

Lohia views Shiva's actions as exemplifying his principle of immediacy which asks that moral justifications be found in the immediate steps one has taken instead of seeking them in either past actions or future outcomes. Taking the morally most appropriate stand in the present without letting the past or the future haunt it, for him, is absolutely essential. Lohia's principle of immediacy wishes of course to break free from liberal and Marxist utopian projects that justify their political action in the present by referring to future outcomes as well as the revivalist politics of religious fundamentalists that justifies revenge in the present by referring to actual or imagined deeds in the past.

Shiva, Lohia observes further, is "not guilty of a single act which can indubitably be described as without justice in itself...Every one of his acts contains its own immediate justification and one does not have to look for an earlier or later act."

In the famous puranic episode of the gods and the demons churning the ocean to get nectar, Shiva, who had no part in the war between these two parties or in their collaborative wish to find immortality through nectar, stepped in to drink the poison emitted from the ocean and saved everyone. His actions, Lohia adds poignantly, "let the story proceed." Again, when a devotee wanted to offer worship only to Shiva and not to Parvathi, his wife, seated beside him, Shiva turned into Ardhanarishwar, part-woman and part man, in response. If these two episodes reveal the exemplary style of Shiva's moral interventions, two other actions of the latter proved less easy for Lohia to justify through the principle of immediacy.

When Shiva cut off an elephant's head to revive the decapitated Ganesha and console his mother, Parvathi, didn't the elephant's mother suffer from grief? Lohia's response: "In the new Ganesh, both the elephant and the old Ganesh continued their existence and neither died." Further, this new being, which meant continued life for both Ganesh and the elephant, went on to prove to be of "perennial delight and wisdom...which only a comic mixture of man and elephant can be."

The other difficult episode for Lohia is the dance contest between Shiva and Parvathi at Chidambaram. Excelling at dance, Parvathi had nearly outdanced Shiva, when the latter raised his leg up high, a move that considerations of modesty made difficult for Parvathi to match. Shiva won as a result. Did he lift his leg high merely to defeat Parvathi? Or, Lohia wonders further, was his move "the result of a natural crescendo of a dance of life that was warming up step by step?" Since "the dance of life consists of bumps which a squeamish world calls obscene and against which it tries to protect the modesty of its women," he surmised, could Shiva have invited his wife to break the moral limits, in the aesthetics of dance as well as elsewhere?

Lohia stayed an atheist till the end of his life. But his great curiosity about the mythological inheritance of India was firmly in place all along. Unlike other atheists, who prefer to either stay indifferent towards religion or strive to demystify it or dismiss it as irrational cultural baggage, Lohia took the mythological imagination of communities seriously without feeling obliged to believe in any religion. He sought in it clues to the cultural psychology of Indians. And, in a display of a still-uncommon creative relationship with the symbolic heritage of the country, he evolved interpretive means from it to better understand Indian society and to craft a rooted democratic politics for it.

Noting that Rama could degenerate into a narrow personality, Krishna into a dissolute personality and Shiva into an amorphous and episodic personality, and that he had no remedies to suggest for pre-empting these possibilities, Lohia proclaimed: "O India, Mother, give us the mind of Shiva, the heart of Krishna and the world and deed of Ram, create us with a non-dimensional mind and an exuberant heart, but a life of limits."

III. The Necessity of an Aesthetic Revolution

An intense curiosity about the cultural world brought a different texture, a different angle, a different keenness to Lohia's political vision. His attention to the noxious politics of skin complexion in India and elsewhere in the world is an illustration.

The debate topics that Lohia listed in 1960 for an "Association for the Study and Destruction of Caste" or "any debating organization" in towns included the following item: "In the opinion of the house, Draupadi and not Savithri is the representative woman of India." A couple of months earlier, Lohia's exciting essay, "Beauty and Skin Colour," had noted:

> The greatest woman of Indian myth was dark. Draupadi also called Krishna has suffered neglect, probably because male vanity cannot reconcile itself to her five husbands and a platonic affair or two in addition. Savitri and Seeta, the chaste and also the fair of colour represent India's womanhood, not

entirely without reason, but unreason ensues when other representatives are excluded.

Exploring social tensions through mythology, Lohia suggested that colour prejudice and a bias against assertive women seen in later times might have let piously virtuous women like Savitri and Sita eclipse Draupadi, who had "ready wit and deep wisdom" and was "the friend, the companion, the heroine" of Krishna during "his years of duty," in the country's cultural memory.

Observing that ancient India saw both fair and dark skin as beautiful, Lohia deplored that, "Succeeding generations have squandered this great maturity of aesthetic judgement." Beauty contests, he noted with sarcasm, had not elected dark skin so far. The dark female child in India grew up with a "diet of anxiety" about skin colour and had fewer opportunities for self-growth than the male child. He added that, "the male has not suffered the same amount of depreciation because of the colour of the skin." The cosmetic industry thrived, he noted further, amidst the cultural fetish for fair skin seen among "the coloured youth."

With an eye on complexity, Lohia observes again and again that the problem is perpetuated by dark-skinned people: "All the world suffers this tyranny of skin's colour, a tyranny made worse because the tyrants do not practise it as much as the slaves who inflict it upon themselves."

Pulling up a brute fact from international politics, Lohia makes a counter-factual observation: "The fair skinned peoples of Europe have dominated the world for over three centuries…If Africans had ruled the world in the manner of the whites of Europe, standards of beauty would undoubtedly have been different…Politics influences aesthetics; power also looks beautiful, particularly unequalled power."

Ever alert to historical ironies, Lohia points to how the European aesthetic regime found an ally with the one prevalent in India: "The worldwide conjunction of fair skin with overwhelming power has received great reinforcement from a specific Indian situation. Those fair of skin or at least less dark have generally belonged to the higher caste."

Like most tyrannies, Lohia asserts, this "largest and widest tyranny" of colour is also built on an error. How is this to end? Lohia is cryptic:

"When would the beautiful women of dark skin assert their supremacy or at least their rights of equality, or perhaps the revolution in this as in other matters will be paved by the tyrants themselves?"

In any case, the primary significance of an aesthetic revolution was never in doubt for Lohia: "An aesthetic revolution in the evaluation of beauty and its relation to the colour of the skin will blow the air of freedom and inner peace over all the world almost as much as any political or economic revolutions."

Colour prejudice as a political problem continued to preoccupy him. In a second, longer essay on this matter, "The Issue of Skin Colour," Lohia used the brutal policy of apartheid in South Africa as a prelude to a discussion of colour prejudice across the continents of the world. Dismissing the idea of a combined military offensive by India, China and Africa against "the white world," Lohia brought the Gandhian principle of non-violence to bear for the work of overcoming racial and colour prejudice. In this complex struggle, he also felt, the ones at the receiving end had clear responsibilities: the "coloured person" had to end his or her desire for imitating those of European ancestry and seek to be their equal and "take equal pleasure in the world around him, of the white as of the coloured skin, in other words, to aim to do the right thing." Overcoming self-loathing and the desire to emulate the other, affirming oneself without resentment or aggression towards the other, and freely appreciating the achievements of humankind without prejudice towards anyone, they were all part of doing the right thing in Lohia's vision of the struggle of the aesthetically dominated.

IV. Privacy as a Political Ideal

'Numerous evils are taking place in the 20th century. But there is one unique quality. Man has never fought against all injustices, everywhere and at the same time, as he is doing today. Seven revolutions (*sapta kranti*) are taking place before our eyes, everywhere and at the same time.'

Listing these seven revolutions in the Socialist Party's Election Manifesto of 1962, Lohia concludes the document with the party's wish to "extend and make victorious these seven revolutions in India and all parts of the world" and its invitation to "every universalist, every world citizen, every human who wants to be a human (to) join in this task". One among the seven revolutions was aimed "against unjust encroachments on private life."

Lohia is perhaps the first thinker in modern India to accord a foundational value for privacy in a political programme. Before moving on to his political regard for privacy, a quick glance at the six other revolutions on his mind: 1. Equality between men and women. 2. Equality of castes (Although confined to India, he notes, caste is "immobile class" and universal in essence) 3. Against foreign rule and domination 4. For the destruction of all conventional and nuclear weapons 5. For economic equality. 6. Against inequality based on race and skin-colour.

"The seventh revolution," Lohia observes, "aims at protecting privacy against encroachment by the collective." The bureaucratic structures of the modern state and market have become massively present in the lives of individuals: "The individual's welfare and happiness, education and health, also his leisure and much of his life and thought are subject to planning of various kinds." True, the individual remains important and his or her welfare may have gone up, but that has also entailed a loss of freedom. Although planning was especially strict in communist countries, "the element of organizational compulsion," in doing good was everywhere and it did not honour the value of privacy.

Planning in the name of the good often forgets, Lohia sharply notes, that there are varieties of the good. Plus the good and the bad are not easy to decide. Being free to choose and make mistakes allow for a better understanding of what makes up the good and the bad. Lohia especially regrets the stranglehold of social realism in USSR which did not allow its people to listen to jazz or enjoy abstract painting. Even in countries like the US, where Soviet style state planning wasn't found and where the freedom of choice was celebrated, "education, information and entertainment stay within a certain framework of permissibility." Lohia's longstanding caution against the ills of both communism and capitalism is alive in his discussion of privacy as well.

The Soviet state had taken over the ownership of all property, but violated the privacy of individuals, be it on the issue of child bearing or in preparing speeches. In the US, where individuals could own private property, a private matter like entertainment was shaped by the state and business interests. The connection between property and privacy, Lohia points out, is not a direct one.

"What then must be done?" Lohia asks before bringing closure to his all-too-brief discussion on privacy. Asking that risks be taken, he offers an illustration: privacy must not be violated with a view to stall the emergence of alternate ideas of property. Modern states must allow for fundamental dissent. "Constitutional and other orderly means are often not enough," Lohia emphasizes, to achieve the seven revolutions. Non-violent means of civil disobedience, of Satyagraha, continue to be crucial for achieving them.

JAYAPRAKASH NARAYAN AND
THE IDEA OF SAMPOORN KRANTI

Jayaprakash Narayan, the Gandhian socialist leader, raised his famous slogan, *Sampoorn Kranti* (Total Revolution), in a speech at a huge rally in Patna on June 5, 1974. The rally is said to have stretched for seven kilometres. Two weeks later, the "gist" of this speech delivered in Hindi appeared in English translation in *Everyman's*, a weekly edited by Jayaprakash Narayan (JP).

Earlier in 1974, JP had accepted the leadership of the student movement in Bihar. He had initially wanted to work with the students as an advisor, but they had not listened to him. The high moral stature of the seventy-one-year-old JP, who had chosen to work, after India's independence, as a social activist, outside electoral politics, had already convinced the students that he was their leader. Their choice proved wise. The JP Movement, as we now know it, found great support across India.

The translation of JP's speech titled, *Towards Total Revolution,* which has retained its spontaneous, spoken form, offers a glimpse of his political passions. The electric appeal the speech must have had on the listeners can also be guessed.

At the very beginning JP clarifies that their struggle was not a "movement," but "a total revolution" for which the protestors had "to make sacrifices, undergo suffering, face lathis and bullets, fill up jails." Although the Patna rally sought the dissolution of the Bihar Assembly, the work required to "achieve that freedom for which thousands of the country's youths made sacrifices," was larger in scope, and needed more time.

JP summed up the situation facing them: "Educational institutions are corrupt. Thousands of youths face a bleak future. Unemployment goes on increasing. The poor get less and less work. Land ceiling laws are passed, but the number of landless people is increasing. Small farmers have lost their lands." Although "a new programme for the future" was expected from him, he could only offer its "main points" now, which had emerged from his discussions with "students, intellectuals and colleagues."

Before sharing the main points, JP dismissed the frequent accusations of communists that his student days in the United States of America had made him an agent of that capitalist country. He shared a stirring glimpse of his student life in USA: "In America I worked in mines, in factories and slaughter houses. I worked as a shoe shine boy and even cleaned commodes in hotels. During vacations, I worked and then three or more boys lived in a single room and we cooked our own food."

Between 1922 and 1929, JP had moved between five universities in America. Financial hardship and shifts in intellectual interests were among the main reasons behind it. He studied science briefly at the University of California, Berkeley, before shifting to the study of chemical engineering at the University of Iowa. He then moved to the University of Wisconsin, Madison, where he studied sociology with leading scholars. Close involvements with radical student groups in Madison and the works of Marx, Lenin, Trotsky, Plekhanov, MN Roy and Rosa Luxembourg, among others, cultivated his passions for Marxism. JP has clarified that he became a Marxist, and not a Stalinist. After getting a BA degree from the University of Ohio, where an American friend arranged for financial support, JP completed his MA from Ohio State University and returned to India soon after.

Sharing Lenin's view that communists in colonial countries had to work with the freedom struggles found there, even if they were led by bourgeois leaders, JP joined the Indian National Congress: "They (the Indian communists) said Gandhi is an agent of the capitalists... But they forgot Lenin." During his work in the freedom struggle and after, Gandhi's ideal of sarvodaya came to matter more for his political thought. His selfless, honest activism earned him admirers throughout India.

Indira Gandhi's unwillingness to understand the seriousness of his struggles piqued JP. He had expected co-operation from her. Instead, she had indirectly accused him—two months before the Patna rally—of taking money from "capitalists" and losing therefore the moral authority to fight corruption. A deeply pained JP responded in *Everyman*'s that it was morally permissible for social workers without an independent means of income to seek the assistance of friends. If that was corruption, he continued, then Gandhi, who had depended on the support of rich patrons, would be the guiltiest of all.

JP's speech at the Patna rally tacitly responded to Indira Gandhi's accusation. His response exemplifies a depth of experience, political seriousness and oratorical style that has clearly become rare:

> There is fire in the hearts of the people. Countless children in Bihar go to sleep without food. I see numerous people getting emaciated. There is a barber from my own village. I was appalled to see how thin he has grown. When I asked Ramsujha Thakur why he was so reduced, he replied that there was nothing for him to eat. I don't know how people manage to live. What do they eat. After the death of my wife, I have to keep account of my expenses and I am amazed at the amount I have to spend on food alone. Without the interest from the Magsaysay Award money and the help of some generous friends, I too would have possibly had to starve.

JP's speech lets us discern only two components of his idea of *Sampoorn Kranti*, both of which related to the polity and were informed by the experience of the preceding five Lok Sabha elections.

The Indian polity, JP felt, had two severe defects.

Elected representatives could hold office for a full five-year term regardless of how well they performed. Finding this unacceptable, JP argued that voters ought to have the right to recall poorly performing candidates. He considered this "an unwritten right" of the electorate. A few years later, JP asked that his proposal not be viewed as "anarchic," and clarified that constitutions across the world had usually resulted out of "revolutionary upheavals."

Next, elections had become very expensive: "Crores of rupees, unaccounted money, is collected form black marketers...Nobody knows how the money is spent and by whom." Election expenses had to be curbed if "a poor candidate, a peasant, or a worker or a party of the poor" had to contest elections.

JP's thoughts on *Sampoorn Kranti* are not found in one place but are scattered across short articles, speeches, interviews, and the entries in his *Prison Diary* (1979). This diary, in his words, was "centrally concerned" with "a theory of a people's movement and its role in a total revolution."

The necessity of violence and the importance of the state for reorganizing society, which feature prominently in discussions of revolutionary politics, are both spectacularly absent in JP's scheme of *Sampoorn Kranti*. A revolution, for him, had to be non-violent. And, social activities had to shape the functioning of the state, not the other way around. Finally, a revolution was "a long-drawn process," not a speedy event. These emphases, which depart fundamentally from conventional ideas of revolution, owe much to Gandhi's philosophical ideas.

In *Prison Diary*, JP specified that his model of *Sampoorn Kranti* was made up of seven revolutions: social, economic, political, cultural, ideological/intellectual, educational and spiritual. These components, he added, were not fixed: the cultural revolution, for instance, could include the educational, spiritual and ideological revolutions. And each of them could be split up further. Economic revolution could be broken up into agricultural, industrial and technological revolutions and the intellectual revolution into scientific and philosophical revolutions.

After outlining what seems a well evolved scheme and insisting that the "technical words" of discussion are "clearly defined," it is unfortunate that JP could not elaborate his scheme any further. The task of reconstructing his scheme of struggle from the several thousand pages of his collected writings and speeches remains to be fulfilled.

Broadcast on radio and television soon after the Janata Government was formed in 1977, JP's *Message to the Nation* affirmed his "faith" in *Sampoorn Kranti* and "pledged" to work for it. It noted the need to preserve the noble parts of "our heritage" and purge the "evil inheritance" of the caste system and the "rotten customs" related to "marriage, birth and death etc."

Evolving appropriate educational and technological arrangements, decentralizing the polity, overcoming communalism and preventing the exploitation of tribals were also at the centre of JP's democratic vision for India. For him, the nationalization of industry and the creation of public sector units did not constitute socialism. In an economic democracy, people had to be more than consumers and workers.

Like Gandhi and Lohia, JP distrusted law and policy measures as means of genuine social and economic transformation. Anti-dowry laws, for instance, had done little to weaken the practice. The true eradication of dowry required individuals to change their selves as part of the struggle.

JP saw his ideals getting shortchanged soon after the Janata Government, which he had termed "a child of the revolution," came to power. On June 5, 1978, the occasion of the fourth anniversary of the Patna speech—"Total Revolution Day"—he rued, after a brief recall of how the movement he had helped build saw a "historic triumph of democracy," through the electoral overthrow of the Congress in 1977: "But it seems that the caravan of total revolution faltered thereafter... The Janata Party Government is treading the same old beaten track which led the Congress government to failure and the nation to the brink of disaster."

Steering clear of defeatism, however, JP felt that the second phase of the total revolution had just begun:

> The caravan of total revolution must not falter any more. Backed by people's and youth power, it must keep moving forward."
> He felt certain that his followers had to concentrate their work in the villages. Noting his ill health made it difficult to provide continued leadership, his anniversary note "call(ed) upon the soldiers of the total revolution to fearlessly and unitedly move towards their goal.

A pragmatist in political action, JP sought to evolve a coherent political vision while keeping the question of strategy open. "Circumstances change," his 1974 Patna speech noted to reiterate the non-necessity of working with "a big, long term programme."

How might JP have thought of total revolution nearly five decades later? The popular—as well as intellectual—amnesia towards JP's efforts to craft a democratic vision that was organic to modern India is a scandal.

IN PURSUIT OF CULTURAL SIGHT

"You are a modern individual. Your wife is a very modern person. The old ornaments that belonged to your grandmother, like ear studs, earrings—did your wife throw them into the fire?"

"No, why would she do that?"

"What did she do with them then?"

"We melted the old ornaments and got new ones made."

"That means: whatever the form of the ornament, its substance is valuable; it is foolish to discard it. Similarly with the Ramayana and the Mahabharata or any other story. They are not to be thrown away. They have to be melted and brought into your literature in keeping with your new aims and desires."

Kuvempu, the Kannada writer, recalled this exchange between a Dravida Kazhagam activist and himself in "A Call for a Cultural Revolution," his famous inaugural speech at a meeting of the Karnataka Writers and the Artists Association in Mysore in 1974.

In a soul-searching address on the writerly imperative given at *Jana Nudi*, a literary convention held in Mangalore, in 2015, Devanur Mahadeva, the famous Kannada writer, held up Kuvempu's analogy to illustrate how to relate with intellectual inheritances from the past.

Mahadeva began with an ironic observation that many writers, including himself, were all "saying the right things." But the social trends arraigned against their wishes were getting stronger. Where were the writers failing then? Had speaking on behalf of equality become a mere skill for them? Or, had their quest gone still, reducing them to being entertainers? It was essential for writers "to explore what it takes to relate to the minds of the community and to make our words the words of the communities."

When Sheldon Pollock, the Sanskritist, had asked him how he, a Dalit, could accept the Ramayana and the Mahabharata, he recalled having replied: "If the mind of the Indian community was laid out like a mat, the Ramayana and the Mahabharata will be seen to have been woven into more than half of it in some way or another." Had the avoidance of these epic poems, he wondered, made us have-nots? "Might we become social drop-outs if we did not attain rebirth by connecting with the mind of the community?"

Young writers, Devanur felt, ought to take history and culture seriously. His invocation of Kuvempu's speech from four decades ago itself was a reminder of the continuity in writerly concerns. And, in keeping with a literary tradition that expected the writers and their work to stay face-to-face with their communities, he suggested that they ought to experience the existential predicament of communities and articulate it in their writings.

The epics, for Devanur, continue to provide a reliable guide for understanding the moral life of Indian communities. The spirit of his discussion can extend to recognize the moral significance of folklore, tribal epics and theological texts from different religious traditions as well.

I doubt Devanur was suggesting the scholastic route of mastering textual traditions for being an effective writer in the present. His demand was more of a general plea that writers creatively engage the moral imagination of communities. Taking the Gita as an example, he asked, can the finer elements of this text be worked with while keeping out its vision of the varna social order?

Engagements with moral inheritances are better done, Devanur insists, like Kuvempu, through images and metaphors, and not literally. He offered an instance—a hurried one, no doubt!—of a three act play to show what such an engagement might look like: In Act One, Lord Rama is distraught upon his arrival in the world, "This isn't the same place where I was born." In the next Act, his devotees strangle his neck and destroy him without leaving a trace. And, in the last Act, a mad bid for power has resulted in hate mongering among communities.

A running concern in Devanur's address was that cultural politics had become reactive and all too often took the form of a counter to the offensives of the fundamentalist forces. Kuvempu's speech had similarly discouraged such a politics: "Get away from the negative attitude (English in the original)."

The issues that Devanur felt ought to be of concern for writers are of equal relevance for scholars of Indian society at large, whose political sensibilities tend to be at a remove from those of the communities they study.

Devanur's address ended thus: "We need to acquire cultural sight by grafting on to the mother-creeper of the community mind. Our words might then become one with those of the community. Yes, we need to meditate to attain cultural sight."

LET US BECOME SHUDRAS

Deploring the growing trends towards 'neo-Brahminism', Prasanna, the reputed theatre director and handloom activist, asks that we strive to become Shudras instead. In his book, *Shudraraagona Banni* (Let us Become Shudras, 2016), he elaborates that "Brahmin" was a metaphor for a life freed of physical labour, whereas "Shudra" stood in for a life that values it. Unlike the science fiction scenarios of the future, where the need for physical labour is often eliminated, Prasanna sees a permanent place for it. Sidestepping the baffling complexity of the global financial system or international relations, he offers passionate reflections on how a simple life which valued physical effort was crucial for averting the ecological catastrophe. They also provide tantalizing glimpses into several moral traditions that valued the ideals of physical work and simple living.

Prasanna notes: "Machine civilization is a peculiar thing. It tries to turn everyone into a Brahmin. Do we need so many intellectuals, traders, artists, middlemen, and entertainers? So many singers, dancers, priests, sanyasis? Since everyone wants to be a Brahmin, agriculture and crafts suffer massively."

SB discusses how physical work had a spiritual focus and integrity for many of the devotional saints in India. Stories from Taoism, Christianity and Sufi traditions also shared this understanding. Even the rich in olden times, Prasanna points out, did not shirk physical effort. Manual work is not to be prized for its own sake. Physical exertion makes humans conscious of the world in a different, self-enhancing way.

If the elite embrace the ideals of physical effort, the consequences will be great. And, manual work will seem less degrading too: "The rich, the Brahmins and the neo-Brahmins need to change first. They must accept Shudratva. If they change, the poor will change, the system will change. Even now, the system means us, isn't it? Not the poor." In a telling metaphor, Prasanna argues, "instead of lifting up those at the bottom, the ones above should step down below."

Prasanna recalls how Ebrahim Alkazi, his teacher at the National School of Drama, New Delhi, awakened him and his classmates to the value of manual work. Alkazi would sweep the room before starting his class. The surprised students then began to do it themselves.

A large poster of Lenin, which Prasanna brought back from a visit to the Soviet Union, hangs on a wall in his house in Heggodu. On it is sketched a speech balloon where Lenin admits, "I like Gandhi." Prasanna explained, "Lenin and Gandhi do not mention each other in their writings. I wanted them to come together." Might the high regard for physical labour found in Gandhi's vision of individual self-reliance have spoken to Lenin?

Prasanna locates his recent concerns within a long tradition of struggle—from Veerashaivas to the Tattva poets to Gandhi—to reorder the cultural values that put intellectual work above physical labour and affirm the virtues of simple living. That tradition becomes a point of entry for thinking about how to sustain ecological sanity in the world. Its ideals, Prasanna believes, can still help rebuild institutions.

Don't the metaphors of Brahmin and Shudra limit the discussion to Hindu society? "No," Prasanna clarifies, "they can be extended to other religions."

THE MATTER OF A MELA

At the meeting held at the Sevagram Ashram six weeks after Gandhi's assassination, in March, 1948, Vinobha Bhave argued that a *mela*, and not a formal organization, was the ideal model for continuing the work of Gandhi in independent India. The discussions at this meeting illuminate the many dimensions of the idea of *mela*.

In arguing that financial reserves were unimportant for carrying on the work of Gandhi, Vinobha pointed out, "The *melas* and gatherings of the religious people of this country have never needed funding."

Maulana Azad, who expressed support for Bhave's proposal, singled out the special freedoms that lay in the experience of a *mela*: "A mela is an open fair, a carnival. No one attending it needs to know the others. No one has responsibility of any kind. An open fair is a throw about of people and purposes."

Mela is usually taken to mean a fair where a large number of people gather and various kinds of goods are bought and sold. A *mela* is also a spectacle to behold and rejoice in.

Held on the banks of rivers, the *kumbha melas* of Prayag, Hardwar, Ujjain and Nasik exhibit remarkable features. They swell up with lakhs of people with the necessary facilities seeming to emerge spontaneously, without much prior planning on the part of any designated authorities. This magical quality indeed is a constitutive feature of a *mela*, as distinguished from a *sammelana*, which is an organized affair.

Not a random coming together of people, a *mela* happens in a designated place and time. The latter details are known to people not as a result of formal announcements as much as in the nature of a detail in an ingrained cultural calendar.

The 1899 edition of the Monier Williams Sanskrit dictionary defines a *"mela"* as "association, assembly, company, society." A crucial feature of the coming together of people in a *mela* is that the participation in it is open to all. Social hierarchies and prejudices do not find space in the imagination of a *mela*. Everyone, in other words, is welcome in a mela. When communal minds ask that Muslim vendors be barred from temple and village fairs, they are finishing off the very idea of a *mela*. A *mela* ceases to be a *mela* if anyone is barred from it.

Interactions in a *mela* are not tightly bound by rules. Things happen, as it were, on their own. There is a freeness to how people interact without the assembly risking slipping into chaos or anarchy. Also crucial: people can come in and leave as they wish.

The 1894 Kannada-English Dictionary compiled by Rev. Ferdinand Kittel extends the range of meaning inhering in *"mela"*: "meeting," "union," "a large concourse of people collected at stated periods for religious or commercial purposes," "a fair," "a band of musicians," "a set of dancing girls, musicians and singers and their performances," and "mirth, merriment, jest, sport, joking fun."

A sense of fun, gaiety, blitheness and festivity are integral to the imagination and experience of a *mela*. This is probably a reason for the word to also refer to performers, musicians and entertainers. While *mela* as a fair or a large gathering brings up the idea of an assembly of people in the abstract, it can admit of gender distinctions when used to refer to a chorus of musicians.

A *mela* can also refer to the union or the conjoining of two objects or people. For instance: "this literary work invokes *shringara rasa* to portray the *mela* of *prakriti* (nature) and *prema* (love)." Indeed, *"melaisu"* (to create a *mela*-like relation) means a bringing together of different elements in a harmonious way and, at times, a sexual union.

Melas are places of general social mixing with scope for promiscuous encounters too. Women who hadn't been able to conceive were known to seek sex freely here. The anonymous nature of the mixing is perhaps reflected in the Kannada word, *"meladava,"* which literally means, a man of the *mela* or a man who has emerged from the *mela*. In the Kannada dictionary compiled by the famous writer, Shivaram Karanth, *meladava* is defined as "a prostitute's son" and "an intimate associate of a prostitute."

It is more common to see the term, *mela*, being used to deride or scoff at a gathering that is crowded or that has turned into a comical affair or a state of confusion. A lineage to the sense of a comic occasion is illustrated by the old Kannada words, *meladaata* (a male buffoon) and *meladaake* (a female buffoon).

Over the decades, the word "*mela*" has become hitched to modest, limited-purpose occasions. Consider the following phrases: mango *mela*, loan *mela*, saree *mela*. In all of these instances, no one is under an illusion about the narrowness of the *mela* experience. A shopping sale organized by an online retailer a few years ago, *The Great Indian Mela* projected a *mela* experience in digital space, among a virtual community of consumers. A sale exclusive to credit and debit card holders, its organizers could at best have been cynical in pitching it as a *mela*.

EXCAVATIONS

A FEW DEVOTEES OF SHIVA

Marayya lived in the town of Kalyana. A virtuous man and an ardent devotee of Shiva, he provided water to thirsty pilgrims. The donations of fellow devotees helped him do his work. Many advised him to also serve other refreshments to the pilgrims: sugarcane juice, buttermilk, ragi gruel, and jaggery-sweetened milk. These drinks, they said, better protected the pilgrims against the heat. Marayya followed their advice and began to serve a variety of drinks to the weary pilgrims. On occasion, the latter would rest for a while and listen to the discussions of the knowledge and experience of Shiva that took place at the water shelter.

Worldly-minded people would also stop by to refresh themselves. Not disapproving of their worldliness, Marayya served them with the same earnestness as he did the devotees. A few among them who enjoyed liquor asked that he serve that as well. Acceding to their request, Marayya began to serve them the intoxicating toddy made from the juice of palm, coconut and other trees. After finishing their drinks, they usually lingered to listen to Marayya's religious discourses and left singing his praises. Marayya always tried to alert them to the dangers of the drinking habit and also offered lofty lessons about the greatness of Shiva.

News that Marayya was serving liquor reached King Bijjala. He summoned his minister, Basavanna, and expressed disbelief that offering liquor could be seen as work and in tune with the morality of Shiva's devotees. Basavanna replied that that was indeed work as it involved the refinement of the soul. If an upper caste person did physical work in the home of an untouchable, he argued further, that work sought to attain the abode of God, and was not aimed at making profits.

Unable to understand such points regarding work, King Bijjala said: "This is not work but immorality. Let me cut off the hands that have served liquor. If, as you say, Marayya is a true Shiva's devotee, he will get them back. Basavanna agreed. The king chopped his hands off immediately. But the pure hearted devotee was not harmed; his hands were restored right away. Convinced that Marayya's work was valuable, the astonished king returned to his palace, singing praises of the former. Since then, Marayya became famous in the world as Hendada Marayya (Liquor Marayya).

*

Making Shiva's devotees laugh was a form of work and happiness was not extrinsic to the pursuit of Shiva's devotion. Maritande was among the several people who did this work. He had spent many years at it.

It rained heavily during one of his visits to a village. The river had flooded and left him stranded in the rain.

Desiring to test his devotion at this time, Shiva appeared before him in the disguise of a devotee. His wife, Parvathi, and a bull had accompanied him. Parvathi was seated on the bull.

Shiva: "Where are you headed?"

Maritande: "I need to visit the neighbouring village for my work. How will you cross this river at this time?"

Shiva: "I'll sit on this bull and cross it. My wife will sit on my shoulders. You seem to be stuck. How will you cross the river?"

Maritande: "I'll sit on your wife's shoulders and get across the river."

Seeing through the answer, Shiva broke into laughter. If the bull could help him cross the river safely, where was the need to make his wife sit on him? She could sit behind him instead. Wouldn't people laugh if they saw her sitting on him?

Maritande had not abandoned his work even under difficult circumstances. His joke had also spared the disguised Shiva from ridicule. A deeply moved Shiva paid him for his work and left with much love towards his devotee.

*

Maadara Dhoolayya worked as a cobbler in Kalyana. He served Shiva's devotees with his earnings. In deep admiration for his work, Shiva appeared before him and asked him to join him in Kailasa, his abode. Dhoolayya declined the invitation, "I don't want to be in Kailasa. I want to be in the service of your devotees here."

Time passed. Shiva wished that the world recognized the greatness of Dhoolayya's work. When Dhoolayya was stitching a pair of sandals, Shiva appeared at the tip of the awl and slowly enfolded him.

*

Marayya and his wife, Lakkamma, were very poor. They did not have enough food to eat; nor clothes to cover themselves. Still, they did not beg anyone for help.

One day, Lakkamma asked her husband, "We need to earn money and serve the Lord, the gurus and the devotees, and find liberation. What work can we do?"

Marayya replied, "You are right. But our work shouldn't mean getting a part of others' wealth. It must be truthful and pure. People drop grains of rice, which the Lord has gifted everyone, on the streets. Let us collect these grains and do our service."

Gathering the grains scattered out of neglect did not impinge on the wealth of others. In going about his work, Marayya even entered people's homes at times and picked up the grains fallen near the grinding stones. No one complained about it. He came to be called Aydakki Marayya*.

Basavanna often hosted large feasts at his house. Marayya collected grains from there as well. He would be able to collect three measures of rice over several hours. Lakkamma would later cook the rice he brought home and serve it to devotees.

Moved to pity to see the hard efforts of Marayya, Basavanna asked his assistants to scatter rice generously on his path. He also asked his two wives to leave some rice around the grindstones.

The following day, Marayya was surprised to see large amounts of rice on his way to Basavanna's house. He collected as much rice

---

* *Aydakki:* Literally, the collected rice.

as he could. He found a lot of rice inside the house too. Collecting three measures of rice within a short period of time, he returned home jubilantly and put the grain in front of his wife.

Lakkamma remained silent. Marayya was surprised at this response. She asked, "How were you able to find this much rice so quickly?" He let her know what he had heard from Basavanna's wives. The latter had given away their husband's scheme for helping him.

Lakkamma became furious, "Basavanna has become arrogant. He thinks we are poor. He does not understand the faith of the devotees. What he has done is like offering salt to the sea."

She continued, "What you have done does not count as work. The rice you have got cannot be offered to the Lord. Take it back to where you found it. Basavanna is haughty that he serves food to a lakh and ninety-six thousand devotees. Invite all those guests for lunch at our home tomorrow."

Marayya did as he was told. Everyone, including Basavanna, accepted the lunch invitation.

Lakamma started cooking preparations for the large gathering.

The following day, the guests were surprised to not see signs of a grand feast. They nevertheless seated themselves down for lunch. When Lakkamma offered the boiled rice to the Lord, its quantity grew and grew until there was enough for the big gathering of guests. Her rice offering had been prepared from the rice grains she herself had collected. Everyone now understood the true significance of *kayaka* (work). Basavanna bowed to the couple before taking leave. Marayya and Lakkamma's toil made the ideal of *kayaka* radiate in the world.

*

Somavve lived in Kalyana. She removed the husk from paddy for a living. Her small income from pounding the paddy and separating out the rice let her live simply and immerse herself in the service of Shiva's devotees.

*

Originating in the 12th century, Lingayat philosophy elevated physical labour (*kayaka*) to a spiritual ideal. The stories of the Shiva devotees found here affirm the spiritual value of work done with selflessness and purity of devotion. I have adapted and translated them from the legendary compiler of *vacanas* (free verse poetry), F.G. Halakatti's *Shivasharanara Charitregalu*—I (Histories of Men Devotees of Shiva, Vol 1, 1944) and *Shivasharanayera Charitregalu* (Histories of Women Devotees of Shiva, 1959). Contemporaries of Basavanna, the twelfth century founder of the Lingayat dharma, all the devotees who appear above have composed *vacanas*.

THE VARIOUS BIRTHS OF GANESHA

Surya-Vinayaka was born on his own (*svayambhu*). He had no parents.

*

After finishing her bath, Parvathi made a human figure from the bathing oil and the dirt scrubbed away from her skin. Ganesha came to life after she sprinkled water from the river Ganga on it.

*

Once Shiva and Parvathi went to rest in a forest in the Himalayas. They saw two elephants making love inside the forest. Their passions ignited, Shiva and Parvathi wanted to enjoy themselves like those elephants. They turned into elephants and made love. This is why Ganesha, the son who was born to them afterwards, has the face of an elephant.

*

A handsome boy emerged out of Shiva's laughter. Noticing Parvathi getting attracted towards him, Shiva turned jealous. He cursed the boy and took away his good looks by giving him an elephant's head and a fat belly.

*

A part of Shiva turned into a handsome being and then emerged from Parvathi's womb.

*

The gods were feeling alarmed: a large number of humans were being allowed inside heaven as reward for their penance. They rushed to Shiva for succour. After listening to their complaint, he turned towards Parvathi. Rubbing some dirt off her body, she made with it a plump figure with four arms and an elephant head. It came to life soon afterwards. Parvathi directed him to place obstacles in the path of the humans seeking to enter heaven through penance. Before he left to carry out his task, Shiva gave him an axe, Parvathi, a bowl of eatables, and Kartikeya, his brother, a mouse to ride on. Other presents also came his way: Brahma, Vishnu, Indra, Kubera, Surya and Chandra gave him, respectively, omniscience, wisdom, good fortune, wealth, and courage and radiance.

*

Parvathi gave birth to a beautiful boy. All the gods came to see him. Except Shani. He had not come due to a curse which made anyone he saw get their head burnt to ashes. When Parvathi heard about this, she felt her son faced no such threat. She pressed Shani to visit her. But, even his hesitant glance at the child—with just one of his eyes—proved his fears right. The child's head went up in flames.

A distraught Parvathi demanded that Shani restore her son's head. Shani expressed helplessness. Not accepting his answer, she asked him to send a servant to bring back the head of the first person he met. But Shani could punish someone only if he or she had erred. His emissary, who went looking for an erring individual, found an elephant sleeping with his face turned northwards. He cut off his head and brought it back to be placed on Parvathi's little son.

*

In the Kritayuga, Vinayaka was born to Kashyapa and Aditi. He doesn't have an elephant's face. A lion is his vehicle in this age. In the Tretayuga, he is Parvathi's son and is known as Mayureshwara. In this age, too, he doesn't have the face of an elephant. And a peacock is his vehicle. In the Dvaparayuga, Gajanana is the son of Shiva and Parvathi. He has an elephant's head and rides a mouse. Known as Dhumaketu Vinayaka in Kaliyuga, his features remain undescribed. He rides a horse in this age.

THE STORY OF GAJAKUMARA

Ruler over half of Bharat Kshetra in the Jambudvipa continent, Emperor Vishnu lived in Dwaravati, a town in Surata country. At this time, King Aparajita was the ruler of Sooradatta country. Conscious of his great strengths, he didn't show much regard for others. Angered at his attitude, Vishnu issued a proclamation: "If anyone in my kingdom can vanquish Aparajita and bring him to me, I'll give him everything he asks for."

Only his brother, Gajakumara, took up the challenge. The emperor lent him all the four divisions of his army to aid him in the battle. Gajakumara defeated Aparajita in a fierce battle and brought him captive, his hands tied tightly at the back. He also brought back bounty: elephants, horses and jewellery. An overjoyed Vishnu asked Gajakumara to name his reward.

Gajakumara replied, "Due to your generosity, I already have most things I need. There is only one thing that I still long for. Barring the queens in your palace, allow me to live with any married woman in this town the way I wish. This is the reward I want."

Vishnu granted his wish.

Gajakumara freely struck relations with the wives of merchants, scholars, peasants and vassal kings in Vishnu's kingdom. His eyes once fell on Vasundari, the wife of Pangula, a goldsmith. Stunned by her grace and beauty, Gajakumara took her home. The separation from his wife deeply pained Pangula. Since he had lacked the courage to respond to the emperor's call to defeat Aparijita, he hid his anger against Gajakumara. Time passed.

One day, Arishtanemi Tirthankara and his followers arrived in Dwaravati to deliver religious sermons. Vishnu and Gajakumara visited the great spiritual leader to pay their respects. In his sermon, Arishtanemi dwelt at length on the suffering that came from being in bad company, and from living with women from clans outside one's own. Gajakumara was transformed on hearing him. All desire left him; luxuries now seemed loathsome. Renouncing all his worldly attachments, he undertook a harsh penance under Arishtanemi's blessings. After twelve years of penance and extensive wanderings, he returned to Dwaravati and stood in meditation inside the Revata grove. His relatives and the good-natured people of the town came by to offer him worship.

Pangula heard about Gajakumara's return. He was delighted that the time for vengeance had finally come. He went over to the Revata grove, taking large iron nails with him. Forcing Gajakumara to lie down on his back, he split him from his chest to his navel. He then impaled him and nailed the skin to the ground.

All this while, the ascetic Gajakumara sought forgiveness and dwelt on matters of faith. After inviting death, he was reborn as Ahamindradeva in Sarvaarthasiddhi, a heaven that was like a cupola to the palace called Deva Loka (celestial abode) with a lifespan as wide as thirty-three oceans.

Bearing in mind the pain of Gajakumara's predicament, the faithful must endure hunger, thirst and heat, achieve death willingly and attain heaven and liberation.

The Tale of Gajakumara appears in Shivakotyacharya's *Vaddaradhane* (Honouring the Elders), a collection of nineteen stories from the tenth century and the first work of prose in Kannada. Bringing the base expressions of human desire into view, these stories cherish worldly detachment, hard penance, forbearance in the face of physical suffering and other Jain values. In each of these stories, which are set in the region of Bharata in the Jambudvipa continent, an epiphanic moment sets the main character on the path to liberation where he endures intense physical pain with great restraint and inner calm. Graphic imaginations of violence accompany these stories exemplifying Jain philosophical ideals. The story of Gajakumara also draws attention to the unforeseeable vastness of the scope of sovereignty. Not offering to fight Aparijata is to be ready to abide by any obligation entailed by the emperor's wish. My retelling of this story has translated and adapted from T. Keshava Bhatta's rendering of the medieval Jain text into modern Kannada prose (Kannada Sahitya Parishad, 1976).

THREE MORAL STORIES FOR CHILDREN

I. Satyagupta and Kamalapeeda

King Satyagupta ruled over Kalinga. Building a large army, he won over many kingdoms. He took care to get his son, Kamalapeeda, a fine education. The son however turned arrogant as a consequence: he came to think he was a bigger scholar than his father. He started speaking to him contemptuously.

One day, Kamalapeeda confronted his father in the royal assembly, "Appajji, you are squandering money on the army." The king replied, "The matter is complex. You are still young. You don't understand political affairs. If I don't provide for the soldiers and look after them now, they will not fight for us at the time of war." His son replied, "Whenever war breaks out, we can toss our money around and find as many soldiers as we want. Just like we find crows when rice is tossed around."

After several days, the king took his son to the terrace at midnight. "Toss a handful of rice now and see if you can attract crows." Kamalapeeda laughed contemptuously, "Do crows appear at night? This only shows the intelligence of those who lack understanding." Hearing these words, his teacher, who was also present, scolded him, "Fool! You abilities are nowhere close to your father's. You haven't understood him at all. Just as rice doesn't make the crows appear at night, money won't help find soldiers at wartime."

II. Susharma, Dharmakushala

A man called Susharma lived in Chidaranyapura on the banks of Tapati river. Dharmakushala was his devoted servant. Susharma was always kind towards him.

One day, Susharma left to do penance for Lord Virupaksha on the banks of Pampa river. Dharmakushala accompanied him. Impressed by his penance, Virupaksha, appeared before Susharma and offered him the boon of *moksha* (liberation). The latter said, "I am now saved. But my servant, who has been loyal to me, also needs *moksha*." When Virupaksha offered to grant *moksha* to the servant in his next life, Susharma replied, "My Lord, please grant me my *moksha* along with him then."

III. The Story of King Canute

A thousand years ago, King Canute ruled England. One day, he and his family were enjoying themselves on the seashore. The courtiers and reciters sang his praises, "O King of Kings, your valour is unmatched in the three worlds. Even this sea will obey your command."

Having his seat face the sea, the king stretched out his legs towards it. He cried, "King of the Sea! My courtiers tell me that you are my servant. You will obey my command then. Shift back a little!"

A tidal wave came towards him just then. It pounded his feet and drenched his clothes before receding.

The king turned to the courtiers and reciters, "I really do have all the qualities you said were in me! Believing you, I thought I was supreme and ordered the King of the Sea to shift backwards. But, a wave disregarded me and pounded my feet. Do you understand at least now? What does it mean to say there is no one above my command?! Only an all-powerful God can command the sea or the mountain to move around, and not mere humans like us. Let the tongue sing praises of God, and not of the sin-filled humans."

*

In Bellary district, around 1820, the children in indigenous schools were taught the two major epics as well as texts like Panchatantra, a set of animal fables meant for royal instruction, and Kanakadasa's Mohana Tarangini. Besides, children from artisanal castes were taught texts like Visvakarma Purana and the Lingayat children Channabasava Purana. It isn't clear from the records what the children in *maktabs* in Bellary were taught, but their counterparts in Bengal read *The Quran* as well as *Gulistan* and *Bustan*, the famous works of the 13th century Persian poet, Sa'di.

In the nineteenth century, the British-influenced discussions on the need for the moral education of children saw compilations of moral stories for children appear across colonial India. Among the earliest among such anthologies in Kannada, *Niti-Chintamani* gathers stories from eclectic sources: the Puranas, local and pan-India historical lore, and, as seen above, even a story from English folklore. Whereas traditional schools taught verse texts, these anthologies are usually found in prose. Although these texts could be viewed as having edificatory content, they are not solely moral texts. And, unlike in the indigenous schools, where the community background of students dictated at times the choice of texts taught to them, books like *Niti-Chintamini* presented themselves as eclectically assembled books of general morals.

In ninety thematic sections with titles such as God is Everywhere, Obedience to Parents, Monogamy, Gratitude, Idle Chatter, and Patriotism, Puttanna sews together old and new virtues for children through didactic stories set in the distant past. Accompanying each of the stories, the black and white sketches graphically aid his moral effort to supply deep time continuities for the selfhood of children.

THE CHESS MATCH

A horse trader from Kabul arrived in Closepet. He wished to sell horses at the military encampment there. A passionate chess-player, he was excited to hear that a soldier there was a chess player.

Tracking down the soldier, the trader invited him to play chess with him. They played several rounds. The horse trader marvelled at the soldier's skills in the game. But the solider merely smiled, "If you want to know what real chess talent looks like, you should play with Bakshi Chamappajji's daughter in Mysore. Women in his house though are behind a purdah and don't meet outsiders. Try your luck. If it works out, you will have played the most fabulous chess game in your life ever."

Intrigued and curious, the horse trader made his way to Mysore. He waited outside Chamappaji's house in the morning and greeted him as he came out of the gate. The sequence recurred over a couple of days. An intrigued Chamappaji called out to him, "Who are you? Is there anything you want from me?"

The horse trader explained everything. Chamappaji replied, "Women live in seclusion in our house. I'm not sure you will be able to play chess with my daughter. But I can check with her and let you know. Please come back in the morning."

Chamapajji let his daughter know about the trader's desire. She readily agreed, "We can have the game tomorrow afternoon. A curtain can be put between us. A small slit can be made in it to let me see the chessboard and you can make the moves for me."

Delighted that his wish would be fulfilled, the horse trader showed up for the game in the afternoon.

He bowed to Chamappaji's daughter behind the curtain before sitting down at the chessboard. Before the game started, she asked her father to ask the trader to pick any soldier-pawn he wished to be checkmated by. Her opponent nervously chose one and was checkmated within a few moves. The bewildered trader exclaimed, "I've never experienced this kind of defeat in my life. Amazing!"

Found in *Nenapugalu* (Memories, 1960), the memoirs of K. Vasudevacharya (1865-1961), the famous composer and musician from Mysore, the incident I have translated above lands us in the company of beautiful surprises.

THE IRISH CONNECTION

Kuvempu had set out to become an English writer in his teens. He published *The Beginner's Muse*, a slim volume of seven English poems, in 1922, while he was still in high school. He would later call these poems "childish and imitative" and wonder why any of the elders who had seen them hadn't tried to instill better sense in him. In a climate of servitude towards the language of the rulers, he surmised, might they have seen writing poetry in English as a sign of talent?

In 1924, the history teacher in his high school advised Kuvempu to show his poems to James Cousins, the Irish poet and theosophist, who was a visitor at Mysore University. After a long wait at the university's guest house, he was ushered inside. Seating himself on a sofa near the Irish poet, Kuvempu explained the reason for his visit and handed him a manuscript of his poems. Cousins flipped through the pages over and over again and looked accusingly at the young writer. A supporter of the Swadeshi boycott of foreign clothes, Kuvempu was dressed fully in khadi. His cap, shirt, jacket and dhoti were all made from khadi.

Cousins seemed disappointed. "What is all this stuff?!" he said. "You are dressed in swadeshi clothes from head to toe, but the poems are not swadeshi. Have you written anything in your language?"

His words humiliated and saddened Kuvempu who was in ready anticipation of praise. Although he had written a short story and a few poems in Kannada, he hit back: "No, I haven't! Lofty sentiments and fine thoughts cannot be expressed in Kannada the way they can be in English. Kannada is a lowly language. Its metrical forms are outdated. The diversity of metrical forms seen in English simply don't exist in Kannada." (He saw these remarks later as "unwise, comical and dishonest").

Cousins became tender and consoling: "It isn't like that. No language is unworthy in itself. It might seem that way until a talented person comes along. The language can achieve any feat in his hands. Bengali was in the same condition as your language. Rabindranath Tagore arrived on the scene. He wrote in new ways. He created new metrical forms. He even won the Nobel Prize. You must do similar things with your language and create great literature. We will then translate it into English, the way we did Tagore's work. English is not your language. You will not be able to create truly creative literature. This is especially so for poetry." Cousins handed back the manuscript to Kuvempu and bid him farewell after a few other words of advice.

A sullen Kuvempu walked out suspecting whether Cousins' solidarity with the Irish struggle against the English was behind his advice. His "inner consciousness," however, accepted the truth of Cousins' seemingly slighting counsel. He resolved to write in Kannada later that day. He did not stop writing poems in English, however, with the hope of being a bilingual writer. His diary shows that he stopped writing poetry in English sometime in the mid-1920s.

James Henry Cousins (1873-1956) was a poet and younger member of the Irish Literary Revival, which was as much a literary movement as it was a political struggle against English colonial rule. Moving to India in 1915 at Annie Besant's invitation, he worked at the Theosophical Society and at Kalakshetra in Madras. He took a deep interest in Indian thought and interacted closely with Aurobindo and Tagore.

Cousins' work in India has been documented. As far as I know, his chance encounter with the young Kuvempu does not form part of it. In retrospect, that meeting probably had a more extraordinary consequence than anything else he did in India.

My account draws from Kuvempu's narration of his encounter with James Cousins in his autobiography, *Nenapina Doniyalli* (In the Boat of Memory, 1980).

AROUND A LAND SURVEY

"Two surveys have been done until now. One every thirty years. This is the third survey," recalled the elders of Bailahalli village. "The agricultural tax went up after each of those surveys."

Gorur Ramaswamy Iyengar (1904-1991), the well-known Kannada writer and humorist, records this response in *Bailahalli Survey* (The Survey in Bailahalli, 1936), a light-hearted record of events that unfold during a village land survey done by the Mysore Government in the mid-1930s.

After the British killed Tipu Sultan and took over Mysore state in 1799, Colin Mackenzie, British cartographer and surveyor, completed the first land survey of Mysore in 1800. For reasons of administrative expedience as well as of commerce, Mysore state, like the governments in the rest of colonial India, carried out several surveys of land, soil and minerals from the late nineteenth century onwards. The maps and tables in the survey reports make the world look neat and precise to a modern mind. But Gorur's account of the land survey in Bailahalli shows the messiness behind them.

The land surveyors usually came from far off Dharwar. The villagers were struck by how they calculated accounts in a mixture of Marathi and Kannada: "Donaane. Charaane. (2 Annas, 4 Annas)."

The Revenue Collector's order announcing the resurvey of Bailahalli had not specified the date of the surveyor's arrival in the village. Five days later, the surveyor arrived along with his friend early in the morning. They had walked from the nearest rail station ten miles away. Ignoring the station master's suggestion that they spend the night at the station, they had made their way to Bailahalli in the dark.

The villagers were not impressed with the surveyor. His soft voice, they felt, meant an inability to command people. He also seemed weary and weak willed. A sense of official authority was lacking in him.

"It is the sowing season," the village headman said. "The farmers will be working in their fields. The survey is better done after the harvesting is done." The farmers might have co-operated, Gorur adds, if the surveyor was domineering.

The surveyor wanted to return to Bangalore the very next day, but stayed back, at the headman's insistence, for a couple of weeks.

Another surveyor showed up a month later. He won over the headman immediately. He wore a coat and a hat of the kind seen on the British officials. A fountain pen and a watch were on him. The short, pot-bellied surveyor was also self-assured. His thick moustache—"on which a lemon could bounce,"—especially impressed the headman.

The village elders acceded to the surveyor's request for recruiting survey assistants from among the village men. Each farmer was asked to assist in the land survey for fifteen days. They were asked to bring along a chain, hammer, pick-axe, pegs, among others.

The request met with reluctance. "Why should we measure land? It is a sin to measure Mother Earth. Our life-spans will shorten. Unfortunate things will happen if we do forbidden things." Apprehensions that the survey meant an increase in tax were also heard.

The farmers agreed to join in the work after much persuasion. The temple priest though asked to be exempted from the survey work as he couldn't come away from his temple duties. Determined to enlist his help, the farmers replied, "We don't have the authority to exempt you. Let's ask God for help in this matter."

The next day, a flower was placed on the temple deity's idol: if it fell on the right, the priest had to join in the survey work; if it fell on the left, he was exempt from it. Since these means did not end in a clear resolution, the priest was now offered the option of cooking the meals for those doing the survey work.

In the mornings, the surveyor slipped into a shirt, coat and trousers and heavy boots and got ready for work. One of his assistants would visit the farmers at their homes to bring them over for work. The surveyor would then try to get them to march in line: "Left. Right. Fall in march."

Slackness in work invited the surveyor's lash. After work ended in the evening, all of them convened near the temple. A sense of solidarity set in soon enough.

From this point on, Gorur shifts the focus away from the survey work and records the surveyor's growing sense of the village realities: the panchayat's style of settling disputes, the local medicinal practices, and the *kolata* dance and the songs, to name a few. The surveyor and the villagers come to share a deep bond over the days.

The survey had taken a couple of weeks to get finished. The surveyor wanted to take time off and visit his brother in Mangalore. The villagers suggested that he ride with the many bullock carts carrying bags of coffee beans across to Mangalore. At first, the surveyor dismissed the idea, "The cart ride to Mangalore down the rough forest ghat takes twenty days." He relented later: the idea of a slow journey seemed appealing.

The villagers received a long letter from the surveyor after he reached Mangalore: he had learnt much from the ride; and he could never forget his experiences in Bailahalli.

GANDHI AS MORAL PRESENCE

On May 8, 1915, Gandhi made his first visit to Bangalore. He and his wife, Kasturba, had arrived from Madras by rail. Since their travel companion, GA Natesan, the famous publisher, was in poor health, they had travelled first class.

DV Gundappa, the Kannada writer, had taken Natesan's help to arrange Gandhi's visit to Bangalore. Donations from Mysore state towards Gandhi's satyagraha in South Africa had been routed through the latter, who co-ordinated the fund raising for it in South India.

Gandhi stepped out of the train holding a small bundle of clothes and a water bottle. His clothes were simple: a thin half-sleeved linen shirt, dhoti and a Gujarati turban. Dressed in a white saree with a red border, Kasturba's appearance, too, was simple. The welcome party therefore had not recognized them straightaway.

The excitement was real: large crowds had turned up at the rail station to see Gandhi. He had returned to India from South Africa only the previous year. But his political struggles in that country had already acquired a presence for him here.

News of Gandhi's displeasure at the grand reception in Madras made the local organizers replace the banners on the streets with festoons made with mango leaves. And a western music band had made way for nadaswara musicians.

A fully decorated horse carriage waited to take Gandhi and Kasturba in a procession towards their host's house. Unfastening the horses from the carriage, a few overzealous students took their place: "Please sit inside. We will draw the carriage." Not going along with their plea, Gandhi asked how far his host's home was from there. "Half a mile," they replied. He said, "Let us all walk then."

Accommodation had been made for the Gandhi couple in the new bungalow of a District Judge. Its housewarming ceremony hadn't been done yet. A comment had come up with regard to this detail: wasn't being graced by the dust from a great man's feet also auspicious?

The guest's diet, the host knew, consisted of groundnuts and fruit. Still, the meal had to be worthy of a grand guest. The host finally decided to serve apples. *What was the need for such an expensive fruit?* An agitated Gandhi then settled for papaya.

Founded by DV Gundappa, Social Club had arranged a meeting on the outdoor premises of the Government High School. A recitation in English of Tagore's poem, "Leave this Chanting and Singing and Telling of Beads," from *Gitanjali* started off the programme. After Gandhi and Kasturba were felicitated, the organizers asked Gandhi to unveil a portrait of Gopala Krishna Gokhale. Before doing so, a visibly delighted Gandhi spoke at length, in English, about the many virtues of Gokhale, who—he reminded his audience—was his guru in his political life. He also let them know that Gokhale loved John Henry Newman's hymn, *Lead, Kindly Light.* This hymn, Gandhi explained, held that great work began with small steps.

On the way back to his host's home, Gandhi asked that they take a route through the poorer areas of the city.

Later, in a lengthy meeting with the notables of the city, Gandhi dwelt on issues that were to preoccupy him till the end: the importance of Indian languages and of local handloom production, among others. War, he asserted, was a manifestation of modern civilization. The removal of untouchability, which was the focal point of his later visits to Mysore state, did not weigh heavily on his mind at this time.

A large meeting was held at the Lalbagh Glass House in the evening. A reading of poems in Kannada, Urdu and Telugu inaugurated the programme. In his speech, Gandhi explained why he hadn't climbed into the carriage: "We should not spoil public servants with processions. Let them work quietly and not hanker after public recognition. They should devote themselves to service knowing full well that people might pelt stones at them for their work and treat them like dirt."

As Gandhi came out of the Glass House, the jubilant crowd outside became restless. A seven-year old-girl, who had also come for a glimpse of the leader, was pushed down by the crowd. Gandhi rushed in to lift her up. The crowds became still as he held her and took her over to her brother.

Arriving from Mysore in the evening, Dewan Visvesvaraya had an hour-long meeting with Gandhi. He then asked the hosts to book first class train tickets for the guests. Gandhi demurred: "Even if I took the first class now, due to your insistence, please know that I will get off the train at the very first stop and move into a third-class compartment." The hosts did not press further. Gandhi was to visit Bangalore on a few more occasions in subsequent years*.

*

"Under Gandhiji's influence, I picketed and campaigned in support of his struggles. I took part in the salt satyagraha. By 1933, I had been jailed a couple of times. Other women protestors had accompanied me. On one occasion, I went on a hunger fast for eighteen days to protest the injustices that women faced inside the jail. Gandhiji visited my town during his Harijan Campaign. Hearing about these efforts, he asked me to come to Wardha…"

—Smt. Mahadevitaayi, Siddapura,
North Kanara District

"Gandhiji's Harijan Campaign passed through Karnataka in 1934. I had come to Motebennur from Kachavi, a village. Gandhiji was visiting there. I had taught little children a few songs of welcome to receive him. Gandhiji asked my husband who I was. He said I was his wife. After the prayers ended, Gandhiji asked us to accompany him. My husband and I got inside the car. Thakkar Bapa, Gandhiji and I sat in the back. My husband sat in the front. I pressed Gandhiji's tired legs. He said to me then, "Your husband is the President of Harijan Seva Sangh. Why don't you raise a few Harijan girls in your

_____

* Note: My translated chronicle above draws from local eye-witness accounts found in Kannada.

household?" I told him I wasn't learned or highly educated. He replied, "Won't you be able to bathe them, comb their hair, wash their clothes?" These I can do, I said. He then said, "Raise two Harijan girls in your house the way you raise your own children." I nurtured Madhura and Tara along with my children as if I were keeping my word to Rama. From then until now, that is for about 34 to 35 years, my husband and I have been doing some kind of service or another for the downtrodden. This was Gandhiji's sevadeekshe (initiation into service) to us. For a few years, we ran an ashrama for young Harijan girls (Harijan Baalikaashrama) which later became Mahila Vidyapeeta in Hubli...

"...Gandhiji was enthusiastic about the activities of this institution. He even wrote letters in this regard. He sent Meera, a Harijan girl from his ashram, to study with us. In 1940, we sent Veeramma, a Harijan girl from Sirsi, to study at Gandhi's ashram in Sevagram. We even got her married to Kariyappa from Sangur at our ashram. The couple are engaged in doing Gandhian work in Sangur even now. We have arranged the weddings of numerous Harijan girls in our ashram. These are due to the influence of Gandhi's sevadeekshe."

—Smt. Nagamma Patil, Hubli

"Between 1936 and 1941, I lived like Gandhiji's daughter at Sevagram. Only God knows how much he loved me! He felt unhappy if he didn't see me every day. Because I was a Harijan girl in the ashram.

"He spun yarn only from the nine balls of cotton he asked me to prepare daily. Keeping aside that yarn, he asked Abha Ben to make cloth exclusively from it. If a dhoti was made from it and presented to him, he would exult, 'Ah ha! This is sacred.'

"I didn't know Hindi. He taught me Hindi at nine o' clock in the evening. And I taught him Kannada. We would retire for the night after a light-hearted talk. If my blanket slipped away from me, he would put it back. He rejoiced in the company of Harijan children.

"Everyone in the ashram woke up at four o' clock in the morning. A bell rang at that time. If I woke up to its sound, Gandhiji would ask me to go back to sleep saying I needed a full night's rest and proceed to his prayers. If I woke up on my own, he would ask me to complete the ablutions, eat my breakfast and then take Hindi lessons from Bhansali Bhai. He advised me to acquire good Hindi from this teacher saying, "My hourly lessons in Hindi are not adequate.

"The lunch bell rang at noon…He (Gandhiji) would sit with us to eat lunch. He made me sit near him. When any visitor asked him to give them prasad, he asked me to give them a fruit. If they insisted that he give it to them, he would say, "Do you know who this girl is? She is my darling daughter.

"The month of May was very hot. The girls in the ashram fought amongst themselves to fan Gandhiji. He would then say, 'Please don't fight. I have entrusted Veeramma with this task. She will fan me.' The girls would become quiet. I would then fan him for two hours. He never asked to be fanned. We did it out of our love for him.

"…He told me stories about his mother's love for him during his childhood. I was a 13-14 year old child at that time…"

—Smt. Veeramma Kariyappa,
Sangur, Haveri District

TALL TALES ABOUT AMBEDKAR

Many years ago, Siddalingaiah, the reputed Kannada poet, folklorist and Dalit leader, met an aged Ambedkarite in Bedikehala, a village in Belgaum district. The old man, who lay on a charpoy, was known to have seen Ambedkar. Siddalingaiah asked him, "What were your impressions when you saw him?" Ill and weak, the old man replied: "Ambedkar had visited Bedikehala. When I went to see him, thousands of people were already standing on either side of the road he was to pass through. Each one of them held a stick in each hand. Fearing someone might pelt stones at Ambedkar or harm him in some other way, they had crossed the sticks, scissors-like, up in the air to shield his passage. Their raised sticks didn't let me get a clear glimpse of him."

*

A VIP once visited Ambedkar's house. He wished to see his large collection of books. Inside the home library, the visitor asked him skeptically, "Have you read all these books?" "Yes," the host said with confidence. The visitor proceeded to pull out a book from one of the shelves and opened a page at random. He asked, "Do you know what appears on Page 59 of this book?" Ambedkar recalled the contents of that page in an instant. Pulling out another book, the visitor asked, "What's being discussed on Page 152 of this book?" Ambedkar knew exactly what that page contained. The visitor didn't give up. He picked out another book and chose another page at random. Ambedkar clearly remembered this page too. This went on until the visitor was left with no choice but to give in. He exclaimed, "You are truly a son of Saraswathi."

*

A foreign reporter arrived in India to interview major political figures. He decided to visit Gandhi first. But Gandhi was already asleep when he got there. He then went over to Nehru's house. But Nehru had also gone to sleep. He visited Sardar Patel next. But Sardar Patel had also fallen asleep by then. It was past midnight when the reporter arrived at Ambedkar's house. But Ambedkar was wide awake and working away at his desk. The reporter asked him, "All the other leaders are already asleep. How is it that you are still awake?" Ambedkar replied, "Those leaders have already awakened their people. They can now afford to sleep peacefully. But my people are yet to awaken. So I have to stay up and keep working."

*

After his wife, Ramabai died, Ambedkar remained unmarried for over twelve years. He would say, "The Dalits consider me as their father. Marrying a Dalit woman again will be difficult as I regard all Dalits as my children." So when he married again, it had to be a woman from another community.

*

I once asked Siddalingaiah, "Can you share a few tall tales about Ambedkar?" (His autobiography, Ooru-Keri, in fact, shares a delightful one, where a young Ambedkar falls into a mound of ash while climbing down a tree and then swears in front of his jeering friends, "I might be a Budisaheb ('an ash-covered Saheb') now, but I will become a 'Babasaheb' one day.") Siddalingaiah, a captivating raconteur, went on to narrate one exciting Ambedkar tall tale after another. I have translated and retold a few from among them here.

A distinct genre of myth-making, tall tales step above ordinary reality to disclose truths and mysteries about social predicaments. Whether self-consciously funny or dead literal in their style of articulation, they do offer a glimpse of the inner lives of communities, their desires, anxieties and hopes.

The folk lives of Ambedkar—and, no doubt, those of several other political leaders—await a careful engagement. The biographer's fixation with facts short-changes the task of unpacking public figures as iconic presence, of getting a sense of the ways in which communities and individuals allow iconic personalities inside their lives.

LOHIA'S TRAVELS IN THE USA

Rammanohar Lohia, the great socialist politician and thinker, visited the United States of America for five weeks, between July 13 and August 20, in 1951. The Foundation for World Government, an American organization, had invited him for a lecture tour. This was his first visit to America. It had got delayed due to his arrest in the Kagodu Satyagraha, a farmers' struggle against high tenancy rates in Karnataka.

An economically fair and culturally just international federation was among Lohia's major intellectual preoccupations. He had recently shared his ideas of the "Third Camp", a coalition of countries outside the orbit of the two principal players in the Cold War.

As the Secretary of the All India Congress Committee, the foreign affairs section of the Congress party, Lohia had been in regular touch with activists in America. He wrote several letters to the President of the American Civil Liberties Union (ACLU), assuring him that he and his colleagues in the party had done what they could to bring awareness about the ACLU's struggles to Indians and asking him to make Americans more aware of the freedom struggle in India. He also corresponded with Black activist groups.

America had long found a place in Lohia's imagination. At the New York airport, upon his arrival, Lohia is known to have repeated the reporter's question, "Why did I come to America?" before replying, "As a boy, I was interested in the deeds of Lincoln and Jefferson, and as I come from the community or caste noted for doing business, I was also interested in Rockefeller and Ford. From there the transition was easy to Upton Sinclair, and to your Clares and Maxines. I have a fascination for the American people and doubts about modern civilization, of which America is the climax. I came to find out which is uppermost, my fascination or my doubts."

This response of Lohia appears early in the day-to-day summary account of his travels in the US found in a short book with a grand title, *Lohia and America Meet*. Published in 1951 and a result no doubt of loving and meticulous care, the daily accounts were put down by Harris Wofford, a lawyer and trustee of the host organization. (An admirer of Gandhi's philosophy of non-violence, Harris was the civil rights expert in Kennedy's administration and a supporter of Martin Luther King, Jr. He later became a Senator from Pennsylvania.)

In his lengthy foreword to the Indian edition of this book, brought out by Snehalata Reddy, the artist and socialist activist, ten years later, Lohia offers high praise and affection for Harris. National barriers, he writes, had broken down in his relationship with him. Harris had been like any "intelligent and sincere young Indian with attachment" to what he stood for. But such an adventure happened "only too rarely" and "if it happened oftener, the world would be better." Just when this compliment is beginning to risk being excessive, Lohia's wit kicks in. Harris, he clarifies, was "not an exact replica of a young Indian devotee": "Harris was mad with me on one occasion (and) called me SOB (son of a bitch in American)." On another occasion, Harris told him that the things he did for him he wouldn't do for the US President before "sheepishly" bringing him a cup of coffee from a half mile away. At the same time, Lohia adds, an Indian devotee would not be "as industrious and as efficient."

At the airport, the State Department had extended "full customs courtesies" to Lohia. He didn't have to get his bags inspected. Had he known of this earlier, he joked, he would have brought along something forbidden.

Lohia shared with Harris the first question posed to him "on American soil." The Immigration Officer had asked him: "How strong are the Communists in India?"

"Not very."

"How many votes will the Communists get?"

"Five per cent at most."

The official appeared relieved. His relief became greater when Lohia revised his estimate: "Probably one percent." When Lohia sought the reasons behind his "obsession" with communism, the official replied that that was what they read about in the newspapers.

The sight of hundreds of cars in the parking lot at La Guardia airport, where he had to take the connecting flight, made Lohia shake his head in disbelief: "Are there that many cars in all of India? How can India and America ever be friends with all this?"

Lohia's five weeks in America were packed. During these travels in mid-1951, from the eastern side of the country across to its western parts, he gave twenty public talks, met prominent political figures, intellectuals and labour activists and also managed to get a sense of the everyday life of American society.

The initial public interactions of Lohia were with Black leaders and activists. In a four-day car trip across 800 miles of the American South, he spoke at numerous institutions, including Highlander School, where Rosa Parks, the person whose refusal to vacate a bus seat reserved for Whites touched off the Civil Rights Movement in the US, later studied, and Howard University, a university for Black students. Alongside sharing his socialist views, he spoke about the virtue of civil disobedience in protesting racial injustices and also about the need for making common cause with the struggles seen in African countries.

A conversation with Einstein at his home in Princeton was among the high points of Lohia's trip. He recalls a humourous moment where the great scientist preferred to view politicians as "criminals" when he had termed them "liars." This bit of exchange had happened in German; but the conversation was mostly in English. (Lohia did his doctoral work in economics at Humboldt University in Berlin between 1930 and 1933.)

In a meeting that lasted a few hours, Einstein had sought Lohia's views on Indian politics and his socialist programmes. He welcomed the abolition of landlordism and the measures for land redistribution and also approved of Lohia's advocacy of the small machine.

Had Einstein's research in atomic energy—"a source of death"— not confined and stifled the human mind? Did he see any scope for freeing thought? Lohia had wanted to know. His travel companion, Harris, has not written down Einstein's reply. We do know though that the scientist enjoyed his meeting with the socialist. While taking leave, Einstein remarked, "It is so good to meet a *man*—one gets so lonely."

On July 31, in an address at *America's Town Meeting of the Air*, a programme in San Francisco, which was broadcast by 275 stations of the ABC network with an estimated 5 million listeners, Lohia argued that both communism and capitalism were doctrines of "centralization and mass production." Decentralization and production with small machines, he continued, alone could make possible a government of, by and for the community and "abolish poverty and attain a decent standard of living."

During his visit to the University of Michigan, Ann Arbor, Lohia was invited by Walter Reuther to meet him in Detroit. Reuther was the President of United Automobile Workers, the legendary trade union with a membership of 12.5 lakh workers at that time. He had famously asked the corporations to "open the books" and allow for a public scrutiny of their costs and profits. Several assassination bids had been made on him.

Inspired by socialist ideals, Reuther had written *Proposal for a Total Peace Offensive*, which proposed that all the countries of the world contribute to a UN fund to help the poorer countries help themselves and also help bring about total disarmament and support a global security force. The US citizens, it noted, should commit to contributing 13 billion dollars annually for a 100 year period (this total sum equaled what the Second World War cost the American people). The friendly and open Reuther, Lohia felt, must have had a "fair amount of peace within himself." Urging him to visit him again, Reuther said, "I work eighteen hours a day, so it doesn't matter to me which of them you come." Lohia loved the earthy style of the union leader.

Lohia went on a long walk through the Redwood forest in California. He relished the night life that the students from Stanford made him experience: an Italian restaurant, a Chinese club and an American burlesque. At a baseball game, he cheered individual players. In Los Angeles, he wished to meet Greta Garbo. The actress was apparently out of town at that time. And, Madame Sekulich, a Yugoslavian socialist, posed a question that left him "without an answer." She had asked, "How was the dawn in India?"

In a letter he wrote to his close friend, Jayaprakash Narayan, from Tokyo, on his way back from the US, Lohia singled out the tendency to see the "angle and argument" of those with whom they disagreed as one of the best things about Americans. "A sound that will last in my mind about the American way of life is the swish of speeding automobiles," he observed. Characterizing the Americans as "really mobile," he hoped—with an oblique reference to the propaganda war under way in their country—that their attitudes would never become rigid.

Throughout the trip, Lohia was dressed in a dhoti, a cotton shirt and a Gandhi cap.

Lohia accepted a lecture invitation to visit the Stephan Poetry Center, University of Arizona, in 1964. His second visit to the US lasted two months. He was now Member of Parliament.

Delivered on May 1, Lohia's lecture, "Indian Politics Today," ranged freely: Nehru had not handled the Chinese aggression properly; the two super powers had to unite to end poverty in the world; India's non-alignment policy was not authentic, both Russia's veto on the Kashmir issue and aid from the US mattered to it; the caste system was a great factor in the country's degradation. The American media covered his speech widely. The most eventful episode of this trip however had to wait a few more weeks.

Lohia's concern for racial equality made him commit to a talk at Tougaloo College in Jackson, Mississippi, a hub of civil rights activism. He was curious, too, about the work of the Student Non-Violent Co-ordinating Committee (SNCC), a group formed by young students to end racial segregation in public places and increase the voter registration among Blacks.

After receiving Lohia at the airport, on May 27, the President of Tougaloo College took him to Morrison's Cafeteria, a chain restaurant in Jackson, for supper. The restaurant manager turned them away since Lohia was not white. On his way out, Lohia told him that he might just return the following day.

According to Edwin King, the College Chaplain at Tougaloo and SNCC activist, Lohia felt that staying quiet about the incident did not accord with his understanding of civil disobedience and that would also mean not showing concern for the experiences of local Blacks.

Lohia's hosts advised him to visit a smaller restaurant of the same chain instead of the one that had turned him away. The latter was in the heart of the city. Visiting there, King explained, was to risk mob violence. Although unafraid of "personal violence," Lohia agreed to keep things "as simple as possible;" if he was violating law, he wished to be arrested. He had, according to King, "risked death as well as arrest."

Lohia let the restaurant know of his plans to visit it. He let the police and the press know as well. Exposing "something foul in American life," his press statement noted, was not the aim. "Foul spots," it added, were everywhere, including in India. Not protesting racial segregation however meant promoting "injustice and tyranny." Since he was acting as a human being and "as though" he were an American citizen, he would not inform the Indian Embassy or the Indian Parliament.

King and his wife, who had driven Lohia to the restaurant, and a few students watched the events from a distance. A local paper carried a lengthy description of the restaurant episode. The unusually detailed news item, King surmises, was mostly due to Lohia being a foreign politician. Otherwise, such episodes were played down in the media. And the police normally beat down the protestors.

Reported in dozens of newspapers across America, a news account offers a glimpse into the tensions of racism and Lohia's moral determination:

"Dr. Lohia appeared at the restaurant—as he had announced he would earlier—in a strange three-quarter length robe and wearing sandals.

As he started to enter, the manager of the cafeteria, Vernon Hill, said, "We don't want your business. This is private property. I'm asking you to leave."

Dr. Lohia replied, "I am not leaving. I tell you with the greatest humility I am not leaving."

Police Lt. C.R. Wilson asked Dr. Lohia, "Did you hear the manager? He is asking you to leave. Now please leave."

When Dr. Lohia was being led to a waiting police wagon, he told Wilson, "Now, brother, your job is over."

"No, it's just begun," Wilson replied.

Dr. Lohia put his arm through Wilson's but the Jackson officer jerked his arm away." (*Source: Daily News, May 28, 1964*)

The police drove Lohia in the police wagon for about an hour before letting him go. In all likelihood, they had been instructed not to put him in prison.

The US State Department sent an apology to the Indian Embassy. Lohia was irritated, "They may go to hell!" The restaurant episode, he reiterated, was a moral, and not a political, issue. The US Ambassador to the United Nations had wished to visit him to apologize for the Jackson episode. If he dropped by to see him, Lohia felt that he would ask him to apologize to the Statue of Liberty instead.

Nehru had died on the day the restaurant had first denied entry to Lohia. Among his sternest critics, Lohia's note of condolence though expressed deep admiration for him: "I sorrow over the death of India's prime minister and the Congress Party's most outstanding leader. I grieve over the passing away of a man who led us with sensitive charm when we were young and he at least had the manner of a revolutionary."

Lohia told King that he wanted to revisit America and work in the Civil Rights movement. That visit did not happen.

A FEW BOOKS

MANASOLLASA

A Sanskrit Encyclopaedia

*M*anasollasa ('The Delight of the Mind'), the early 12th century instruction for kings written in Sanskrit, whose authorship is attributed to King Someshvara III of the Chalukyas of Kalyana, opens up nothing less than a cosmology for modern readers.

The kinds of fishes and their habitat and the means of catching them, the means of hunting animals, the varieties of rice and edible meats, the types of charity, the means of having a luxurious bath, the variety of storytellers and storytelling, the variety of dance and music and medical treatments and sports and dozens of other subjects are classified and described along with moral commentary. After classifying women into three kinds, for instance, the text recommends that kings avoid the third kind barring exceptional circumstances. If a Shudra woman was beautiful and talented in the arts, the kings could feel free to marry her. Disclosing social tensions some more, the king is advised to abstain from the company of sinners, wicked people, immoral people, Chandalas and *antyajas* (the latter two categories would correspond to "Dalits" in contemporary usage).

Practical advice, pictures of fantasy and rules for moral conduct are all interwoven in the classificatory universe of *Manasollasa*.

A chapter on the pleasures of a royal bath begins thus: "I'll now describe the grand luxuries of a bath. The king must build a bath house to the east of his palace. It must have pillars of gold and a platform made with pure crystal and a dazzling glass floor. The walls must be coloured with blood red powder. A marvellous arch made from silk

cloth should stand outside. Its brilliance should rival that of a rainbow."
The kinds of flowers and fragrant oils required for the royal bath and
the kinds of assistance that wrestlers and beautiful maidens extend to
the king during his bath are then listed.

The section on the pleasures of the throne notes that a spacious
throne with legs made from the wood of *sampige,* mango, jackfruit
and *atthi* trees is ideal for a king. Another section, "The Amusement
of Magic," affirms that a hand smeared with the fat of a frog would
not burn in fire and that one could walk on water with feet smeared
with ghee.

While *Manasollasa* affiliates itself with ancient Sanskrit texts
at times—for example, it asks that Sama Veda be uttered before
commencing the work of elephant training—M.M. Kalburgi, the editor,
notes that it does not mention Vedic deities or the Vedic practices of
yagna and shores up the imagination of a Dravida culture. The styles of
sculpting idols and building temples described here, he further notes,
also derive from Dravida traditions.

Having addressed itself to kings throughout, *Manasollasa's*
concluding part though insists that the book's scope was universal. It
congratulates itself as a kamadhenu-like shastra (science), since anyone
hearing it "would acquire an interest in matters of religion (*dharma*),
become deft at statecraft and clear sighted in issues of political morality
(*rajaneeti*) and capable at offering service, become skilled in literature
and an expert in logic, acquire knowledge of prosody and figures of
speech and gain knowledge of the *shastras* and become skilled at horse
riding and elephant riding and acquire special knowledge of wrestling
and understanding in matters of war and skilled in the knowledge of
music."

The five major sections of *Manasollasa* offer concise elaborations
of the virtues a king needs to cultivate in himself, of the measures he
needs to take to make his rule stable, and of the variety of sports and
other joyful pleasures found in a stable kingdom.

Dwelling on the virtues of an ideal king, the first section discloses
a lineage for the imaginations of political authority seen in India. The
first subject addressed in the 308 brief declaratives found here pertains
to the ideal of being truthful. Falsehoods uttered out of lust, greed, fear

and anger count as sinful. The violations of oaths taken in the presence of God will count as falsehoods. Speaking falsehoods leads to hell and will be hated by the people: they are repugnant and sinful; they must therefore be abandoned.

Proper modes of relating to the other are elaborated next. Harassing, tormenting and hitting others, stealing money from them and such like acts are known as the betrayal of the other (*paradroha*); slandering, rumour-mongering, scolding and frightening others and torturing their mind amounts to *paradroha*; taking away the homes, farms, clothes, grains and cattle of others is *paradroha* too. *Paradroha* therefore is not be tolerated. Since that leads to a terrible hell, it must be given up. The king ought not to chase after the wives of others, widows, sisters, mothers-in-law, daughters. Having relations with such women reduces the lifespan.

Showing the influence of Jain vegetarian ideals on the conceptions of *sattvik* food, *Manasollasa* asks that the king abstain from eating garlic, onions, radish, chicken, pork. The flesh of tigers, foxes, wolves, crows, monkeys, bears, lions, elephant, camels, pigeons, parrots, swans, nightingale, eagles, dogs, insects, domestic animals (except goats and sheep), lizards, frogs, snakes, mongoose, iguana and crocodile are to be avoided too.

Essential virtues need to be cultivated within the self. Anger destroys the intelligence, wealth and the honour of one's clan, it needs to be given up. Envy should not be directed at those who are prosperous, beautiful, generous, artistic and virtuous. Anyone who praises himself is akin to a living person being dead. Self-praise results in suffering in the other world.

A historian of manners will learn from *Manasollasa* that the relatives from the father's and mother's clans were to be addressed sweetly. They had to be offered comfortable seats. They also had to be given a proper share in the gold, jewellery and clothing.

A few excerpts from *Manasollasa* reveal the moral priorities in administering a state:

> The king ought not to hate other Gods or show contempt for them. He must fold his hands at the sight of a temple or a deity. (105). A king who has cultivated such feelings of a believer and

has equal regard towards all Gods, will obtain the most proper wealth from the blessing of all the Gods (106).

When a person in a wretched condition of being poor utters "*dehi*" ('give me alms') to seek compassion, he is known as "*deena*" (135). A king has to give such a person the things he asks for with a mind that is kind and free of selfishness (136).

A king must strive to protect those suffering from disease through the use of *tantra, mantra* and medicine (137). Offering food, drink, chairs and beds, he must care for them deeply (138). He must appoint doctors who have mastered surgery and medicinal knowledge and are skilled at conjectural reasoning and have a healing touch and speak affectionately (139). Different kinds of medicine must be made available for them. Active, duty-minded assistants must be made available for them (140).

A person who seeks protection from tigers, lions, elephants, robbers and enemies is known as a refugee (*sharanagatha*). The life and wealth of the person seeking refuge must be protected. The protector of refugees will earn a long life and is worshipped by people. When the prescribed *yagnas* and the protection of the frightened people are performed even to a small extent, it results in special gifts (305-308).*

---

* The Kannada translation of this two-volume work of cosmic taxonomy in Sanskrit, which is divided into five major sections consisting of twenty chapters each, was undertaken by twelve scholars under the supervision of Professor M.M. Kalburgi and published by Karnatak University, Dharwar in 1998. Their work is based on the edition of *Manasollasa* prepared in 1925 by Gajanan Shrigondekar, a Sanskrit Librarian at the Central Library, Baroda. Kalburgi suggests that *Manosollasa* comes close to the genre of encyclopedia and is among three such works found in Karnataka. This book refers to itself by two other titles: *Raja Manosollasa* (The Delight of the Minds of Kings) and *Abhilashatartha Chintamani*. The latter title, Kalburgi explains, means that the text is a gem like work on a favoured subject. The English translations of the excerpts found in this chapter are mine.

HALF A LIFE FROM MUGHAL INDIA

In lines that Freud might have liked, Banarasi remarks that his book, *Ardhakathanaka* (Half a Tale), has recorded episodes from the outward life as it was impossible to report all that happened: "Even in the tiny span of a day, a man passes through myriad states of consciousness... A man's life has much that is subtly secret and profoundly beyond grasp."

Considered the earliest example of an autobiography from the country, *Ardhakathanaka* is a panoramic account of a Jain merchant's experiences in seventeenth century North India. Banarsi wrote it in 1641 when he had turned fifty-five years old and completed half of the one hundred and ten years that an old Jain tradition took to be the human life span. Hence the title, *Half a Tale*.

Banarasi was born in 1586 into a Jain merchant family which claimed descent from Rajasthan. A priest had suggested that he be named after Banaras, the town where Lord Parsvanatha was born. His family lived in Jaunpur, a town about a hundred kilometers from Banaras. Not showing interest in the family's jewellery trade, Banarasi read widely and wrote love poems in his youth. Lath notes that he rejected the ritualistic side of Jainism and came to lead Adhyatma, a movement which asked for a more contemplative orientation to Jainism.

Ardhakathanaka is in the nature of a confessional: moral self-evaluations accompany its narration of events alongside. This mode of life narration, Mukund Lath, the translator, informs us, is among the acts of self-purification seen in Jain tradition.

In his early life, Banarasi steals from his father to give presents to his lovers. He lifts food from a plate of offerings made to the deity.

His greed makes him fall for a false sanyasi who teaches him a mantra which if chanted for a full year would ensure a gold coin at his doorstep daily. These narrations are on the way to his final realisation of the truth of the Jain principles of right knowledge and conduct.

Vivid glimpses of Jain ethics are seen throughout the book. Banarasi regularly asserts that joy and sorrow follow each other and that one must not expect otherwise. Indeed, for him, equanimity, a state that rose above joy and sorrow, was necessary to cultivate. It is perhaps this conviction of his that does not let either joyfulness or sadness overwhelm the narrative anywhere. The deaths of his nine children are simply stated as facts. Death simply meant that the soul had left the body. He compares the death of his second son to a parrot that flies away leaving behind an empty cage.

The author's metaphysical journey however does not overwhelm the riveting details of trade, travel, poetry sessions, encounters with political authorities and pseudo sanyasis, among others.

The young Banarasi is passionate about women and studies. The alarmed elders of his community tried to get him to change. "A merchant's son should tend his shop. Don't forget that a man who is too studious has to beg for his food."

Revealing of the support Jain merchants could fall back on within their community, the loss-making Banarasi comes to find extraordinary kin support for his trading ventures in different towns. And, without exception, he makes good in due course the loans with the correct interest. He does succeed in making profits on one occasion, but does not disclose his gains. Profits, he states, were among the nine items that ought not to be discussed openly.

Ardhakathanaka discloses the deeply uncertain conditions under which trade occurred in medieval times. A change of Governors in Jaunpur could mean fear or relief depending on their personality. The arrival of a bad Governor saw traders fleeing the town with their belongings. The nature of insecurity inhering in social life those days becomes dramatically obvious at the news of Akbar's death:

> The whole town was in a tremor. Everyone closed the
> doors of their house in panic; shopkeepers shut down their

shops. Feverishly, the rich hid their jewels and costly attire underground; many of them quickly dumped their wealth and their ready capital in carriages and rushed to safe, secluded places. Every householder began stocking his home with weapons and arms.

Rich men took to wearing thick, rough clothes like those worn by the poor, in order to conceal their status, and walked the streets covered in harsh woollen blankets. Women shunned finery, dressing in shabby lustreless clothes. None could tell the status of a man from his dress and it became impossible to distinguish the rich from the poor. There were manifest signs of panic everywhere although there was no reason for it since there were really no thieves or robbers about.

The description of the fear of anarchy in Jaunpur conveys the very real possibilities of violence in the absence of political authority. Succession struggles could indeed be a prolonged affair. Mukund Lath informs us that Jahangir took over the throne within ten days of Akbar's death, the news of which brought great relief all over town.

Banarasi concludes his account thus: "I would like to extend my good wishes to all who may read my story or listen to it or recite it to others." The pleasures of *Ardhakathanaka* are very many.

Mukund Lath has beautifully translated the 675 Hindi verse stanzas found in *Ardhakathanaka* into modern English prose. He has modified Banarsi's third person narrative to a first person one to retain "the spirit of the original." Lath's extensively annotated translation provides a rich context for understanding the literary and social dimensions of Banarsi's book. A more recent English translation by Rohini Chowdhury retains the book's original third person account. The availability of both of these translations is a treat.

GANDHI'S TRACTS OF FREEDOM

Gandhi wrote *Hind Swaraj (HS)* over ten days in November, 1909, during a return trip on the sea from England to South Africa. He wrote with his left hand when his right hand was too tired to write. Suresh Sharma and Tridip Suhrud, the editors of a recent edition of *HS*, remark that the pages written with his left hand—38 out of the total of 271 pages—"strangely bear a hand more firm and clear." Gandhi translated the Gujarati original into English the following year. This is the only work of his that he himself translated.

HS sees Gandhi reflecting on the meaning of true freedom—true self-rule—as distinct from the limited views of freedom as formal freedom from British rule. Self-rule, for him, meant freedom from the European idea of modern civilization, which had enslaved the minds of so many fellow-Indians who otherwise wished that the British left India. Gandhi was free of this ambivalence. He wanted Indians—and, indeed, the Europeans themselves—to be free of it too. Hence, *HS*, a text that sought to correct a distorted vision, to rebuild civilizational confidence.

In his foreword, Gandhi states that his views in *HS* "are mine, and yet not mine. They are mine because I hope to act according to them. They are almost a part of my being. But, yet, they are not mine, because I lay no claim to originality. They have been formed after reading many books. That which I dimly felt received support from these books." The latter consisted of the works of Tolstoy, Ruskin, Thoreau and Emerson and the Bhagavad Gita, the Ramayana, and the Upanishads. His views, Gandhi also clarifies, were shared "by many Indians not touched by what is known as civilization" and "by thousands of Europeans."

"To make it easy reading, the chapters are written in the form of a dialogue between the Reader and the Editor." Besides easy readability, the dialogue format has allowed for an exciting narrative style replete with dramatic elements and rich metaphors.

HS takes on a fundamental question: what is self-rule? Its engagement with this question clarifies, over twenty short chapters, that the attainment of self-rule was more than ending British rule: it required a thoroughgoing setting aside of modern civilization itself.

In contrast to modern civilization, which Gandhi characterizes as being chiefly preoccupied with "bodily welfare,"—the attainment of more comfortable homes, faster machines and speedy air and rail travel—true civilization pointed at right morality. In his famous definition: "Civilization is that mode of conduct which points out to man the path of duty." Unlike the familiar discussions of "civilization," which classified the world into different civilizations and catalogue the differences in terms of cultural artefacts, Gandhi distinguished "modern" and "true" civilizations on the basis of morality alone.

The observance of morality in true civilization, Gandhi elaborates, is essentially about the exercise of self-restraint, about abstaining from self-indulgence, about mastering "our mind" and "our passions." This, he claims, defined morality in Indian society. In offering this view, he put an ascetic model of the self at the centre.

An integral part of his vision of self-rule, Gandhi's distinct readings of the Indian past both set aside the British misdescriptions of India and demystified the claims of modern civilization.

In response to the powerful British accusation that India was a stagnant society that had not changed over time, Gandhi pointed at the experiential wisdom of settled life-practices:

> It is a charge against India that her people are so uncivilized, ignorant and stolid, that it is not possible to induce them to adopt any changes. It is really a charge against our merit. What we have tested and found true on the anvil of experience, we dare not change. Many thrust their advice upon India, and she remains steady. This is her beauty; it is the sheet anchor of our hope.

Again, showing indifference to the modern fetish for technological innovation, Gandhi argued that, "we have managed with the same kind of plough," and "the same kind of cottages" for centuries not because "we did not know how to invent machinery, but (because) our forefathers knew that, if we set our hearts after such things, we would become slaves and lose our moral fibre." "They saw that our real happiness and health," he continued, "consisted in a proper use of our hands and feet." In his picture of India's past, physical labour found primary social value. Put differently, a value symbolically associated with the Shudras took centre-stage in his view of Indian civilization.

The ancestors, Gandhi further noted, discouraged the formation of cities, preferring instead to build villages where the vices of urban life were absent. The amoral professionalism of lawyers and doctors in modern societies lets them profit unethically, respectively, from litigations and from the willful abuse of the human body. Lawyers and doctors did exist in India in the past, but their occupational status was not very high. And, in any case, the "vakils and vaids" did not rob people; they were considered the latter's "dependants," and not their "masters." He also asserted that "Rishis and Fakirs" enjoyed a higher social status than the kings in India. In identifying this civilizational current, he valued the moral reserves of a society that let it stay immune to the authoritarian worship of state power.

Gandhi's desire to view ethics, rather than history, as a guide for living wisely in the present appears surfaces over and over. Engaging the problem of unity between Hindus and Muslims, for example, he likened it to a fight between brothers in a family which is resolvable.

Light moments surface in the middle of serious discussions. In arguing that British held on to India for commercial reasons, Gandhi recalls that the South African President, Paul Kruger, when asked whether there was gold in the moon, had replied that "it was highly unlikely because, if there were, the English would have annexed it."

The continuous appearance of metaphors enlivens the arguments. Pointing to the ill effects of machinery, Gandhi says, "Machinery is like a snake-hole, which contain from one to a hundred snakes." And, using violent means to achieve freedom was "the same as saying that we can get a rose through planting a noxious weed." And the easily corrupted institution of Parliament was "simply a costly toy of the nation." And his well-known pointer to the ephemerality of modern civilization is also here: "European civilization is a nine days' wonder."

What about the problems of child-marriage, temple prostitution and animal sacrifice? These were, for Gandhi, "defects" that were not to be "mistaken for ancient civilization." Attempts to remove them, he pointed out, have been made before and will continue to be made. The past, he implied, was not defined by an uncritical acceptance of injustice. In a gesture of concession*, Gandhi admitted the potential of modern ideas to also aid in self-criticism: "We may utilize the new spirit that is born in us for purging ourselves of these evils." The removal of untouchability which became a chief activist, concern of Gandhi in subsequent decades, does not find discussion in *HS*.

Gandhi's chastisement of modern Indians for being in a relation of alienation and elitism with the rest of society continues to sting. Noting that English notions of civilization hadn't reached many parts of India, he rues, "Those in whose name we speak, we do not know, nor do they know us." "Those," he adds, "who love the motherland are better advised to go into the interior that has not yet been polluted by the railways and to live there for six months."

Written in 1941, and revised in 1945, *Constructive Programme: Its Meaning and Place* (CP), Gandhi's final political tract was written when his engagement with Indian social and political life had become more extensive.

If he was found holding differing views on an issue, Gandhi had asked that the more recent among them ought to be taken as valid as his views were evolving always. His last tract lets us encounter therefore his most considered reflections on the issues he saw as important for the country.

Although Gandhi's foreword notes that *CP* was meant for everyone, the rest of the tract explicitly addresses Congressmen. Towards the end,

---

* Anthony J. Parel, the editor of *Hind Swaraj and Other Writings* (1997), has identified this moment as the only one in the entire discussion where Gandhi makes a concession to modern liberal thought.

he remarks that *CP* was not written "on behalf of the Congress," but was a response to the request of his fellow-members at the Sevagram Ashram, who wished to know how the constructive programme related to civil disobedience.

The 31-page tract discusses the constructive programme, which Gandhi feels is more properly called the "construction of Poorna Swaraj or complete independence by truthful and non-violent means," under eighteen subjects. All of them are equally important, he insists, and their order of appearance did not imply their order of importance. The constructive programme trained individuals for civil disobedience and kept them in a state of "readiness" for that mode of dissent.

In his discussion of "Communal Unity," the first among the subjects discussed in *CP*, Gandhi observes that "heart unity," between individuals of different faiths mattered more than "political unity." The key requisite for achieving heart unity (*sad bhavana*) was for an individual "whatever his religion may be, to represent in his own person Hindu, Muslim, Christian, Zoroastrian, Jew, etc." Departing further from liberal thought, Gandhi asks that we build friendships with those from outside one's religious faith.

"Removal of Untouchability" comes next. Gandhi advises that, "every Hindu should make common cause with them ('Harijans') and befriend them in their awful isolation—such isolation as perhaps the world has never seen in the monstrous immensity one witnesses in India." Although this was a difficult task, he argued, embarking upon it was necessary "before we can reach the summit and breathe the fresh air of freedom."

Adivasis are sixteenth on the list; but Gandhi hastens to assure us that "they are not the least in point of importance." His disclaimer notwithstanding, there is no forgetting that the subject of tribes had not preoccupied him the way caste and religion had. He indeed admits his insufficient knowledge about tribals in *CP*: "Our country is so vast and the races so varied that the best of us cannot know all there is to know of men and their condition." How might India have gained had Gandhi integrated the tribals in the freedom struggle?

Engaging the issue of women's equality, Gandhi writes that "woman has been suppressed under custom and law for which man was responsible," and that she has "as much right to shape her own destiny as man has to shape his." Viewing rights as corollaries of duties, he adds that "as every right in a non-violent society proceeds from the previous performance of a duty, it follows that rules of social conduct (between women and men) must be framed by mutual co-operation and consultation. They can never be imposed from outside." For him, the practice of acquiring freedom was a contextual one, where the exercise of freedom unfolded with reference to the locally prevalent social arrangements.

Deploring economic inequality, Gandhi writes that a "violent and bloody revolution" was sure to follow if the rich didn't give up their wealth and power voluntarily and share them for "the common good."

A new model of education had to impart "all that is best and lasting in India" and keep children "rooted to the soil with a glorious vision of the future," and nourish the Indian languages.

Prohibition (of alcohol), Khadi, Small Village Industries, Village Sanitation, Kisans, Labour (Unions), Adult Education, Students, National Language, and Education in Health and Hygiene find discussion in *CP* as well. The discussions are always complex. Weaving khadi, for instance, is as much about undoing the divide between manual and intellectual labour as it is about achieving self-reliance and decentralizing the economy.

In *CP*, Gandhi's focus is on building Indian society, and not its polity. His longstanding suspicion of the ability of political institutions to build a durable, non-violent, community life is firmly in place. He is confident in fact that the process should be the other way around: "Imagine all the forty crores of people busying themselves with the whole of the constructive programme which is designed to build the nation from the very bottom upward."

In his foreword to *CP*, Gandhi says that his list of subjects was not a closed one. If readers felt that a subject essential "in terms of Independence" had been omitted, he invited them to add that to the list and let him know about it.

"...AND THE BEAUTIFUL TREE PERISHED"

What was education like in India in the past? A vague awareness of ashramas where young boys were sent to learn from gurus exists. Or a politically complacent, or charged, view might hold that only upper caste children accessed education while the rest were excluded. Indeed, the latter memory has given rise to caste pride among the upper castes and caste resentment among the lower castes who have felt wronged in this matter. Such a memory has also led many to feel ambivalent about the consequences of British rule. True, they exploited us, but didn't they open up education to everyone?

Dharampal's book, *The Beautiful Tree: Indigenous Education in the Eighteenth Century* (1983), unsettles simplified views of India's educational past. Dedicated to the memory of Jayaprakash Narayan, who showed "unflagging interest and guidance in this work," this book owes its research curiosity to Gandhi's unwillingness to believe that education was not generally available in the past in India. Its title was drawn from Gandhi's 1931 speech at Chatham House, London, titled, "The Future of India," where he argued forcefully:

> India is more illiterate than it was fifty or a hundred years ago... because the British administrators, when they came to India, instead of taking hold of things as they were, began to root them out. They scratched the soil and began to look at the root, and left the root like that, and the beautiful tree perished. The village schools were not good enough for the British administrator, so he came out with his programme. Every school must have so much paraphernalia, building, and so forth.

His wish, Dharampal explains, was to understand Indian social institutions in the late eighteenth and early nineteenth centuries, and not to "decry" British rule.

Indigenous education was imparted in *pathshalas, madrasahs* and *gurukulas.* To point to their widespread presence, Dharampal quotes Sir Thomas Munro, the Governor of Madras: "Every village had a school." He notes further: "Education in these traditional institutions—which were actually kept alive by revenue contributions by the community including illiterate peasants... These institutions were, in fact, the watering holes of the culture of traditional communities. Therefore, the term 'school' is a weak translation of the roles these institutions really played in Indian society."

Earlier studies of the pre-British education system had not accessed, Dharampal notes, the Madras Presidency Indigenous Education Survey which collected data between 1822 and 1825. A chief source of evidence for his study, this survey compiles the responses of the District Collectors (DCs) of all the 21 districts of the Madras Presidency. The DCs were asked to disaggregate the students and teachers into male and female and identify their castes and religion as well. The forms sent to the DCs listed the following categories of students: (i) Brahmin scholars (ii) Vaishya scholars (iii) Sudra scholars (iv) Scholars of all other castes and (v) Muslim scholars. The category 'all other castes,' according to Dharampal, implied those castes considered below the Shudra and is likely to have included those termed as the "scheduled castes" today. He observes that the castes considered Sudras and those below them "predominated in the thousands" in the indigenous schools.

Students usually started education between the ages of five and eight. The duration of their study was anywhere between five and fifteen years. It was a long day at the schools: they started early in the morning around six a.m. and closed at sunset with one or two intervals for food. Different kinds of books were used to teach reading, writing and arithmetic.

The district collector of Bellary listed the school books in use under five separate categories: A. Most Commonly Used (*Ramayana, Mahabharata*) B. Used by Children from Manufacturing Classes

(*Visvakarmana Purana, Nagalingana Katha*) C. Used by Lingayat Children (*Girija Kalyana, Chenna Basaveshwara Purana*) D. Lighter Literature Read (*Panchatantra, Mahatarangini*) E. Dictionaries and Grammars Used (*Nighantu, Shabdamanidarpana, Vyakarana*). The madrassahs in Rajamundhry used books in Arabic and Persian such as the Quran and Gulistan.

The school teachers were from various caste backgrounds too. An 1836 British report on the schools of Bengal Presidency noted that while most teachers were from upper castes like Kayasthas and Brahmins, a significant number came from lower castes, six from the Chandals, a Dalit caste.

Higher learning was imparted in "colleges" or in settings like *agraharas*. Dharampal notes that institutions which taught theology, metaphysics, ethics and law using Sanskrit texts like Vedas, Puranas, and Dharmashastras were "limited" to Brahmins. Students from a variety of caste backgrounds, on the other hand, were involved in higher learning in subjects like astronomy and medicine.

Only a few girls, mostly from Muslim and lower caste families, attended schools in Madras Presidency. It was more common for girls to be taught at home by parents, relatives or paid tutors. Only in the Malabar and Vishakapatnam did a large number of girls, who were from upper caste and Muslim families, attend school.

The indigenous schools declined with the erosion of local revenue support due to the British tax policies.

There might have been arbitrariness in how the DCs fit local castes into master all-India *varna* categories like Brahmin, Vaisya and Sudra. An account of how power mattered in the interaction of castes with the school system is missing in *The Beautiful Tree*. And there is no forgetting that not all knowledges mattered equally in the country. Still, Dharampal's observations are valuable. Although a knowledge of Sanskrit was a monopoly of the Brahmin castes, that did not exhaust the entire experience of formal education. And, teachers and students came from various social backgrounds. (Let us leave aside, for now, the rich forms of literacy existing outside formal training).

Dharampal's research should shake up our imagination of India's educational past.

THE SCAVENGER OF THE COSMOS

Written in his mid-twenties, Kuvempu's first play, *Jalagara* (The Scavenger, 1928), continues to hold out a special significance. An early enactment of his philosophical ideal of vishvamanava, the play also reveals the poet's creative engagement with tradition. But, first, a quick outline of *Jalagara*.

The play opens with Mother Earth ushering in a glorious dawn. An untouchable scavenger is then seen at work in a village. His song of admiration for the splendour of the sun quickly reveals a mature, sophisticated mind. A farmer passerby asks him to accompany him to the fair being held near Shiva's shrine. The scavenger declines to join him: the priests, he replies, wouldn't let him come anywhere near the shrine. Enchanted by the scavenger's songs from afar, two learned Brahmin priests withhold their applause however after discovering that the voice belonged to a low caste man. Poets, scholars, sculptors, singers and yogis, they smugly contend, can never be born among the Shudras.

In the evening, on his way back from the shrine, the farmer, who was ecstatic about the ritual pomp, has only coconuts, flowers, *kumkuma* and camphor to show from his visit. "Haven't you brought back Shiva?" The scavenger is unimpressed.

Later, when the scavenger beseeches Shiva to reveal himself, the Lord appears in the guise of a scavenger. "You look human but seem to be superhuman. Your eyes shine brighter than the stars. Who are you?" Noticing the scavenger's bewilderment, Shiva says, "Don't be afraid, brother. I'm your relative." He continues, "I'm of your caste (*jati*). I'm a scavenger. A scavenger of the world. I swallow the sins of the world.

Beauty flourishes in the world due to my scavenging work. The radiant moon, the roaring oceans, the clear rivers, the majestic forests, all of them are in my debt. They call me Rudra at times and Shiva at other times, but they are hesitant and afraid to call me a *jalagara*."

"I had never heard this about you. Scholars and learned people describe you in other ways."

"Their descriptions are imaginary and deceptive. My true form will terrify them. You are the only one to have worshipped me in my true form in your work. My dear brother, I'm not the Shiva found in the shastras and in poetry. I'm not the erotic Shiva who cavorts with Parvathi on a silver mountain. I'm the scavenger who climbs the heap of filth built up in the cosmos and dances on it. The true Shiva is a scavenger. I appeared unattractive to the learned scholars and priests. So they tried to change my looks. The priests don't let me inside the shrine before placing a moon and Ganga on my head. The real Shiva is never ever inside a shrine!"

"Where else are you?"

"I reside in the hearts of the poor who keep the streets clean. I move alongside the farmers ploughing the land. I hold the hands of the crippled, the blind, the orphans and the suffering people and care for them. Come, my brother. You are my true devotee. You have become me. I have become you. You are Shiva!"

"I'm Shiva! I'm Shiva!"

The village scavenger merges into Shiva's embrace.

*

Kuvempu's style of invoking the figure of Shiva in his play does several things. As with his predecessors in the folk tradition, it releases Shiva from the dominant theological imaginations and makes him intimately available to powerless people. It shakes up the moral stupor of the powerful groups too in asking them to shift out of ritual worship and imagine their relation with God in morally daring and socially sensitive ways. Further, Kuvempu is working within the reality of God. His recomposing of the world picture—in order to both make theology open its eyes to the new demands of social justice and make the pursuit of God an individual act and not parcelled along caste, religion or any other community lines—does not proceed therefore in an iconoclastic manner, from a point outside religion.

The rhythmic verse form of *Jalagara* appears to place faith in the capacity of humans to replace an undesirable social order. Minor characters—an idealist youth who admires the tireless work of the sweeper, two young men who boldly dismiss religion as originating from an encounter between a thief and a fool but are lacking in sympathy for a starving beggar, a few boys who are blissful in their stupidity, among others—disclose the diverse currents within the social map, keeping the course of future events open.

IN SEARCH OF DIGNITY AND JUSTICE

Earlier this year, the central government reported that nearly 350 sanitation workers had died over the last five years while cleaning the sewers in Indian cities. This detail conveys though an arid sense for this saddening feature of Indian society. A book of photographs, *In Search of Dignity and Justice: The Untold Story of Conservancy Workers* (2014), by the reputed Mumbai-based photographer, Sudharak Olwe, which offers rare glimpses into the lived worlds of the sanitation workers in Mumbai, is therefore a valuable gift. Sudharak decided to publish this book in 2014, when he heard that three workers had died from inhaling the poisonous gases inside a sewage pipeline in Mumbai. Until then, he had only held exhibitions and workshops with the black and white photographs he had shot over fourteen months between 1999 and 2000.

After learning that the workers who collect garbage, descend the manholes to service the sewage system and manually clean the public toilets were from the Mahar caste, which happened to be his community as well, Sudharak began to detail their lives through photographs. It took time to earn the trust of the workers whom he accompanied through the day, from their homes to their place of work and back. The workers had refused to think that the photographs might change their lives in any way.

The black and white photographs quietly show the sanitation workers being as serious as anyone else about work, the grimy landscape of their everyday work realities and the milieu of their family life. Not seeking to shock or evoke pathos and abstaining from any overt activism, the photographs convey the truth of their life worlds with great love and understanding. They elicit empathy.

The short essay and the notes by Sudharak that accompany the photographs gently draw attention to the deadening life circumstances of the sanitation workers. They inhabit tiny congested quarters inside dilapidated buildings meant only for sanitation workers. These are "like ghettos," Sudharak observes, "where the workers are physically, socially and culturally segregated from the larger population." On many an occasion, following the death of a sanitation worker, both his widow and his siblings make competing claims on the tiny service quarter. It is common to find a couple of families sharing the same quarter. "The toll taken by the constant fighting, aggravated by the violence of alcohol," he writes, "can be seen on the face of every man, woman and child."

The sanitation workers hate the degrading work. Each one of them needs alcohol to be able to do the work. Alcoholism is rife among the workers as a result and hurts their health and family life. Most men don't expect to live long. And widows do not remarry since that makes them ineligible to get their deceased husband's job as well as to stay on in the service quarter.

Since the children of the workers often drop out of school in the absence of a supportive social milieu, Sudharak and his friends organized a photography workshop for them over the weekends to help prevent them from getting into sanitation work. A few of them now work as full-time photographers in Mumbai.

Mechanization of sanitation work does not make the work less degrading as it doesn't eliminate the need to go down manholes or come in physical contact with sewage matter. Besides, Sudharak adds, any measure that doesn't also keep the children of sanitation workers away from the line of their parents' work just isn't good enough.

HUNDRED-MILE COMMUNITIES

" A 100-mile radius is roughly the distance where the land, the people, the climate, and the market are equally familiar to all, where there is a sense of community, and where one can walk, or bicycle, or drive, and still feel close to home ... The 100-mile community weaves together decentralization, locality, scale and livelihoods."

Found in *Anubandh: Building Hundred-Mile Communities* (2015), a book by Ela Bhatt, the founder of the famous Self-Employed Women's Association (SEWA), these sentences form part of a passionate argument for rebuilding local economies.

Bhatt's idea of a hundred-mile community was inspired from discussions on meeting one's food needs within a hundred-mile radius that she heard in Canada. Most villages in India, she wondered, do indeed meet their food requirements locally, but their spatial isolation had unfortunately meant economic vulnerability and not a source of strength.

For Bhatt, the word, *anubandh,* affirms that an awareness of social interconnectedness leads to ethically minded action:

> The problem is not with the products; they certainly enrich our lives. The problem is our relationship with them. Whatever we consume, and whatever we produce, sets in motion a chain reaction that impacts the world around us. By taking conscious charge of our role as a link in this chain, we embody and perpetuate the world we live in, for better or for worse. I call this linked relationship with the world, *anubandh*...

In an interview, Bhatt clarified that 'anubandh' was not a solution, but "a way for us to think about what we do and plan ahead... what will be the impact of my action or decision on another person, the community, ecology and natural resources...When we buy vegetables from a street vendor, what is the impact on his life; or the impact on a mall owner on buying vegetables from his mall?"

The concise social, economic and ecological profiles of ten villages in Gujarat, which form the first part of Bhatt's book, convey the graphic diversity in the agro-climate, occupations, food, clothing and housing found in them. Recalling the experiences of SEWA as illustrative materials, she shows that new markets for local crops can be created locally, that the existing skills among women can find an income with the right linkages to nearby urban markets, that new water conservation techniques can remedy the situation of water scarcity, that new economically viable initiatives can be launched in villages.

In enabling local communities to regain and sustain their strength, co-operative ventures take on great significance. Co-operative ventures, ecological care and the sharing of risk are more easily seen in small scale social settings:

> If we had to witness the consequences of our actions, we would not find it easy to shrug our shoulders and dismiss people as casualties. We should realize that their loss eventually has an impact on ourselves as well. The closer the distance between the producer and consumer, the producer and the raw materials, the government and the governed, we find greater the accountability. It is after all difficult to chop down a forest, pollute a river or exploit the workers in your own community.

Bhatt's argument is many layered. Education is a lifelong affair; not to be mistaken for formal degrees, it is the pursuit of knowledge for a life that is creative, co-operative and filled with happiness. And, clarifying that she was not anti-technology, she welcomes technology "that empowers people in an equitable way, respectful of both human and environmental needs."

Bhatt's ideas for rebuilding small scale communities can appear simplistic. The interlinked fate of currencies and stock markets across countries often suggest that effective attempts at democratic reform can only be global or macro-level in scope. Anticipating this line of concern, Bhatt writes:

> Anubandh and the building of 100-mile communities may sound impractical or a little too simplistic to counter the world's problems. I suggest we begin by building an active relationship with the world around us. We do it in a way that the food we eat, the clothes we wear and the objects we surround ourselves with in our daily lives not only reflect our own values but also activate the values of our society. This is a two-way process.

She reposes faith in the power of individuals to remake their worlds in an ethical fashion and their wholesome effects on the actions of others. If individuals act differently, society will have been altered. The healthful transformations are not merely about the substitution of one's lifestyle: they ask for sustaining the vitality and autonomy of rural communities.

The cities do not find a separate discussion. The massive power of the state or the harms of communal prejudice do not find an explicit engagement either. Gandhi, whose writings on "panchayat, Swaraj, khadi and the village economy" Bhatt acknowledges as "lifelong guides and sources of inspiration" engaged them head-on. Does she presume that the idea of anubandh, which asks that people stay aware of their inter-relatedness, has in-built ethical space for addressing these difficulties?

Ela Bhatt's ideas of anubandh and hundred-mile communities expose the moral hollowness of how development is talked about in our times. Her quiet celebration of a decentralized society, where local communities stay self-reliant and manage adversity on their own should provoke introspection everywhere.

THE RAMAYANA ON THE
HUMAN CONDITION

A s Rama, Sita and Lakshmana made their way through the forest, a great variety of trees, creepers, insects, worms, animals and birds met their eyes. Sita declared that she had spotted twenty-one different birds. When asked to identify those birds, though, she was able to name only six of them. Lakshmana teased her, "Show them to me." "Lakshmana, you are really a fool," Sita retorted. "Are they the court priests of Ayodhya to stand in line whenever summoned?!" She then exclaimed, "Look, a bird with a red beak and a yellow neck is behind that branch!" Lakshmana looked and looked, but only saw an endless green.

Sita, the daughter of the earth, was better at making a life inside the forest than the city-bred Rama and Lakshmana. She identified tubers and roasted meat in fire with ease.

*

Found in theatre director, writer and activist, Prasanna's book, *Moola Ramayana–Part 1* (The Original Ramayana, 2019), my translation of the passages above are part of his retelling of the initial days of Rama's exile in the forest which gently foregrounds details glossed over in the epic's mainstream versions.

Emphasizing that Rama Rajya is nothing other than Grama Rajya, a decentralized kingdom of villages, Prasanna points out that the epic rails against a machine-driven urban civilization. No better proof exists for this claim than the depiction of Lanka as a city with flying objects and magical communication. Besides, Ravana's army has sophisticated armaments while Rama and his army fight with bows and arrows, sticks and stones.

His retelling, Prasanna notes, kept the epic's original intent as well as the contemporary context in mind. Rama and Sita, in his view, are metaphors for *Purusha* (Human) and *Prakriti* (Nature). The Ramayana does not wish for their separation and regards the latter as demonic. The pain in the separation of lovers is easy enough to see but not in that of *Purusha* and *Prakriti*, which then allows for arrogance to rise and generosity to shrink, for cities to dominate villages, for cleverness to take priority over wisdom.

The limitations of Rama, Prasanna clarifies, are not the limitations of the Ramayana. The epic's greatness consists in fact in the revealing of Rama's limitations. If he is viewed as God and not as a human with frailties, the hierarchies of caste and gender and the other critical matters found in the epic disappear into the background without appearing a problem. This observation of Prasanna is less about denying Rama the status of God than it is about grasping the significance the epic sees in the relation between *Purusha* and *Prakriti*.

Written a few years ago, Prasanna's provocatively titled essay, "Ramayanavembudu Yedapantha (The Ramayana is Leftism)," opens thus: "Putting it in a modern vocabulary, Valmiki is a committed writer. The Ramayana is a committed work of art." Many of the values cherished by the leftists, he wrote, can be found in the Ramayana.

Just as the seas in the Greek epics, the forests perform a crucial role in the Ramayana. The epic however is a story of a civilization, and not a forest tale. The forest setting suggests Valmiki's interest in showing how civilization is integrally bound up with nature (*prakriti*). When this bond is weakened, laws become harsh, etiquettes increase, the number of shrines multiply: civilization becomes diseased. Prasanna observes that Ravana, the asura king, and his city, Lanka, exemplify this disconnected state.

It is usual to imagine the asuras as big bodied and unkempt people who harass the sages in the forests. But most of the asuras in the Ramayana reside in the city of Lanka. The handsome Ravana, a Brahmin, is famous as a good administrator, a brave warrior and a lover of the arts. The company he kept—his wives and children and court poets and military officials—were people like him. The picture of the excesses of urban Lanka becomes available through the eyes of Hanuman. A drinking revelry had concluded inside Ravana's palace. Disorderliness was everywhere: the musicians had hugged their instruments in a lovers' embrace; expensive clothes and ornaments were strewn on the floor; half-eaten meat dishes had spilled out of golden plates; fruits had rolled out from their baskets. The throne, the carpets, the mattresses, all of them were in an untidy state. Ravana was asleep, Prasanna observes, as if he was the very Lord of Disorderliness.

Forced out of circumstances to live in a forest, Rama, Sita and Lakshmana had accepted their life in an ashram with dignity. Dozens of ashrams are found in the Ramayana. Those living in them are not forest dwellers, but those who have come from outside the forest, from society (*nadu*). Their lives exemplify simplicity as well as a model of civility and authentic living. Not only do the residents of the ashrams seek knowledge, Prasanna reminds us, they also work hard and strive to attain simplicity in living. They are not always, he adds wryly, chanting mantras and pouring ghee into a fire.

Servants don't exist in the ashrams. Everyone has to work there. They collect firewood and conserve food. They keep the premises clean. The elderly need to be cared for too. Prasanna reminds us about the many misconceptions that exist about the ashrams. The deer in the ashrams, for example, are not present as decorative animals. Instead, they have come there seeking protection from the wild animals in the forest.

Lanka and Ayodhya are the only cities that appear in the epic. While Lanka stands for a highly advanced city, Ayodhya is an incomplete one. Ayodhya is filled with disputes and family intrigues. It becomes complete, Prasanna observes, at the end of the epic, after Rama returns from exile. If Rama hadn't been exiled in a forest, he wouldn't have transformed into a *maryada purushottama*: his dislike of authority-mongering, his ready abdication of power, his happy embrace of a life without privileges in the forest are what made him an honourable person. In the absence of these virtues, he would have remained a Dasharatha-like king.

Rama is at times cruel and insulting towards Sita. The pursuit of wealth and hierarchies in social relations seem ever-present in the epic. Civilization appears inevitably an unfair arrangement. Eliminating its ills might be impossible, the Ramayana seems to suggest, but regulating them is necessary. The epic admits to these difficulties, Prasanna remarks, but we are unwilling to do so.

Valmiki, the author of the Ramayana and a hunter by occupation, subjects a fellow hunter, who kills the pair of mating Krauncha birds at the beginning of the epic, to a curse. This decision of Valmiki, for Prasanna, demonstrates the need for humans to curb the wild instincts inside them. The tragedy is that such a noble epic, he regrets, is being put to inhuman ends.

Ayodhya Kanda, a brilliant play that Prasanna wrote and directed for the stage in 2022, wove in several everyday moments to make the epic more alive to the contemporary moral imagination. Mantare, for instance, remarks that the work she, a lower caste servant, had had to do to manage the three hundred conniving wives of Dasharatha had made her hunch-backed. Calling out the deep damage done by patriarchy, she jokes that these queens stayed within the dark indoors like termites and had turned into child bearing machines instead of blooming like flowers.

Two new characters appear in *Ayodhya Kanda*: Shambuka's wife, Ganga, who is a palace servant, and his unnamed father. Both of them Panchamas, or, Dalits, in modern usage, their presence puts a new moral energy to work in the play. At one point, Ganga likens her husband to Rama since he too left unhesitatingly for the forest, to do penance, to gain knowledge.

The characters in *Ayodhya Kanda* speak 'chaste,' 'colloquial' as well as Dharwar-style Kannada in the most unselfconscious manner, the way conversations are so naturally multilingual in the country. In a delectable moment, Dasharatha recalls the joyful exclamations made in Hindustani, Bengali and Telugu by different visitors to his court when they learn of Rama's anointment as his royal successor.

Prasanna's novel readings of the overfamiliar ancient text establish a different kind of proximity for it with contemporary times. Enriching the thinking about the human condition, they bring the epic to fresh relevance.

PERSONALITIES

TO THE OCEAN OF STRUGGLE, FLOW
A THOUSAND RIVERS

*W*ho were among the earliest upper caste individuals to work for the Dalit cause in Karnataka? I happened to ask Siddalingaiah, the Kannada poet and Dalit leader. He admired four individuals in particular for their courage and commitment in engaging with the realities of untouchability.

*

Born into a family of Gauda Saraswat Brahmins in South Kanara in 1859, Kudmal Ranga Rao grew up to become a conscientious lawyer. He is known to have come under the influence of Brahmo Samaj, a branch of which had been founded in Mangalore in 1870. He founded several schools and hostels for Dalit boys and girls across South Kanara and also helped find housing and farm land for Dalit families. He and his family had to endure, as consequence, immense hostility from the upper castes.

In keeping with Ranga Rao's wish, the members of *Thotis*, a Dalit caste which did sanitation work, carried his body to the cremation site. An express desire of his was to see an educated and prosperous Dalit individual drive off in a car in his presence, leaving a cloud of dust around his head. This wish of his is inscribed on his tombstone in Mangalore. Over-earnest as it might seem, what might Ranga Rao have wished for in that utopic scene? His idea of modern society as one where education and the owning of a personal car did not remain the preserve of the upper castes is clear. The experience he sought for himself in his scene of utopia though is intriguing. Did he think that

Dalits needed opportunities to humiliate the upper castes for caste equality to be truly realized? Did upper castes need to experience humiliation to truly understand the pain of untouchability?

*

By the start of the twentieth century, the Mysore state had built nearly thirty Panchama schools, as they were then called, for Dalit children. Finding teachers for these schools was however not easy. Talakadu Range Gowda worked as the headmaster at the Panchama boarding school in Malvalli for more than three decades. He would often be on the lookout for Dalit boys who were grazing cows and sheep or collecting firewood in the forest. Following them home, he would then persuade their families to send them to his school. The latter initially suspected his motives. They feared that their children would be sacrificed at the Krishnarajasagara Dam that was being built at that time! Abandoning such fears soon enough, they began to marvel at the man's goodness. They often came to school to listen to him teach.

On Sundays, Range Gowda bought combs, castor oil and soap for his students in the nearby town of Mandya and personally ensured that his students remained tidy. The first generation of Dalit graduates, MLAs, and MLCs include many of his students. They remember him with affection as the "Dalit Vidya Guru." They are putting together a commemorative book on him.

*

Gopalaswamy Iyer came from an affluent family in Bangalore. His father was a Deputy Commissioner. Influenced by Annie Besant's theosophy, he devoted himself to the uplift of the Dalits. When he was in charge of a Panchama hostel in Bangalore, he meticulously maintained a register of the home addresses of the hostel children. He would send postcards with the exam result to the students and urge them to return to the hostels and resume their studies. For those who had passed the tenth standard, he offered to find college admission or jobs as school teachers and clerks.

When the owner of the hostel building asked Gopalaswamy Iyer to shift his hostel elsewhere, the latter conveyed the desperate need for finding an alternate building to Sir CV Raman, the Nobel-prize winning physicist. The physicist immediately offered his bungalow in the city to be used as the hostel until another building was found. Gopalaswamy Iyer, who was close to the Mysore royal family, escorted the first Dalit to the Mysore Durbar in the mid-1930s. Intense dislike for his work with the Dalits made his relatives abuse him as Panchama Iyer.

*

Kaka Kharkanis, a Gandhian, did much work to educate Dalit girls in Bijapur in the 1930s. When no one was willing to rent him a building to run a hostel for them, he built a couple of storeys on his house to accommodate them.

Remembering the work of these individuals is to partake in the memories of being together across the difficult lines of caste. And, to aspire to make society habitable. As the famous closing lines of Siddalingaiah's poem, "A Thousand Rivers," say:

"To the ocean of struggle,
flow a thousand rivers."
("Horatada Sagarake/Saviraaru Nadigalu").

THE GANDHI OF MALNAD

The Auxiliary Nurse Midwife positions had received applications from numerous candidates. A few of them had submitted a recommendation letter from the district-in-charge minister. Only two among those could be accommodated. So the selection committee dropped in on the minister to ask how they ought to decide. The minister said, "I feel that you should offer them to those among them who are qualified and poor. The nurses who work in rural areas must have a certain kind of caring sensibility. Serving pregnant women and new mothers there is better done by those with similar life experiences."

H.G. Govinde Gowda (1926-2016) belongs among the most illustrious political figures seen in the country. He came to be known as the Gandhi of Malnad* around the time he first contested the Karnataka assembly elections in 1983, following three decades of selfless work in Chikmagalur district. The subsequent fifteen years in the state's politics saw him set lofty standards of honest, constructive work.

Born into a small agriculturist's family in Hinachi, a village in Chikmagalur district, in 1926, Gowda lost his mother at an early age and completed his schooling under the warm guardianship of a family relative. He felt grateful to his school teachers who took their work seriously. Their conscience, Gowda noted poignantly later, wouldn't let them take their salaries otherwise. He did not join his friends when they spun tops or played other games as he sold goods in the market on holidays.

---

* The Malnad region, a forest region with high rainfall, comprises the districts of Chikmagalur and Coorg and parts of Hassan and Shivamogga districts.

During the Quit India movement, Gowda mobilized local student groups to join the struggle. Self-reliance, non-violence, a simple lifestyle, anti-untouchability, among other Gandhian values, had appealed to him greatly. He always wore a khadi shirt and pyjamas. He and his classmates waited eagerly for the Kannada translation of the *Harijan* weekly to arrive in the town. He frequently responded to the nationalist calls for satyagraha.

Gowda stopped pursuing his intermediate degree in early 1948. It is possible that the assassination of Gandhi, which, in his words, "left thousands of youths like him orphaned," made him discontinue his studies. He then set up a provision store in Koppa town. Being a trader, he observed, let him remain independent. His fairness, political seriousness and sensitivity towards the poor made the store a hub for discussions and advice-seeking for people from surrounding villages. His wife, Shantha, has recalled a delectable slice of memory from this time: during school exams, Gowda gave free pen ink refills to students.

Under the mentorship of Kadidal Manjappa, the reputed Gandhian Congressman, Gowda joined the Congress Party*. The large number of his local admirers helped him win the municipality elections in 1952. In his two-term, eight-year long tenure as President of the Koppa Municipality Board, he did much to secure the town's well-being: laying down a cement road that is still functional, installing an overhead tank to supply purified water, bringing in electricity, to name a few of the most remembered among his initiatives. He dropped in on restaurants and barber shops to ensure that the utensils and the razors and scissors had been cleaned with hot water. Always careful with finances, Gowda chided the office attendant if he brought in an extra cup of coffee to a meeting: "Can't you count how many are here before you bring us coffee? Does money shower on the municipality?"

Moving up to the next administrative level, Gowda got elected as the President of the Koppa Taluk Development Board for two terms

---

* Most remembered for the land reform measures he initiated in favour of the tenancy farmers in the 1950s, Kadidal Manjappa, a lawyer by profession, was Revenue Minister and then Chief Minister of Mysore state (later renamed Karnataka) for a brief period in 1956.

between 1960 and 1968. In this phase, he got schools built in most of the villages in the taluk. He also got many roads and bridges built in rural areas. These would, he felt, make it easier for girl children to attend schools.

Dedicated and selfless work over the years brought him an intimacy with the local people and the issues confronting them. Gowda's life in politics exemplifies a robust model of grassroots leadership. All shops and other commercial establishments in Koppa and the small towns in its vicinity stayed closed on the day he was cremated.

The Congress party's manner of handling the 1969 Presidential elections left him disappointed. In the mid-70s, he led the JP movement and headed the Raitha Sangha, the farmer's organization, in Koppa. Fielded as a candidate from the Janata Party, he won the very first assembly elections he contested from Sringeri in 1983.

Gowda was minister of primary education twice, once in the mid-eighties and a second time in the mid-nineties. Taking to his work with a natural flair, he went on to offer a new direction for his department, shore up the staff morale and restore public faith in the work of the government. His fair and transparent recruitment of over a lakh teachers for the state-run primary schools, which brought down the imbalance in the teacher student ratio, is remembered until now. But there were other special deeds: he abolished the oppressive practice of declaring ranks for students in the tenth standard exams; he commissioned fine anthologies of children's fiction for classroom use; he gave constant attention to the upkeep of the school infrastructure; he ensured the timely distribution of school textbooks and uniforms; he brought in Nali-Kali, an innovative model of activity-based learning, in schools. These along with numerous other measures saw a decline in school drop out rates and an increase in student enrollment in government schools. Assisted by a terrific group of officers at all levels, Gowda threw himself passionately into the work. "Twenty-four hours," he said, "weren't enough."

Just about every contributor to *The Gandhi of Malnad* (2000), the mammoth felicitation volume for him, has shared anecdotes that reveal his social concern, uncompromising honesty and principled conduct. Many have testified that it was impossible to ask him for a favour that meant a setting aside of the proper procedure. The devout Gowda however was not a rigid puritan and had great warmth and openness of feeling. Even his rivals found it tough not to admire him. Indeed, his virtues saw him being admired across different castes and religions.

In an interview he gave in 2000, Gowda deplored that the spirit of self-sacrifice had declined in the country in recent years. A blind mimicry of Western countries, he felt, was also a key problem: initiatives that were in consonance with India's cultural realities were what were needed.

Govinde Gowda was grateful that the autonomy he enjoyed during his ministerial tenures let him stay true to his principles. His own moral assertiveness in the middle of the realpolitik pressures had perhaps played a bigger part.

U.R. ANANTHAMURTHY

The Attractions of Metaphor

D uring my first meeting with U.R. Ananthamurthy (1932-2014), when I was a college student, he had advised that I read without rest, like a caterpillar devours leaves.

As it became clear subsequently, living metaphors meant a lot to him. Metaphors were essential for the life of politics; they might even "open the heavens."

Lohia compared the work of politics, U.R. Ananthamurthy (URA) recalled to me once, to that of keeping the floor clean. It meant continuous effort. There was no point, Lohia's metaphor implied, in hankering after a utopia where politics was no longer necessary. He was dismissing communist or liberal fantasies of a society without politics. Being in politics was to be committed to being in a process without end.

URA fondly remembered Gopala Gowda, the famous socialist leader and his mentor and friend, say: "There are people who have reached the shore, and there are people who are yet to reach the shore. I want to do politics for those who haven't reached the shore." He shared another instance to express his admiration for Gopala Gowda's metaphoric imagination. Finding the Indian communists' demand for complete class equality dogmatic, the socialist had remarked: "The communists won't share the earth until they are done sharing the sky."

Basavalingappa, the distinguished Dalit political leader, had once told URA that when upper-caste persons climbed on the back of Dalits in a crowded audience to get a glimpse of the theatre performance, the latter used to consider that a part of the performance but had now stopped thinking that way. URA considered this description "a great metaphor" of political awakening among Dalits.

How does one be creative and yet do work that is seen as belonging to tradition? The relationship between tradition and creativity was indeed a chief intellectual preoccupation of URA. His essay, "Tradition and Creativity (1990)," recalls: "Some time ago, during a visit to Germany to participate in an international book fair, I had the good fortune of listening to (Kapila) Vatsayanji giving a beautiful metaphor for tradition. The metaphor is that of a hookah. Someone says:

> 'This hookah has been in our family for nearly three hundred years.'
>
> 'Three hundred years! This same hookah!'
>
> 'Yes, but when the bowl became very old and worn out, we changed it. And then, the pipe became too rough and rigid, so we changed it too. But we still have the same hookah.'"

Metaphors bore the imaginative potential of a culture. Indian languages continued to allow, URA felt, for the natural use of metaphors in a way that contemporary English, which has "become analytical" and is "being used increasingly as a vehicle of the technological age," did not. He invoked the metaphor of *jeernagni* (digestive fire) to describe Kannada's capacity to absorb elements from outside its cultural world and make it its own.

The frontyard and the backyard were among URA's favourite metaphors for understanding the dynamics of culture. His father, he wrote, transacted with his friends in the frontyard: it was the world of men and authority; it was the place of political and spiritual discussions. Whereas his mother and the women of the village met in the backyard: it was the world of gossip and secrets and the sharing of joys and sorrows. If he hadn't overheard the conversations in the backyard, URA felt certain that he wouldn't have become a writer. He had also joked that writers are made in the backyard of civilization whereas "the frontyard produces only professors!"

The metaphoric couplet of the frontyard and the backyard travelled freely to stand in for the West and India, Sanskrit and Indian bhashas, upper caste and lower caste literature. The frontyard was the world of the powerful whereas the backyard was the world of the dominated which nevertheless retained vitality and creative ferment. URA's view that dominant perspectives have not gone unchallenged in the country and that those conflicts and negotiations have enriched its cultural world made him regard India as a civilization than as a nation with a uniform culture.

In the last years of his life, the growing frenzy for development in the country and the rise of the Hindu right-wing worried him. The earth, he said, was not an *akshaya patra* that supplied resources endlessly. His remark that he didn't wish to live in an India where Narendra Modi was the Prime Minister was read literally by the right-wing attackers who didn't want its metaphoric side to trouble their conscience.

THE FIGURE OF O.V. VIJAYAN

It was in the mid-1990s that I met O.V. Vijayan (1930-2005), the great Malayalam writer. Needing a break from New Delhi, where he had lived for over two decades, he had decided to spend a few months with his nephew, and my dear friend, Paul Vinay Kumar, in Bangalore. This proved a piece of wonderful luck.

Until then, I had known of O.V. Vijayan only through *Outsider*, his trenchant column in *The Illustrated Weekly of India*. His description of caste, in one of his columns, as a "choreography of prejudice," had stayed in my mind.

Slight in build, and simple in appearance, Vijayan wore a thin white cotton kurta over a *mundu* that stopped just above his ankles. I never saw him wear anything else. His long hair, which reached down to his shoulders, and goatee made his sharp features look even sharper. He moved and spoke slowly (Parkinson's disease had already set in). He was an intense presence.

Rarely did Vijayan initiate a conversation. He was perfectly willing, though, to respond to questions. Since I was curious about his opinions on the writers I liked or didn't like, the meetings unfolded easily. A student of English literature at Madras Presidency College, he regretted that he still hadn't read Conrad's *The Heart of Darkness*. "Where do the ducks go in winter?"—Holden Caulfield's question to the cab-driver as they drove past Central Park in Salinger's *The Catcher in the Rye*, seemed profound to him.

Vijayan's wife, Theresa, who had taught ancient Greek and Roman philosophy at Daulat Ram College in New Delhi, would join us whenever she had the time. Caring and generous as a host, she was constantly alert to the demands of Vijayan's health.

My luck continued. Vijayan and Theresa moved from Delhi to their house in Secunderabad during my MA days at the University of Hyderabad. Since I knew that they liked meeting me, I would go over to their house frequently.

Vijayan cared only for literature with philosophical and spiritual depth. Many writers fell short in his estimate: "They remain at the level of social concerns." Dostoevsky, Faulkner and the French existentialists were among those he liked. Of the three early icons of Indian writing in English, Raja Rao seemed the only relevant one. He saw his own allegorical stories of state tyranny in *After the Hanging and Other Stories* (1989) as being only "concerned with power and terror." (Incidentally, he must be among the few Indian writers who did fine translations of their own writings into English). Clearly, the other stories in the book that overcame that "obsession" and "explored the need to flow along with life, in the spirit of the stream" mattered more. Indeed Vijayan's complaint against Marxism was that it made no room for spirituality.

A card carrying member of the Communist Party, Vijayan quit the party and its ideology in 1958, when the Soviet Union executed Imre Nagy, the Hungarian leader. If not for this decision, he has observed, his first novel, *The Legends of Khasak* (1969), which explores the place of cosmic mystery and points to the limits of rational thought, would have suffered. English reviewers outside Kerala had been quick to term Khasak, Vijayan's literary creation, as the Macondo of Kerala. Vijayan sneered that *The Legends of Khasak* appeared two years before the English translation of Gabriel Garcia Marquez's *One Hundred Years of Solitude* came out.

Vijayan considered Narayana Guru his Guru. He shared several anecdotes to illustrate the virtues of a spiritually serious life. One of them was about how Ramana Maharishi, who was suffering from throat cancer, had asked, a few hours before his death, whether the peacock in the ashram had been fed.

A break with communism and a passion for transcendental issues did not mean a turning away from the brute social realities. Viewing himself as a Third World cartoonist, Vijayan clarified that the child in his cartoons had been fed "the boiled roots of grass." "This tryst with grass" made him want to repudiate "all those who lied about the tryst with destiny." His work calmly exposed the "native rapacities" at work in India. "War and security," he felt, had turned "decolonization into a confidence trick." The modern world with its annihilationist weapons weighed heavily on his mind. "We are living under ceasefire conditions."

A reflective account of Vijayan's thirty-five year career as cartoonist—he worked for *Shankar's Weekly, Patriot, The Hindu* and *The Statesman*—as well as a rich selection of his cartoons can be found in his *A Cartoonist Remembers* (2002). *Tragic Idiom* (2006) offers another set of his cartoons. The no-holds-barred cartoons and essays in these two books bring independent India under a unique moral scanner. Never settling for the soothing platitudes of democracy, they unmask contemporary evil with raw honesty and intense courage.

RAMCHANDRA GANDHI

A Philosopher's Sojourn in the City

Philosopher Ramchandra Gandhi's brief stay in Bangalore in 2003 must surely count among the moments of surprise in the city's history. He had taken up a two-year visiting faculty position in the philosophy department at Bangalore University in late August of that year. Siddhartha, the founder of Fireflies ashram, Siddalingaiah and I rushed excitedly to meet him at the university guest house on the evening he had arrived. Dressed in a bright orange cotton kurta, a grey haired, bespectacled individual of medium build and height and with a slight stoop and mildly ruffled look overall, greeted us warmly. He was looking forward to being in Bangalore after having lived in Delhi for so long; he had ties with South India through his mother, who was C Rajagopalachari's daughter. His chief concern at the moment was to find local accommodation: the faculty house given him was too large for a single person.

I offered to help Ramu Gandhi (1937-2007) find an apartment in my neighbourhood which was close to the university. He had suggested that I address him as either Ramu or Ramuji; I chose the former since the suffix "ji" didn't come naturally to me. During the three months that he lived in Bangalore, he moved houses twice and was unhappy with the third. Ramu Gandhi was a slightly restless individual, no doubt, but the problem was real each time and couldn't have been known beforehand: the unco-operative auto drivers who made his university commute a hassle, loudspeakers that disturbed the evening, an overcurious family of the landlord.

I had only known of Ramu Gandhi as the author of *Sita's Kitchen: A Testimony of Faith and Inquiry*. Written before the Babri Masjid demolition, this book recognized a different ethical demand in the Ayodhya crisis with the help of a Buddhist tale where the Buddha asks a few rich young men to search for their self instead of seeking revenge on the prostitute who had robbed them of their jewels. In a postscript to this book, Ramu Gandhi had observed: "Rama Bhakti in India today needs enlightened trusteeship, not manipulation by the politics of historical revenge." He had just finished another book called *Svaraj: A Journey with Tyeb Mehta's 'Shantiniketan Tryptich.'* He had previously published, *The Availability of Religious Ideas* and *I am Thou: Meditations on the Truth of India*. He wished to complete the manuscript of *Muniya's Light* in Bangalore.

Ramu Gandhi's course at the university focused on the ideas of who he called "the sapta rishis (seven sages) of modern India," which included Ramakrishna Paramahamsa and Ramana Maharshi, his two gurus, and Swami Vivekananda, Aurobindo, Mahatma Gandhi, Narayana Guru and J. Krishnamurthi. He passionately held that their ideas could regenerate intellectual and political life in India.

A dozen interested people from the city and a couple of university faculty attended Ramu Gandhi's stimulating lectures week after week. The lone faculty member in the philosophy department would dutifully arrange for a big-sized audio recording equipment to be placed beside the lecture platform. Not a single student from the university came to class. (The philosophy department did not have any students). While this absence was probably due to intellectual lethargy, Ramu Gandhi wondered if the faculty members had advised students to avoid his classes, mistaking him to be a right-wing conservative. His exasperation grew stronger when the posters on his lecture on the Mandukya Upanishad appeared without the symbol "Om." He had explicitly wished that this symbol appear on the poster since the Mandukya Upanishad elaborated the meaning of Om.

Ramu Gandhi quit his visiting position at Bangalore University within four months of taking it up. A few months later, he wrote from Delhi: "I miss Bangalore and deeply regret not having had the capabilities to transform adversities into opportunities."

Ramu Gandhi's unexpected presence in the city had aroused curiosity in local intellectual circles. Gauri Lankesh, the editor of *Lankesh Patrike*, invited him to write a column for her weekly. He agreed to write one titled, *Sanmathi*. (He did not write it in the end.) Gauri suggested that I interview him and publish it in Kannada translation in her weekly*. Ramu Gandhi's responses addressed the religious violence of our times with distinct courage and philosophical creativity. For him, the questions, *"Who am I? Who are we?"* demanded a deeper response than saying we belonged to this or that social community. A secular politics that satisfied itself only with the pursuit of civil liberties or the egalitarian distribution of public goods could never be adequate. Larger, transcendental concerns had to guide our political imagination and struggle. This was why he felt that the Spanish film maker, Luis Bunuel's critique of bourgeois society could never attain the depths of the Russian director, Andrei Tarkovsky's critique of modern civilization.

Ramu Gandhi liked watching films. He wished to see the newly released, *Boom*, since Amitabh Bachhan acted in it. Twenty minutes into the film, we decided to leave the movie theatre: the film was incredibly crass. On the way out, he remarked: "Amitabh is a great actor. Look at his eyes. He is not happy doing these roles." A couple of months later, Ramu Gandhi expressed interest in watching Girish Kasaravalli's *Dweepa* (The Island, 2002) which was being screened at the Bangalore International Film Festival. It turned out that we had to settle for the un-subtitled version of the film as the subtitled print had not arrived in time. He was furious: "I feel cheated as a viewer of international cinema!"

Being with Ramu Gandhi was to partake in constant reflections that ranged from everyday sociology to constructive philosophy. He expressed amazement at how urban India had managed the issue of caste hierarchy with caste-neutral terms of address like "uncle" and "aunty." He had proffered a creative recipe in ethics for guiding inter-religious life: "Whatever your conception of religion, add non-violence

---

* *The Hindu* carried this interview with the title, "Ethics, Ecology and Enlightenment," after he passed away in 2007.

to it. It will then be free of any impulse to dominate other religions and change its outward forms."

Ramu Gandhi had found an existential anchor in the world of Advaita Vedanta. It was not an escape however from the hard challenges of our times. He tried to establish the relevance of Advaitic thought for engaging contemporary social and political issues. His philosophical passions were accompanied by a close grasp over the goings on in the Indian polity. He was aware of the fine points in difficult matters like Kashmir and Pakistan. His concern for democracy had led him to campaign against Indira Gandhi in Chikmagalur when she contested the parliamentary elections from there in 1978.

When Ramu Gandhi visited Heggodu to give a talk at Ninasam's annual culture workshop, the entire village had shown up to see Mahatama Gandhi's grandson. Although he never seemed to let this fact of kin weigh on him much, social occasions must have forced him to reckon with it frequently. In the interview I did with him, he admitted that "he ignored the discomforts of special attention" that such occasions brought and viewed the fact of being Gandhi's grandson as "a blessing" which meant "an urgent invitation to inquire into the meaning of truth and non-violence."

THE ETHICAL STANCE OF
KADIDAL SHAMANNA

A few years ago, Kadidal Shamanna (b. 1938), the beloved farmer leader, declined the Karnataka government's invitation to inaugurate the Dasara festival. Chief Minister Siddaramaiah had phoned to invite him personally. He couldn't accept the invitation, Shamanna said, at a time of worsening drought and increasing farmers' suicides in the state. The government had reasoned differently: it is fitting that a "progressive" farmer inaugurated the Dasara at a time of agrarian crisis. As a reminder of his uninterest in religious rituals, Shamanna suggested that it was better that a believer in Chamundeshwari, the presiding deity of the Dasara festival, offered the inaugural worship. His gesture shone through in its ethical seriousness.

An incident found in Shamanna's gripping memoir, *Kadatoreya Jadu* (The Trail of a Forest Stream, 2011), underlines the irony of his present predicament. In his undergraduate days in Mysore, he and his friends were arrested for waving black flags at the Maharaja's elephant procession during the Dasara. They had felt—owing to the influence of a local Lohiaite—that such a procession had no place in a democracy.

Shamanna's subtle wit, compassion and moral sincerity have always lent a unique charm and depth to his politics. And his search for beauty in the world of birds and animals have shown another endearing side to him. Besides nature photography, Hindustani music remains a passion. In 1962, he had moved to Bombay to be a student of Pandit Ali Akbar Khan, the great sarod player.

Sparkling accounts of early socialist politics in Karnataka and its powerful offshoot, the Karnataka Rajya Raitha Sangha (KRRS), which led the strong farmer's movement in the state during the eighties are found in Shamanna's memoirs.

After a short stint as a school teacher in the late 1960s, Shamanna became a farmer due to an unusual circumstance. When he sought the socialist leader, Gopala Gowda's help in finding a lecturer's position in a local college, the leader reminded him of a public meeting where they had both proclaimed the virtue of a person having only one job. Having multiple jobs, their argument held, deprived others of employment and concentrated wealth among a few. By this token, landowners hankering for jobs in the government, for instance, were guilty. Abandoning his desire to be a lecturer, Shamanna decided to cultivate the farm his family bought for him near Shivamogga.

Shamanna's efforts at organizing local farmers took on greater intensity after moving to his new farm. He became famous for urging local farmers to opt for the simple Mantra Mangalya weddings devised by Kuvempu. Couples in inter-caste marriages leaned on him for moral support. In the late 1970s and the 1980s, as a highly committed member of the KRRS, he organized several farmer rallies and mobilized protests against the government's brutal crackdown of farmer protests and the harsh official loan recovery raids on their homes, among others.

In the early 1980s, the work on a bridge near Thirthahalli had been completed. The local Congress party workers barricaded the bridge entrance until Gundu Rao, the Chief Minister, was able to inaugurate it. Three months passed before local individuals willing to fund the inaugural ceremony were found. The CM was rumoured to arrive in a helicopter to inaugurate the bridge. The local Inspection Bungalow began to be renovated for his visit. Realizing that the expenses of the CM's visit would outweigh the bridge construction costs, Shamanna and his fellow activists wrote a letter to the CM suggesting he abandon his visit. They did not get a reply. Two days before the official inaugural, they invited one of the workers who had built the bridge to inaugurate it. Five hundred local supporters followed the worker who was seated in a decorated bullock cart. The bridge was now free to be used. The CM canceled his visit.

In a memoir where he steadfastly avoids presenting himself in heroic terms, Shamanna cheerfully claims sole credit for the green khadi shawl that the farmers of the KRRS came to wear on their shoulders. When the KRRS leaders felt unsure about adopting the shawl, Shamanna explained, "instead of identifying oneself as the brother of this engineer or that doctor, a farmer should introduce himself as a farmer. A symbol is needed to make this happen. The green shawl is that symbol. This is a movement for self-respect." The green shawl became a charged symbol of a politically awakened farmer.

The well-being of farmers continues to matter for Shamanna. He hopes that the factions of the KRRS will come together and resuscitate a glorious social movement.

THE IMPORTANCE OF PROFESSOR KALBURGI

The murder of Professor M.M. Kalburgi (1938-2015) at the hands of right-wing Hindu extremists has meant the loss of a scholar who exemplified a grand research tradition where philology, history and literature walk together. National and international media had been quick to view the tragedy as the murder of a rationalist and an atheist—he was a devout Lingayat, in fact—at the hands of religious bigots.

Kalburgi had worked extensively on Lingayat philosophy, classical Kannada literature, and the folklore of North Karnataka. *Marga* (The Way), the four-volume anthology of his writings, gathers a rich range of essays in these areas, an engagement with which is essential for getting a good sense of contemporary Karnataka. As the hostile reception to Kalburgi in the past had shown, a discussion of medieval India will not remain only a historical discussion: medieval society, unlike in Europe, is a living presence in the country. It is indeed strange to see the medieval world successfully exiled from so much of the academic work on contemporary India.

During his tenure as the vice-chancellor of the Kannada University at Hampi, Kalburgi was keen on making up for the modernist intellectual bias of its faculty and get them to engage pre-modern literature and history. He edited the massive fifteen volume compilation of *vacanas*, the free verse poetry composed by Lingayat saints and devotees from the 12th century onwards. At the time of death, he was supervising the mammoth Kannada translation of twenty-one volumes of Persian manuscripts written during the Adil Shahi rule in Bijapur (1489-1686).

The work of Kalburgi, who taught at Karnatak University, Dharwar, is testimony to the valuable scholarship that has emerged from the state-run universities in the country. Much of this work has happened without the support of large research grants or the formidable library support of the kind found in universities abroad. The presence of serious scholars in non-metropolitan universities cannot be valued enough. Keeping scholarly discussions decentralized, they have guarded against homogeneity in research concerns. Kalburgi's work also attests to the enormous research freedom found in state universities.

Kalburgi's scholarly writings disturbed the stable official memories of Lingayat institutions. He would, for example, present facts to show that the Lingayat dharma was not part of Hinduism. Since his claims were backed by his formidable hold over the *vacanas*, such findings angered the Hindu right wing as well as many of the Lingayat mathas, some of whom had openly wished that it was better that he died. In the late eighties, the anger of the established Lingayat orthodoxy became so great that they forced him to retract his claims that the father of Basavanna's nephew, Chenna Basavanna, was a lower caste man. The Hindu right wing had attacked him viciously when he questioned the sanctity of idol worship in Hinduism.

Only humanities scholars and creative writers have elicited discussions that stir the moral selfhood of communities in the country. For all their care about data and method and analytical rigour, the work of social scientists usually fails to engage the moral imagination of communities. The scholarly contributions of Kalburgi are doubtless a precious intellectual inheritance.

D.R. NAGARAJ

The Wonder of Retrieval

During one of D.R. Nagaraj's visits to our home, I had held out towards him my new acquisition, a copy of Vaclav Havel's *Living in Truth*. He took it from me saying, "This has an exciting essay, 'The Power of the Powerless.'" On another occasion, it was *The Essays, Articles and Reviews of Evelyn Waugh*. Pushing up his black, square horn-rimmed glasses on his nose bridge, he exclaimed: "Oh! I learnt the niceties of English from Waugh." I was finishing high school during this time, the late eighties. My father, who had studied and taught English literature before joining the Karnataka civil services, and D.R. Nagaraj (DRN, 1954-1998) had met through common friends.

The range of DRN's reading was absolutely stunning. Primarily a Kannada literary critic, his passions moved across Indian, English, American, European and African literatures. Indeed, literature from any part of the world. Indian and Western philosophers and political thinkers also grabbed him. His recall of books, writers and literary episodes had an endearing nerd-like quality. And, the joy he felt about ideas was independent of anything else.

DRN would narrate one of the case dreams from Freud's *The Interpretation of Dreams* to show his excitement about the great psychoanalyst's method. His review of Mao's biography written by his personal physician opened with "Among the tallest revolutionary leaders of the twentieth century, Mao didn't have the habit of brushing his teeth in the morning: he only rinsed his mouth with tea."

True, literature could have a political side, but the power of the literary imagination soared above it. While referring to Kannada writers who he felt had "written more authentic stories" on matters of concern to Dalit and feminist movements than the latter's ideologues, he noted, "Literature probably has its own way of ditching ideology."

After being beholden to the socialist ideas of Marx, Lohia and others in his youth, DRN had struggled to break out of their influence. The great folk epics of Male Madeshwara, Manteswamy and Junjappa, the vacanas of Allama Prabhu and the poetry of Rumi, the Persian poet, offered him new angles to regard the socialist ideals, helping shake his ideological fixity to an extent. The folk epics showed the radiant literary and aesthetic creativity as well as the intense critical sensibilities seen among the lower castes, a fact that appears counter-intuitive to fossilised histories of caste relations where the upper castes triumph in all instances. DRN had joked once, "Do you think a Shudra landlord would let molten lead be poured in his ears as penalty for overhearing the Vedas? *Manusmriti* is an ideological fantasy of the orthodox Brahmins. It isn't a document of how things actually were."

Not proposing a diminished place for the power of Brahmin culture, DRN was asking instead that the cultural experiences of lower castes be properly understood. An attention to how the social worlds of castes and religions in India cross-fertilized each other all the time while institutional memory erased the history of that co-influence was needed for overcoming of what he termed "cultural amnesia."

Mystical traditions which revealed hitherto hidden relationships in the world through metaphors, also fascinated DRN. A sense of vismaya (wonder) and a relish for metaphors, which modern scholarship so easily dispensed with, better aided the work of overcoming cultural amnesia.

The hundreds of books that emerged in the wake of Edward Said's *Orientalism* concentrated their energies on how European thought dominated social life in colonized countries. The hundreds of ways in which small communities retained their creativity amidst colonial rule though met with virtual neglect. For instance, the Kannada poets of the early twentieth century appeared to DRN like a tiny bird that had reached for twigs, feathers and leaves from anywhere to build a nest amidst a storm: "They saved Kannada poetry from the vulture that was colonialism."

For modern minds like him, DRN confessed, history was like a mother's saree in whose folds frightened children sought refuge at the sight of violence. Having seemed opaque at first, Rumi's poetry later proved to be like 'a seed that waits patiently in the folds of darkness to burst through the cracks at some point and flourish as a plant.' His celebration of Rumi though kept doubt within view. In his introduction to *Vasanta Smriti* (Memories of Spring, 1992), his translation of Rumi's poems, he wondered whether his reading had politicized the Persian poet.

In April 1997, while I was studying sociology at the University of Pittsburgh, I attended a lecture by Salman Rushdie. In the overcrowded lecture hall, Christopher Hitchens had introduced him. "Here is the real thing!"

At some point during his scintillating talk, Rushdie coolly claimed that the best of contemporary Indian writing was happening only in English. It was hard to believe he had said that. In the post-lecture question-and-answer session, someone in the audience asked him why Indian language writers weren't creating good literature. The reply had come swiftly: "Oh, they write about bride burning, about heroism in villages."

"People like Rushdie simply don't think that creative possibilities exist in Indian languages!" DRN's expression of incredulity during a past conversation came sailing in.

I phoned DRN to report Rushdie's remarks. He was then a visiting professor at the Department of South Asian Languages and Civilizations at the University of Chicago. After commiserating with me for a while, he noted that only the Kannada proverb, "Indifference is the best remedy for arrogance", could help in this situation.

DRN took absolute delight in the words he chose to make a point. Two instances have stayed with me in this regard: "Fight the libraries of the West!" and "critical intuitionism." The first remark of DRN asked that the West's archival might and its cultures of hyper-specialisation ought not to intimidate Indian intellectuals. They even posed a threat to creativity. At the University of Pittsburgh, I had enrolled in a course, "Democracy and Difference," with Iris Marion Young, the political philosopher. Her *Justice and the Politics of Difference* had already become famous. And she had turned out to be a warm and friendly presence in the class. Everyone was in awe of her. When I shared my excitement with DRN over the phone ("We are reading John Rawls, Charles Taylor"), he listened for a while before remarking quietly, "These things can become sterile after a point."

DRN didn't advocate a scholastic return to old Indian texts. He put his faith instead in what he called "critical intuitionism," where imagination and intuition enjoyed a prime position as sources of creativity and knowledge. DRN's view on why colonialism didn't make the nineteenth century yogis in Karnataka nervous is illustrative: "They considered state power and historical actors to be like nature: erratic and beastly at one time; and friendly, generous, and benevolent at another." Falling back on his critical intuition, he stayed away from the routine academic certitudes about how the colonizers broke the self-confidence of the colonized.

At a time when critical commentary is becoming flattened across countries—scholars in Bengaluru, Kolkota, London, New Delhi and New York often read the same books and share similar intellectual problems—DRN wrote as if one's local world mattered for the way one thought and wrote about society. He freely ransacked and localised ideas, images and expressions from everywhere to keep the discussion fresh. To recall a minor instance: asserting the purity of cultural identity, he noted, led to the "bonsaization" of one's experience, which pre-empted, especially in the case of activists, the emergence of a rich political struggle.

An awareness about the interdependent evolution of our cultural selves, DRN held, enabled a more expansive relation with one's experience. In these days, when dissent is being streamlined along narrow sectarian identities, his caution against self-insularity, against self-segregation, against the amnesia of the co-evolution of cultural selfhoods, is even more urgent. In the preface to *The Flaming Feet*, he admitted that he had not given up on the "idea of a common humanity." The idea that something essentially human lay beneath cultural differences probably stayed with him till the end.

When I visited DRN in Chicago, during his first visit to that city in 1996, he exclaimed, "Chicago, Chicago! It's done now. I want to get back." He was referring of course to the fetish for Chicago that the figure of AK Ramanujan had given rise to in Kannada intellectual circles. Being at Chicago was now a been-there, done-that detail.

A few days later, at an academic conference in Chicago, the moderator was seeming strict about rationing time across the panellists. DRN broke the tedium mischievously: "Just this morning, I read that the Regents of the University of Chicago are committed to the policy of affirmative action. Since I come from one of the most backward castes in India, you will have to give me extra time. Otherwise, you will incur the wrath of the University Regents!"

While walking through the corridors of the old university buildings, DRN pointed at their architectural design: "The whole thing is fake Gothic." Founded in 1890, the University of Chicago's buildings in the initial phase mimicked the English Gothic style used at Oxford University several centuries earlier.

DRN relished the special attention his colleagues gave him, but living in Chicago had its costs: "It is deathly quiet here. I miss hearing the abuses on the street." The silence of the university apartment and the extra-cold Midwestern winter proved too much for him. He was happiest to be in Bangalore.

THE HUMANISM OF SIDDALINGAIAH

Indispensable for a scholar of contemporary morality, Siddalingaiah's work elaborated a rich vision of humanism. His debut book of poetry, *Hole-Maadigara Haadu* (The Song of the Holeyas and Madigas, 1975) expressed the suffering of Dalits with a fury and imagery wholly unfamiliar in modern Kannada poetry. Owing to an early attraction to the class analyses of Marxism, his poetic focus though was not solely fixed on the Dalit experience. The famous poem from his debut anthology, *Nanna Janagalu* (My People), for instance, summons the experience of several kinds of toiling labourers without referring to their community identities. The title poem of his second book of poetry, *Saviraru Nadigalu* (A Thousand Rivers, 1979), which viewed society as a place of struggle and likened it to a vast ocean formed by thousands of rivers, offered a vision of deep political and cultural plurality. Sung with revolutionary fervour at political rallies and street processions organized by Dalit Sangharsh Samiti, the poems from these anthologies were integral to the political consciousness emerging among the Dalit communities in post-Independence Karnataka.

A rage towards the exploitative social order didn't mean though a simultaneous rejection of tradition in Siddalingaiah (1954-2021). A scholar of Kannada literature, he identified moral lineages in the past to his political concerns. His well-known poem, *Chomana Makkala Haadu* (The Song of Choma's Children, 1979), asks the country where everyone knew of Choma, the Dalit protagonist in Shivarama Karantha's tragic novel, *Chomana Dudi* (Choma's Drum, 1933), to listen to the stories that his children wish to narrate in the present. Another poem, *Tabarana Haadu* (Tabara's Song, 1983), which bemoans the fate of the poor under a callous government, remembered Tabara, the guileless office attendant who turns insane trying to get his official pension in Purnachandra Tejasvi's short story, *Tabarana Katha* (The Story of Tabara, 1974). Clarifying that the school of Bandaya (Protest) Literature, which his poetry is seen to belong to, was not the first to embrace a pro-people stance, he saw predecessors for the latter in Pampa, the tenth century Jain poet, who claimed that the human community was one, the Shaiva composers of vacanas and Kanakadasa. Siddalingaiah argued that Kannada Dalit writing was not separate from Kannada. Observing that Dalit writers were custodians of the humanistic thought found in the Kannada literary tradition, he advised them to cultivate a close understanding of this moral legacy. It was their responsibility, he felt, to lend voice to everyone's suffering.

The breadth of Siddalingaiah's political and moral vision—as well as that of the two other co-founders of the Dalit movement in Karnataka, Devanur Mahadeva, the writer and B. Krishnappa—made a difference to the character of Dalit activism in the state. The founder-activists invited well-wishers from non-Dalit communities to participate in their organizational efforts. Their regard for the significance of Ambedkar for the Dalit movement didn't mean an avoidance of Gandhi, Lohia or Marx. And, all through their political work, their faith in non-violence was unwavering.

Ooru-Keri (1996), Siddalingaiah's celebrated autobiographical account of his experiences from childhood until the start of adult life, showed a fundamental shift of tone in his writerly voice. His miniature sketches of his family relations, his hostel, his friends, his schoolteachers and the various people in the slum he grew up in are suffused with light-hearted wit and a meditative quality.

In Siddalingaiah's autobiography as well as in his speeches and conversations, the moments of wit were occasions for a communion, an opportunity for exploring common grounds of being together. They loosened hardened sensibilities. They also undid the political tedium, and made reality a bit more bearable, achieving a prelude perhaps to starting things anew.

The philosophical implications of *Ooru-Keri* are profound. In a social relation between the dominant and the dominated, modern social thought presumes that the latter can acquire recognition as an equal only through a struggle with the former. Siddalingaiah offers a powerful alternate perspective. He affirms his selfhood without a trace of resentment towards the vicious social games while also quietly doubting the value of the very things prized in those games. A philosophy for a liberation of the self is tacitly present in his autobiography.

Ooru-Keri is also a consideration of the ethics and aesthetics of memory. Why must we remember painful incidents? How should we remember them? Engaging these questions tacitly, it suggests that a struggle for social justice is not complete if the hearts of the hard-hearted are not changed. Addressing everyone as a member of a moral community, the entire autobiography is a gentle moral suasion.

Poet, folklorist, orator, teacher, legislator, administrator and co-founder of the Dalit movement in Karnataka, Siddalingaiah's many layered engagement with the life of Karnataka eludes easy characterization. I was among the hundreds of his friends and well-wishers who wished to see him return home safely from the hospital two years ago. He was struggling against COVID complications. In his death, a rare voice fell silent.

KSHEERASAGAR

A Friend of the Adivasis

"A festival called Haadi Habba was recently celebrated in Balle haadi (settlement). At this festival, the son of the headman got possessed by the ancestral spirit. He started abusing the Forest Department and the outsiders for evicting them, and cried that they had sullied the Gods. Saying this, he started banging his head on the stone idol as a protest against displacement. Blood started flowing from his forehead. He fainted. The people of the tribal settlement applied some medicine on the wounds."

Ksheerasagar (1949-2021), an activist and organic farmer based in HD Kote, recalled this painful episode in an essay on adivasis that he had sent in belatedly for the *Seminar* issue on Karnataka that I guest edited in 2010. Noting the dire predicament of adivasis—hundreds of families evicted by the government to create the Nagarahole National Park were yet to find rehabilitation, a tiny two percent of over a lakh of adivasi students who studied at the government-run Ashrama residential schools had passed the tenth grade, the communities who recently got themselves falsely classified as Scheduled Tribes had cornered the benefits that legitimately belonged to the adivasi communities, including election victories in all the sixteen assembly constituencies reserved for adivasis in the state—he had written in earnest: "The Government of Karnataka should take up the cause of the tribal people as its first and foremost priority." A committed activist for the adivasi cause, Ksheerasagar died from brain haemorrhage in 2021.

Ksheerasagar came from a Marathi speaking family from Hunsur that had traditionally done the work of measuring and surveying land. While doing his college and post-graduate studies in Mysore—he did his master's in philosophy—he came in close contact with the young socialist and civil liberties activists of the city. After working with a Bangalore-based NGO that focused on land reform issues, he moved to HD Kote, where his wife had found a job as a teacher in a nursery school. He fell in love with the local adivasi communities, in particular, the Jenu Kurubas, the most numerous among them, and spent the rest of his life trying to understand their culture and aid them in various ways.

Between the mid-eighties and 2000, Ksheerasagar worked for Fedina Vikas, an NGO that worked for adivasi welfare in HD Kote. During this period, he along with his colleague, Nanjundaiah, and the members of Budakattu Krishikara Sangha (Association of Tribal Agriculturists) helped the local adivasi communities reclaim over 12,000 acres of land that had originally belonged to them. The slow, tense and risky experience of working through the bureaucracy, the courts and local vested interests can be guessed. Other tasks were achieved alongside: securing government pensions for the elderly adivasis, the promotion of water harvesting methods in the newly reclaimed land.

Siddhartha, the founder of Fedina Vikas and a dear friend, had introduced me to Ksheerasagar during a visit to HD Kote twenty years ago. Both of them had worked closely on many occasions, including, most spectacularly, the successful halting, in the mid-90s, of a project of the Tatas to build a five-star hotel inside the Nagarahole forest. The slim, medium-built Ksheerasagar was shy and friendly and self-effacing. His genuine care and understanding towards the well-being of adivasis stood out through the entire meeting.

Ksheersagar's written works show his awe and love for the sophistication with which the adivasis made their lives inside the forest. As a non-adivasi who had learnt much from having worked with them, he wished that other non-adivasis also recognized the rich knowledge that they had formed over the ages. Published in English as *Playing with the Children of the Forest* (Translator: Nandini Srinivasan),

Ksheerasagar's book conveys a sense of the food gathering practices and of the local animal and plant world that he obtained during his visits to the forest in the company of adivasi children. "The main hope of the book," he wrote, "is that curiosity and wonder about the mysteries of nature become an integral part of (school) learning."

Ksheerasagar's writings, including a novel, capture in graphic detail the forest milieu of the adivasis of HD Kote. He also prepared a detailed report on how the adivasis met their food requirements through the year. His idea was to demonstrate to the government that evicting them from the forests meant uprooting them from a highly evolved means of finding food. He was keenly involved in the work of compiling, *Jenu Nudi Kaliyaaku*, a book that introduced adivasi children to the Kannada alphabet and offered elementary language lessons with words and references taken entirely from their cultural universe. His column, *Harisarodala Dani* ('Nature's Inner Voice'), in *Samyukta Karnataka*, a Kannada daily, conveyed his intense romance with birds and butterflies. Most recently, in over forty columns written for *Andolana*, the Mysore based newspaper, he did fascinating profiles of a living adivasi elder every week.

Wide ranging, understated and selfless, Ksheerasagar's work among the adivasis needs to be celebrated.

THE GESTURE OF NISSAR AHMED

Hardly had the news of Nissar Ahmed's death come, people started reaching for his poems turned into song: *Nityotsava* ("The Eternal Celebration"), a paean to Mother Kannada, *Kurigalu Sir Kurigalu* ("Sheep, Sir, we are sheep"), a satire on how the rulers and the ruled had lost a sense of direction, *Yella Maretiruvaga* ("When everything has been forgotten,") a wistful recall of a past love affair.

Unlike his modernist peers in Kannada literature, in the 1960s, Nissar Ahmed composed lyric poems. As he repeatedly recalled, "communicating" with the ordinary people was important for him. Not wanting commercial Kannada film songs to dictate popular tastes, he personally produced, *Nityotsava*, an album of his poems set to music by Mysore Ananthaswamy in 1978. The songs caught on. The world of light Kannada music embraced other poems of his in subsequent years and Nissar Ahmed was everywhere: school and college day functions, inaugural ceremonies, radio and television programmes. The Kannadiga NRI households he visited during his trips abroad, he has recalled, unfailingly had the *Nityotsava* audio tape with them. He remained grateful for the affectionate place Kannadigas made for him in their minds.

While the metaphors and cadences found in his poems on love, nature, the Kannada land, historical personalities, among others, show how much of an insider he was to Kannada society, Nissar Ahmed's poems which express his feelings of alienation from the same society show the relationship to be a troubled one. His 1968 poem, *Nimmodaniddu Nimmantaagade* (Being with you, and yet not be one of you) is a powerful instance. Its opening stanza goes thus: "Being with you, and yet not be one of you/To not give in when pulled/and to stay distinct/Despite being rooted in this soil/to have to raise my head as an alien, you see/It's a very tough task." Although the narrator's identity remains unidentified, the poem is pitched towards the dynamics of exclusion from the nation. After ruing that "the cat hidden inside" the words of the dominant community had scratched at his integrity and spilt blood, Nissar Ahmed concludes: "The investigation done in my own presence/for elements of nationalism in the spilt blood/Facing that moment with a false smile/It's a very tough task." Relentless and unsparing, the murderous potential of the dominant community's suspicion of religious minorities can be felt beneath the poem's gentle irony.

Another poem, *Anaataru* (Orphans, 1972), also holds out a bleak vision. Addressing himself to a patriot, the poet hints that he hasn't been able to afford to send his children to school and that their future lay in a remand home. Economic hardship, he connotes darkly, will likely push his children into petty crime. Another powerful poem, *Savatiya Makkala Hage* (Like Stepchildren, 1982), asks a mother to not "regard" and "torment" Muslims like they were "her step children." Clarifying soon that the mother it invokes is India, the poem shares an anguish about the many discriminations facing Indian Muslims. While asking for their difficulties to cease, the poet also asks the mother to forgive "the misguided ones."

In a wide-ranging conversation recorded with Kannada literary critic, Rahamath Tarikere, in 2001, Nissar Ahmed repeatedly disavows any interest in taking a conflictual stance in his writings. "If we are pained about something, we need to share it with others and try to make them see it," he said. "I don't wish to criticise others." His poems which bemoan social orthodoxy among Muslims, like *Amma, Achara Mattu Naanu* (Mother, Orthodoxy and I, 1970) also share this non-confrontational stance. They are content to point at a difficulty and put their faith in the possibilities for reconciliation.

Appearing among the columns he wrote for *Tushara*, the popular Kannada monthly magazine, during the early 90s, his essay on the Hadiths ended with the hope that it spurred readers to want to become aware of the life and thought of Prophet Mohammed and the life-affirming philosophy of the Quran. His poems on the Ugadi festival, the mischievous deeds of the child Krishna, and many others reveal his strong acquaintance with Hindu culture. And his moving poem, *Shilube Yeriddaane* (He Has Ascended the Cross, 1982), which sees Christ being crucified daily in courts, factories, prisons, hospitals and in the tiny dark homes of Dalits, shows a familiarity with Christian theology as well.

Nissar Ahmed's writings reveal a reaching out to the communities around him. They oblige us to return the gesture.

NADOJA SARA ABOOBACKER*

Sara Aboobacker (1936-2023) and her husband, an engineer with the government, moved to Bangalore in 1981. He had been transferred from Mangalore. One day, as she was heading out of a public library in Halasur, *Lankesh Patrike*, which was dangling in a roadside stall, caught her eye. She bought a copy of the eight-page Kannada weekly launched the previous year and pored through it at home later that evening. The editorial, which asked the various socially marginal communities to work together, piqued her. Her experiences in her hometown, Kasargod, where strife wasn't seen between these communities, made her view the matter differently. She wrote down a rejoinder to the editorial and sent it to the weekly.

The stories and articles Sara submitted to newspapers had gone unaccepted all along. Things panned out differently now. Her article appeared in full on the first page of *Lankesh Patrike* the following week with the headline: "A Muslim Woman Responds." After publishing a few more of her articles, its editor, P. Lankesh, the famous Kannada writer, urged Sara to consider writing a short story or novella. His invite, she recalled later, made her feel like a sprinter who hears the start whistle at an athletic race. She wrote her debut, and most famous, work, *Chandragiri Theeradalli* (On the Banks of Chandragiri, 1982), in the space of a week.

---

* Nadoja: Literally, a teacher of the land, the phrase was used by Pampa, the 10th century Kannada poet. The Kannada University, Hampi, offers an annual award titled, Nadoja, to people who have made distinguished contributions to society. Sara Aboobacker won this award in 2006.

Lankesh offered to serialize this novella in his weekly. But Sara felt unsure. She dashed to her hometown and ran her newly composed story by her younger brother. He as well as several other relatives felt that it had to be published. Sara enquired whether an Islamic moral injunction that a divorced woman can reunite with her former husband only after being married to another man ('nikah halala') was still practiced. While not a frequent occurrence, she learnt, a couple of instances had occurred in recent years. Although this injunction might exist to deter hasty divorces or to punish men for being flippant with divorce, it nevertheless, she held, left women deeply vulnerable and was better dropped. She decided to publish her story. Its appearance in *Lankesh Patrike*, she would affirm later, launched a fulfilling writing career.

Sara's novella was based on a true incident from three decades ago. A recently married thirteen-year-old servant girl at Sara's home got divorced following her husband's invocation of *talaaq* three times. An elderly man had wished to marry her soon afterwards. On hearing about this, her former husband wanted to remarry her. The kazi at the local mosque suggested that the girl marry the elderly man temporarily ('for only a day') and remarry her former husband after divorcing him. But the girl refused to go along with the pragmatic solution and suffered greatly in her new marriage.

Chandragiriya Theeradalli, where Nadira, the divorced female protagonist, meets a different tragic fate, is a passionate portrayal of the sinister ways in which religious, patriarchal and economic forces hold down women in a lower-class Muslim community in Kasargod. The source of instant literary acclaim as well as censure from local Muslim orthodoxy for its forty-six-year old author, this novella offered a rich fare: the brilliantly sketched micro-scenarios, the effortlessly captured multi-lingual world of Kasargod, an unceasingly intense prose narration and an earthy moral energy.

Appearing in quick succession, Sara's novella and sparkling autobiographical essay, *Muslim Hudugi Shaale Kalitaddu* ('A Muslim Girl Goes to School'), which are rooted in the experiences of a Muslim community, nudge the readers to imagine analogous predicaments in their own communities*.

---

* Vanamala Vishwanatha's English translation of the novella and the essay (*Breaking Ties*, 2001) retains this narrative virtue.

Sara Aboobacker, whose family spoke Malayalam, ended up studying at a Kannada medium school because it was close to her home. This historical accident has proved fortunate for Kannada, and Indian, literature. Her voice, which embodied a wish that literature enhances understanding between communities and help them share their sorrows and joys, has proved to be unlike any other.

PUNEETH RAJKUMAR

The Last Kannada Icon?

Everyone knew that Puneeth Rajkumar (1975-2021) was a superstar. Little could anyone tell however that he had also emerged as the biggest living icon of Kannada society. The shock and grief felt across Karnataka at the news of his tragic death two years ago brought home this truth.

Illustrating the unique ways in which the public self and the private self stay inseparable in India, the loving regard for Puneeth rested on a sense for both his on-screen and off-screen persona.

His film characters invariably youthful, Puneeth's earnestness towards the dance and fight sequences was impossible to miss. While his fit body, hair style and clothes bespoke a middle-class respectability, his winsome smile and righteous anger left no doubt that his heart beat for the people at the bottom. Being a dutiful son, brother, friend and lover, being respectful towards the elderly, being comfortable with religion without being orthodox, taking pride in Kannada identity, unaccepting of social elitism and snobbery are among the core virtues radiating across the film characters played by Puneeth over the last two decades.

He was a hero who held his individual passions in deference to the community. He could be trusted to not betray the Kannada community in a modern world and ensure its continued existence. His characters moved through modern landscapes affirming with confidence the virtues of honesty, courage, fidelity and social dutifulness. Puneeth's films could therefore earn him a massive following across the cities, towns and villages of the state even when every film he did in his adult life was set in urban settings.

Puneeth's death instantly summoned memories of the several film roles he had done as a child, many of them alongside his father and legendary Kannada film icon, Dr. Rajkumar. The film images and voice of the child actor recalled the older phase of cinema communion with Puneeth, making the loss of his life feel deeper.

It must be noted that Puneeth inherited the aura that his father had acquired around himself over his lifetime. Indeed, in so many films, the characters played by Puneeth step out of the narrative to announce the actor's relationship with Rajkumar, blurring the lines between the film and reality momentarily and allowing a glimpse of the thick relationship he enjoys with the Kannada community through his father, whose films have contributed heavily to the modern Kannada sensorium through their images, songs and dialogues. In a poignant instance: when someone asks Puneeth's character whether he was a doctor, he replies smilingly, "No, but people used to call my father 'Dr.' Who knows? In the future, they might call me 'Dr.' too!"

Apart from a couple of films with graphic violence, Puneeth's films were seen as wholesome: the entire family, as the common remark goes, could watch them together. Testifying to the somewhat loosened up social orthodoxy inside and outside the Kannada film industry, his characters ate meat freely and, on a rare occasion, even smoked cigarettes and drank alcohol. And at times—in *Milana* (2007), for example—the community presence in his films could be thin in the tradition of films made in the wake of Yash Chopra's *Chandni* (1989) and *Lamhe* (1991), where the focus is almost wholly on the romance of the couple with everything else muted.

Puneeth's anchoring in *Kannadada Kotyadipathi*, the smash hit game show modeled on *Who Wants to be a Millionaire?*, and his presence in various public occasions revealed him as affable, good-spirited and down-to-earth, not unlike the characters he portrayed in his films. In *Dr. Rajkumar: The Person behind the Personality* (2012), a charming coffee table book that he co-wrote, Puneeth credits his father for instilling these qualities in him early on in his childhood.

Puneeth Rajkumar was in the prime of life when he collapsed

from a fatal heart attack. He was expected to foster a tradition of small budget, high quality Kannada films. With millions of others, I can only say: "He ought to have been with us today."

A FARMER CALLED NARAYANA REDDY

It hadn't been easy to find Narayana Reddy's phone number.
"Hello."

He didn't sound like an old man. I had heard about his farm since my school days in the eighties. It was now 2017.

I was discussing Fukuoka's *One Straw Revolution* in my class and the students, I felt, would gain from meeting a farmer who worked with the cult Japanese natural farmer's ideas. But visiting campus from his farm near Doddaballapura was quite a commute. I asked hesitatingly if he could give a talk in my class.

"I can come, but not until next week." He was committed to two programmes.

"Can you give me your address? We will arrange for a cab."

"Tell me where your campus is. I'll get there by bus."

"A cab will be more comfortable."

"No, no! A bus is comfortable for me. I'll get a bus to Majestic and then take a bus going towards Hosur. It shouldn't take me more than three hours."

Before hanging up, he said, "Please let me know the parts of the book you are discussing in class. I would like to read them before my visit."

The eighty-two year old Reddy was a thin, dark man with sharp features. He was in a half sleeved white shirt and white *panche* with a thin cotton towel thrown over his left shoulder. His hair oiled and neatly combed and side-parted, he was the archetypal farmer of the southern plains.

His hour long talk complicated the archetype. He laid out his early life experiences, his adventures in natural farming and advice for living responsibly, all in fluent English. His pride in being self-made in full evidence, it was an inspirational talk of the serious kind.

When he was a young boy, Reddy had felt like seeing a train after he was done grazing his sheep. His father beat him for returning home late. It made him run away to Bangalore and find a job as a cleaner in a restaurant. He was soon "promoted to the kitchen." Over the next few years, he passed his matriculation; he had learnt typewriting alongside. He became an office attendant and then a manager. He lived frugally the entire time: he spent very little on food; and a gunny sack was his "bed as well as quilt." The money he saved over twelve years let him buy farm land in his native village in Varthur.

In the arid region, Reddy grew ragi and maize. "The first mistake I made was to go to an agricultural university." With their advice, he continued, "I quadrupled my yield with chemical farming. I got the best farmer of the country award in 1976." Still, the expensive farm inputs meant he was losing money overall. After six years on the farm, he felt like moving into business. But a chance meeting with a NASA scientist at Sri Sathya Sai Baba's ashram changed everything. The American, who was now doing organic agriculture in San Francisco, gave him a copy of Fukuoka's *One Straw Revolution*. The cult book, which he read several times, made him rethink the idea of farming entirely.

Everyone felt he was foolish to give up chemical fertilizers and pesticides. With only his wife by his side, Reddy stuck to his plans. The yield was very low in the first year. But, in the second year, it was close to what he used to get earlier. There was no looking back from then on. After irrigation became locally available, Reddy began to grow coconut and sapota.

Reddy dwelt at length on the wisdom of natural farming. It was enough to stop the weeds from blocking light to the main plant. Eliminating them was a mistake as they protect the soil moisture and enhance its fertility and act "as a friend to the main plant."

And, while termites might be enemies inside the house, they were friends on the field. They eat dead leaves and dying plants and trees and convert them into manure. They never eat a living organism!

Agricultural science, Reddy argued, had spread many false ideas about farming. The research in our agricultural universities is mostly funded by multi-national companies like Monsanto and Syngenta. What else can you expect then? he asked matter-of-factly.

He was witty. "Even Kashmir apples aren't good enough for the Bangalorean!" he remarked while deploring we got food from across long distances and worsened global warming. "We get apples from Washington, New Zealand, China."

Friendly rebukes were also handed out. "Grains and fruits are seasonal. Mango is to be eaten during April, May, June, not in other months." Lots of preservatives, he added, are used in mango soft drinks. Fruits ought to be had in their season: he struck at the consumerist hubris of wanting access to everything all the time.

When Fukuoka came down to Bangalore, during his visit to Shantiniketan in 1988, a local NGO took him to Reddy's farm in Varthur.

"The happiest day of my life was when he came to my farm. I didn't know he was coming. My most valued teacher is Fukuoka. I got the gift of meeting him personally. You are lucky you have his book. Distribute it among your friends. His message is for humanity."

Students mobbed him with questions after the session. I tried to rescue him, "You should leave before the traffic gets bad."

"No, I have time. I don't need to go home now. I'm taking the night train to Gadag. The irrigation minister has organized a farmers' meeting there."

AUTHOR'S NOTE AND ACKNOWLEDGEMENTS

Portions of this book have appeared in *Bangalore Mirror* and *Deccan Herald* over the last few years. I wrote for these newspapers with the wish to engage a set of readers regularly and find for myself a stable community of readers. At the same time, I had wanted all along to bring these pieces together in a book—in particular, the ones whose underlying instincts give them a coherence in collected form—because they would engage new readers elsewhere.

When I revisited the pieces while putting this book together, I found myself editing them closely all over again. I took off some parts, added new parts and polished just about everything else to make the prose better, to make the points more precise.

Mahesh Balasubramaniam invited me to write a column for *Bangalore Mirror* and set me on a weekly writing rhythm. I'm grateful to Mahesh and Ravi Joshi, his successor at the paper. I'm also grateful to S. Raghotham, editor at *Deccan Herald*, who asked me to do a column for his paper. I'm thankful to both of these papers for permission to use my writings that originally appeared there.

Barbers and Hairstylists had appeared in *The Hindu*, *The People Without a Stereotype*, *Ambedkar's Ideal of Maitri* and a segment of *The Passions of Lohia* in *Outlook* and *The Matter of a Mela* in *Keywords for India: A Conceptual Lexicon for the 21st Century* (Editors: Rukmini Bhaya Nair and Peter Ronald de Souza, Bloomsbury). I'm grateful to all of them.

I am thankful to Easterine Kire for permission to retell the story, *The Monkey-Husband*, found in her *Naga Folktales Retold* (Barkweaver and Keviselie, 2009).

Vikas Kumar was often the first reader for what I wrote and cares for them as much as I do. I have also run my writings by Manu Chakravarthy, whose comments proved valuable always. Srikanth Sastry has offered sharp feedback on my work. Laura Brown shared superb comments on the book manuscript. Harsh Sethi and Tridip Suhrud gave helpful feedback on the book draft at short notice. My warm thanks to them all.

I'm grateful to my dear friend of many years, Paul Vinay Kumar, for presenting the idea of this book to the publisher at Simon and Schuster.

It has been fabulous to work with Himanjali Sankar, editor and publisher at Simon and Schuster. Her patient and close involvement has mattered a lot for this book.

Many thanks to Pinaki De for the beautiful book cover.

Sanjay Reddy, Shankar Ramaswami and Peter Ronald de Souza have engaged parts of this book in valuable ways. Syed Akbar, Madhulika Banerjee, Prathama Banerjee, Prashanta Bhat, K.M. Chaitanya, Frank Cody, D. Govindaraju, Rajeev Gowda, Govindraj Hegde, Amar Kanwar, Ashwani Kumar, Srikanth Mallavarapu, Bishnu Mohapatra, Harish Narasappa, Rakesh Pandey, Aroon Raman, Sumathi Ramaswamy, Supriya RoyChowdhury, Mohan Rao, Sharmila Rudrappa, Pam Sanath, Prithvi Datta Chandra Shobhi, Siddhartha, Shreelata Rao Seshadri, Dilip Simeon, Pattabhi Somayaji, Aseem Srivastava, Uzramma, A.R. Vasavi, Vishala Varanashi, Ashutosh Varshney, Dhulipala Venkat and Paul Zacharia have shared enthusiasm for my work. I'm thankful to them.

The loving affection of my relatives has nurtured me. My mother, Subhadra, my sister and brother-in-law, Sanchayana and Manu, and my nephew, Sumedha, and niece, Saanvi, have shown a different order of affection. Thank you all.

Megha, Advaya and Tunga were wonderfully supportive as I agonized over my writing tasks week after week. Thanks, thanks, thanks!

ABOUT THE AUTHOR

Chandan Gowda is Ramakrishna Hegde Chair Professor of Decentralization and Development at the Institute for Social and Economic Change, Bengaluru. He has edited *Theatres of Democracy: Selected Essays of Shiv Visvanathan* (2016), *The Way I See It: A Gauri Lankesh Reader* (2018) which later saw Hindi, Kannada, Malayalam, Telugu and Tamil translations, as well as *A Life in the World* (2019), a book of autobiographical interviews he did with UR Ananthamurthy. His translation of UR Ananthamurthy's novella *Bara* (2016) was shortlisted for the Crossword Book Award for Translations, 2017. He is currently co-translating and editing *Daredevil Mustafa*, a short fiction anthology by Purnachandra Tejasvi and *The Greatest Kannada Short Stories Ever Told*, and co-editing *The Rammanohar Lohia Reader*.